English Pronunciation in Use

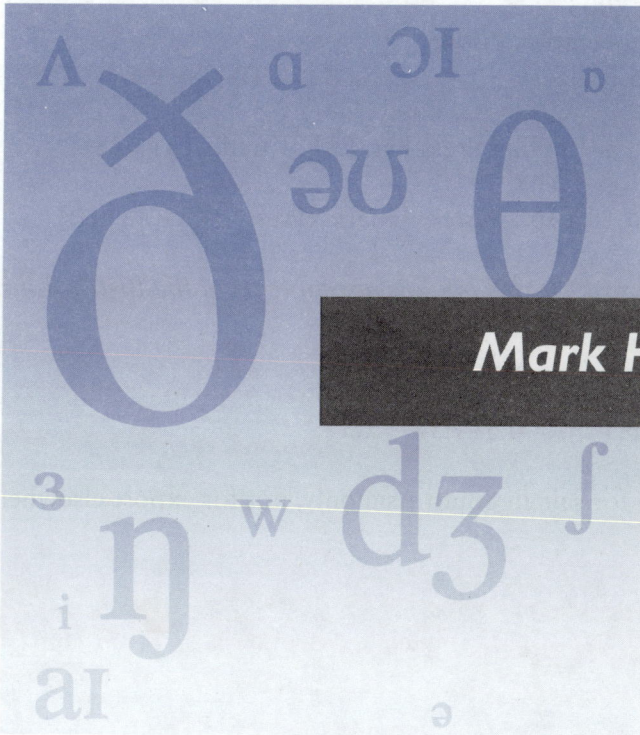

Mark Hancock

CAMBRIDGE
UNIVERSITY PRESS

PUBLISHED BY THE PRESS SYNDICATE OF THE UNIVERSITY OF CAMBRIDGE
The Pitt Building, Trumpington Street, Cambridge, United Kingdom

CAMBRIDGE UNIVERSITY PRESS
The Edinburgh Building, Cambridge CB2 2RU, United Kingdom
40 West 20th Street, New York, NY 10011-4211, USA
477 Williamstown Road, Port Melbourne, VIC 3207, Australia
Ruiz de Alarcón 13, 28014 Madrid, Spain
Dock House, The Waterfront, Cape Town 8001, South Africa

http://www.cambridge.org

First published 2003
First South Asian edition 2004
Reprinted 2005 (twice)

Printed in India at Replika Press Pvt. Ltd., Kundli 131 028

Typeface Sabon 10/13pt. *System* QuarkXPress® [KAMAE LTD]

A catalogue record for this book is available from the British Library

Book	0 521 54770 9
Book + CD	0 521 54771 7
Book + Cassettes	0 521 54772 5

Special edition for sale in South Asia only, not for export elsewhere.

Contents

To the student   5
To the teacher   7
Map of contents described in phonological terms   9

Section A Letters and sounds

1	*Bye, buy* Introducing letters and sounds		10
2	*Plane, plan*	/eɪ/, /æ/	12
3	*Back, pack*	/b/, /p/	14
4	*Rice, rise*	/s/, /z/	16
5	*Down town*	/d/, /t/	18
6	*Meet, met*	/iː/, /e/	20
7	*Carrot, cabbage*	/ə/, /ɪ/	22
8	*Few, view*	/f/, /v/	24
9	*Gate, Kate*	/g/, /k/	26
10	*Hear, we're, year*	/h/, /w/, /j/	28
11	*Wine, win*	/aɪ/, /ɪ/	30
12	*Sheep, jeep, cheap*	/ʃ/, /dʒ/, /tʃ/	32
13	*Flies, fries*	/l/, /r/	34
14	*Car, care*	/ɑː(r)/, /eə(r)/	36
15	*Some, sun, sung*	/m/, /n/, /ŋ/	38
16	*Note, not*	/əʊ/, /ɒ/	40
17	*Arthur's mother*	/θ/, /ð/	42
18	*Sun, full, June*	/ʌ/, /ʊ/, /uː/	44
19	*Shirt, short*	/ɜː(r)/, /ɔː(r)/	46
20	*Toy, town*	/ɔɪ/, /aʊ/	48

Section B Syllables, words and sentences

21	*Eye, my, mine* Introducing syllables	50
22	*Saturday September 13th* Introducing word stress	52
23	*Remember, he told her* Introducing sentence stress	54

Syllables

24	*Oh, no snow!* Consonants at the start of syllables	56
25	*Go – goal – gold* Consonants at the end of syllables	58
26	*Paul's calls, Max's faxes* Syllables: plural and other –s endings	60
27	*Pete played, Rita rested* Syllables: adding past tense endings	62

Word stress

28	*REcord, reCORD* Stress in two-syllable words	64
29	*Second hand, bookshop* Stress in compound words	66
30	*Unforgettable* Stress in longer words 1	68
31	*Public, publicity* Stress in longer words 2	70

Sentence stress

32	DON'T LOOK NOW! Sentences with all the words stressed	72
33	THAT could be the MAN Unstressed words	74
34	I'll ASK her (Alaska) Pronouns and contractions	76
35	She was FIRST Pronouncing the verb be	78
36	WHAT do you THINK? Auxiliary verbs	80
37	A PIECE of CHEESE Pronouncing short words (a, of, or)	82
38	Pets enter, pet centre Joining words 1	84
39	After eight, after rate Joining words 2	86
40	Greet guests, Greek guests Joining words 3	88

Section C Conversation

41	Could you say that again? Understanding conversation	90
42	'Was that the question?' he asked. Reading aloud: 'pronouncing punctuation'	92
43	A shirt and a tie / a shirt and tie Grouping words	94
44	Ehm … Showing that you want to continue	96
45	Well, anyway … Telling a story	98
46	I mean, it's sort of like … Understanding small talk	100
47	Right, OK … Understanding instructions	102
48	'Like father like son' as they say Quoting speech	104
49	He will win Introduction to emphatic stress	106
50	Schwartz … Pedro Schwartz Emphasising added details	108
51	I think you're in my seat Emphasising important words	110
52	Chips or salad? Emphasising contrasting alternatives	112
53	Fifty? No, fifteen! Emphasising corrections	114
54	Look who's talking! Introducing tones	116
55	Here? Yes, here! Asking and checking tones	118
56	Where were you born? Tones in asking for information	120
57	We're closed tomorrow Tones in new and old information	122
58	Oh, really? Continuing or finishing tones	124
59	It's fun, isn't it? Agreeing and disagreeing tones	126
60	It was brilliant! High tones	128

Section D Reference

D1	Introduction to phonemic symbols	130
D2	Pronunciation test	137
D3	Guide for speakers of specific languages	141
D4	Sound pairs	144
D5	Sentence stress phrasebook	161
D6	Glossary	162
	Key	166
	Acknowledgements	200

To the student

English Pronunciation in Use is a book to help students of English to work on pronunciation, for both speaking and understanding. It is written mainly for students of intermediate level.

What will I need?

You will need a cassette or CD player to listen to the recorded material that goes with this book. It will be very useful if you have equipment to record your own voice, so that you can hear your own progress. This symbol (A1) indicates the track number for recorded material i.e. CD or cassette A, track 1.

Also, when you are studying individual sounds, it is sometimes useful if you have a mirror. With this, you can compare the shape of your own mouth to the mouth in diagrams like this one from Unit 8.

See page 163 for a labelled diagram of the mouth and throat.

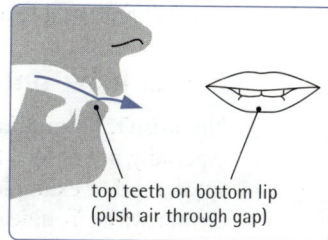

top teeth on bottom lip
(push air through gap)

How is *English Pronunciation in Use* organised?

There are 60 units in the book. Each unit looks at a different point of pronunciation. Each unit has two pages. The page on the left has explanations and examples, and the page on the right has exercises. The 60 units are divided into three sections of 20 units each. Section A is about how to say and spell individual sounds. Section B is about joining sounds to make words and sentences. Section C is about pronunciation in conversation.

After the 60 units, there is a fourth section, Section D, which contains the following:

- Introduction to phonemic symbols
- Pronunciation test
- Guide for speakers of specific languages
- Sound pairs
- Sentence stress phrasebook
- Glossary

At the end of the book there is a Key with answers.

With the book, there is also a set of four cassettes or CDs, one for each section of the book.

What order shall I do the units in?

It is better if you balance the work that you do from the three sections: first, do a unit from Section A, then a unit from Section B, then a unit from Section C, then another unit from Section A, and so on.

So, for example, you could begin like this:

Unit 1, then Unit 21, then Unit 41, then Unit 2, etc. At the end of each unit, you will find a note telling you where to go next.

If you have problems in hearing the difference between individual sounds in Section A of the book, you will be directed to one of the exercises in Section D4 *Sound pairs*.

You may want to focus your work more closely. If so, here are more ideas:

- Do the *Pronunciation test* in Section D. Count your score for each section. If you did specially well in any one of the sections, then you may want to miss the units in that section of the book.
- Look at Section D3 *Guide for speakers of specific languages*. Find your own language (the languages are in alphabetical order). The notes there will tell you which units are less important for speakers of your language and which sound pairs in section D4 are recommended.

Do I need to know the phonemic symbols?

It is possible to use this book without knowing phonemic symbols. However, it is useful to learn them because they make it easier to analyse the pronunciation of words. Also, many dictionaries use phonemic symbols to show pronunciation. In Section D1 *Introduction to phonemic symbols*, you will find a table of the phonemic symbols, plus a set of puzzles to help you learn them.

Is this book only about pronunciation in speaking?

No, it isn't. Pronunciation is important for both listening and speaking. In many of the units, especially in Sections B and C, the pronunciation point is more important for listening than speaking. For example, when they are speaking fast, many native speakers join words together in certain ways. You need to be able to understand this when you hear it, but it does not matter if you do not speak in this way. People will still understand you. Pronunciation points like this are shown with a grey background and this sign:

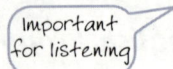

> Important for listening

It is your choice whether you want to just focus on listening, or whether you want to try to speak that way too.

What accent of English is used in this book?

For a model for you to copy when speaking, we have used only one accent, a Southern British accent. But when you are listening to people speaking English, you will hear many different accents. If you are not used to these, it can be very difficult to understand what is being said. For this reason, you will hear a variety of accents in some parts of the listening material for this book.

What is the *Sentence stress phrasebook*?

It can help you to speak more fluently if you say some very common expressions with a fixed pronunciation, like a single word. In Section D5 *Sentence stress phrasebook*, some common expressions are given, and they are grouped together by the way they sound: by their *sentence stress* or *rhythm*. You can practise listening and repeating these to improve your fluency.

What is in the *Glossary*?

In this book, there are some words which are specific to the subject of pronunciation. You can find an explanation of the meaning of these words in Section D6 *Glossary*.

How should I use the recordings?

When you are working with the recording, you should replay a track as often as you need to. When you are doing an exercise you may also need to pause the recording after each sentence to give you time to think or to write your answers. When you are instructed to repeat single words there is a space on the recording for you to do so, but if you are repeating whole sentences you will have to pause the recording each time.

To the teacher

Although *English Pronunciation in Use* has been written so that it can be used for self-study, it will work equally well in a class situation. In a classroom context, the learners can get immediate guidance and feedback from the teacher. Also, they can practise some of the dialogues and other exercises in pairs. You can direct students with particular pronunciation difficulties to do specific units on their own.

In order to simplify the jargon in the book, many of the terms you may be familiar with are not used. For example, the term *initial consonant cluster* is not used. The unit on initial consonant clusters is called *Unit 24 Oh, no snow!: Consonants at the start of syllables*. The following is an explanation of how the book is organised, ending with the map of contents described in phonological terms.

Section A aims to cover the sounds of English and their main spellings. The units are organised by letters rather than sounds. The intention is that this would be a more intuitive route in for non-specialist users. At the same time, this organisation helps to highlight sound–spelling regularities in English.

The vowels are covered first via the five vowel letters of the alphabet, and their 'long' and 'short' pronunciations, for example the letter A as in *tape* or *tap*. The remaining vowel sounds are presented as vowels which typically occur before a letter R. The consonant sounds are presented through either their most common spelt letter, or by one of their main spellings. The ordering of these units is more or less alphabetical.

The units in Section A are not presented as minimal pairs. Vowels are paired according to their spelling, not their potential for being confused with one another. Consonants are paired mainly where they share the same place of articulation. The units were not organised as minimal pairs for two reasons:
- Any sound can form a minimal pair with a number of other sounds, not just one. Organising units according to minimal pairs would therefore lead to a huge number of units and a lot of duplication.
- Many minimal pairs will be redundant for any given learner, so learners need to be selective. Potentially confusing minimal pairs are gathered together in Section D4 *Sound pairs*. Learners are encouraged to select from these according to their own needs.

Alternatives are included for those areas of pronunciation which are especially susceptible to variation across different varieties of English. For example, where there is a letter R with no vowel after it, many speakers do not pronounce the R and many other speakers do pronounce it, and both varieties are presented.

Many vowel sounds are treated as local variants of vowel + R. For instance, the diphthong /ɪə/ is initially presented not as a sound in itself, but as a variant of /iː/ when it occurs before R or L.

Some of the pronunciation points in the book are potentially irrelevant to some learners. For instance, for learners whose aim is mainly to communicate with other non-native speakers of English, accurate production of the sounds /θ/ and /ð/ is probably not necessary. Research suggests that where speakers substitute these sounds with other approximations such as /t/ and /d/, communication is not impeded (Jennifer Jenkins: 2000)*. In many such cases, readers are advised of this fact in the units. These pronunciation points are nevertheless included. My feeling is that a distinction can be drawn between what we *aim* for and what we *settle* for. Thus, a learner might *aim* for /θ/ and *settle* for /t/ (or /s/).

Similarly, even in cases where a learner does aspire to communicate with native speakers, there are many pronunciation features where receptive competence would be sufficient. For instance, such a learner would need to understand speech with weak forms, but not necessarily produce it. This is indicated in the units by a grey background shade and the sign 'Important for listening'. Nevertheless, there may be exercises which ask the learner to produce such features. I have observed that in many cases, there is no better awareness-raiser than to *attempt* to produce, even if the aim is receptive competence.

Section B focuses on pronunciation units which are bigger than individual sounds. The units are in three blocks, dealing in turn with syllables, word stress and sentence stress. As the title of the section suggests, these features are looked at more or less in isolation from a communicative context. For instance, in the case of word stress, it is the form as it may appear in a dictionary that is dealt with here. Similarly, in the case of sentence stress, we focus on an unmarked form in Section B. For example, 'What do you think?' is presented with the stress pattern OooO. In a specific conversational context, this same sentence could be said with the stress pattern ooOo, but sentences in conversational context are dealt with in Section C rather than Section B.

Section C focuses on pronunciation features which emerge in the context of conversation. These include discourse organisation, prominence and tone. Note that there is a lot of grey shading in this section, indicating material that is more important for listening than for production. It is felt that while productive mastery of many features of intonation will be beyond the reach of many learners, they may nevertheless benefit from a receptive awareness of them.

Note: The material in Section D3 *Guide for speakers of specific languages* is based on the pronunciation notes in *Learner English* (Michael Swan and Bernard Smith: 2001)**. Nevertheless, I have had to extrapolate from the information presented there, as many of the minimal pairs presented in this book are not specifically mentioned in the pronunciation notes in that book.

*Jenkins, J. 2000 *The Phonology of English as an International Language*. Oxford: Oxford University Press.
**Swan, M. and B. Smith 2001 *Learner English* (Second Edition). Cambridge: Cambridge University Press.

Map of contents described in phonological terms

A Letters and sounds	B Syllables, words and sentences	C Conversation
1 Introduction to vowels and consonants	21 Introduction to syllables	41 Repair strategies
2 The vowel sounds /eɪ/, /æ/	22 Introduction to word stress	42 Pronouncing punctuation
3 The consonant sounds /b/, /p/	23 Introduction to sentence stress	43 Grouping words: chunking
4 The consonant sounds /s/, /z/	24 Syllables: initial consonant clusters	44 Keeping your speaking turn: floor holding
5 The consonant sounds /d/, /t/	25 Syllables: final consonant clusters	45 Discourse markers in story telling: back-channel responses
6 The vowel sounds /iː/, /e/	26 Syllable structure and –s endings	46 Discourse markers: 'throw away' words
7 Weak vowels /ə/, /I/	27 Syllable structure and –ed endings	47 Discourse markers: signalling next stage: change-of-state marker
8 The consonant sounds /f/, /v/	28 Word stress: two-syllable words	48 Pitch in pronouncing direct speech
9 The consonant sounds /g/, /k/	29 Word stress: compounds	49 Contrastive stress
10 The sounds /h/, /w/, /j/	30 Word stress: suffixes with penultimate stress	50 New and old information
11 The vowel sounds /aɪ/, /I/	31 Word stress: suffixes with ante-penultimate stress	51 Emphatic stress on important information
12 The consonant sounds /ʃ/, /dʒ/, /tʃ/	32 Sentence stress: short imperatives	52 Contrastive stress on alternatives
13 The consonant sounds /l/, /r/	33 Sentence stress: unstressed words	53 Contrastive stress: correcting
14 The vowel sounds /ɑː(r)/, /eə(r)/	34 Sentence stress: weak forms of contractions of pronouns	54 Introduction to tone: intonational idioms; fall and rise tones
15 The consonant sounds /m/, /n/, /ŋ/	35 Sentence stress: weak forms of contractions of be	55 Intonation: open and check questions
16 The vowels sounds /əʊ/, /ɒ/	36 Sentence stress: weak forms of contractions of auxiliaries	56 Tonic stress placement
17 The consonant sounds /θ/, /ð/	37 Sentence stress: weak forms of articles, prepositions and connectors	57 Intonation: old and new information
18 The vowel sounds /ʌ/, /ʊ/, /uː/	38 Linking consonant to vowel	58 Intonation: continuing or finishing tones
19 The vowel sounds /ɜː(r)/, /ɔː(r)/	39 Linking vowel to vowel	59 Intonation: opinion, disagreement, tag questions
20 The vowel sounds /ɔɪ/, /aʊ/	40 Assimilation and elision	60 High tones: evaluative comment

1 Bye, buy
Introducing letters and sounds

A

In writing, words are made of letters. In speech, words are made of sounds. Letters are not always the same as sounds. For example, the words *key* and *car* begin with the same sound, but the letters are different. We can see this clearly if we read the two words in phonemic symbols: /kiː/, /kɑː/. In the examples below, word pairs have the same pronunciation but different spelling:

buy	bye	sun	son
weak	week	weigh	way
too	two	write	right

⚠ Note: There are some exercises to help you learn the phonemic symbols in Section D1.

B

There are two kinds of sounds: consonant sounds (C) and vowel sounds (V). For example, in *duck*, there are three sounds, consonant–vowel–consonant (CVC). The number of sounds in a word is not usually the same as the number of letters. We can see this if we write the word using phonemic symbols (see Section D1). For example, *duck* is /dʌk/.

C

Writers often play with the sounds in words. For example, if they are finding a name for a cartoon character, they might:
- repeat the first sound, for example **D**onald **D**uck.
- repeat the final sound or sounds (this is called rhyme), for example **R**onald **McD**onald.

🎧 **A1** Listen to these examples of names and expressions with sound-play. Notice that the writer is playing with the *sound*, not the spelling. For example, in **D**ennis the **M**enace, the last three sounds of the words are the same, but the spelling is completely different.

Mickey **M**ouse
Rudolf the **r**ed-nosed **r**eindeer
Dennis the **M**enace
Bugs **Bu**nny
news and **views**
rock and **r**oll
wine and **dine**
While the cat's away, the mice will **p**lay.

D

There are probably some sounds in English which do not exist in your language, and others which are similar but not exactly the same. This can make it difficult to hear and make the distinction between two similar words in English.

🎧 **A2** Listen to these pairs. Are any of them difficult for you?

boat – vote   hit – heat   so – show   sung – sun   wine – vine   wet – wait

⚠ Note: To find out which sounds are usually easy or difficult for speakers of your language, see Section D3 *Guide for speakers of specific languages*.

Exercises

1.1 In this story, there are 12 incorrect words. The correct word is pronounced the same as the incorrect one, but the spelling is different. Correct them using words from the box.

| son | some | meat | way | threw | pears | sent | ~~week~~ | buy | piece | road | two |

week
Last ~~weak~~, I cent my sun Jamie to the shops to bye sum food. He got a peace of meet and too pairs. On the weigh home, the bag broke. The food fell onto the rode and got dirty. In the end, Jamie through the food in the bin.

1.2 How many sounds are there in each word? Write the order of consonant sounds (C) and vowel sounds (V).

EXAMPLE
night ......*CVC*...... (three sounds: first a consonant, then a vowel and finally another consonant)

1 dog ....

4 gorilla ....

2 rabbit ....

5 snake ....

3 frog ....

6 bee ....

1.3 Listen to these possible names of cartoon animals. Do they have the same first sounds? (Write A.)
(A3) Do they rhyme? (Write B.)

EXAMPLE Sam the lamb ....*B*....

1 Phil the fox ....

5 Polly the parrot ....

2 Mary the canary ....

6 Deborah the zebra ....

3 Ida the spider ....

7 Myrtle the turtle ....

4 Claire the bear ....

8 Kitty the cat ....

1.4 Listen to these sounds. Do you have a similar sound in your language? If you do, write a tick (✓).
(A4)
1 /ʃ/ (<u>sh</u>oe) ....

5 /dʒ/ (<u>J</u>une) ....

2 /ɜː/ (g<u>ir</u>l) ....

6 /əʊ/ (s<u>oa</u>p) ....

3 /æ/ (h<u>a</u>t) ....

7 /θ/ (<u>th</u>ing) ....

4 /z/ (<u>z</u>oo) ....

8 /l/ (<u>l</u>ife) ....

Now go to Unit 21

2 Plane, plan
The vowel sounds /eɪ/ and /æ/

When you say the letters of the alphabet, A has the long vowel sound /eɪ/. You hear this sound in the word *plane*. But the letter A is also pronounced as the short vowel sound /æ/, as in the word *plan*.

A A5a • Listen to the sound /eɪ/ on its own. Look at the mouth diagram to see how to make this long vowel sound.

A5b • Listen to the target sound /eɪ/ in the words below and compare it with the words on each side.

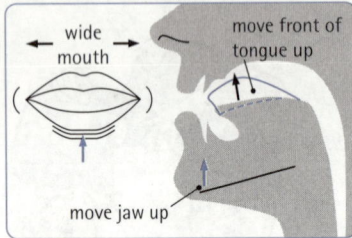

target /eɪ/

meat	**mate**	met
come	**came**	calm
white	**wait**	wet
buy	**bay**	boy

A5c • Listen and repeat these examples of the target sound.
play   played   plate
grey   grade   great
aim   age   eight

"The rain in Spain falls mainly on the plain."

B A6a • Listen to the sound /æ/. Look at the mouth diagram to see how to make this short vowel sound.

A6b • Listen to the target sound /æ/ in the words and compare it with the words on each side.

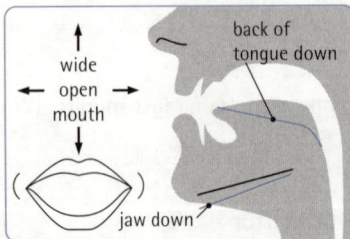

target /æ/

mud	**mad**	made
sing	**sang**	sung
pen	**pan**	pain
hot	**hat**	heart

A6c • Listen and repeat these examples of the target sound.
bank   bag   back
can   cash   catch
ham   has   hat

"The fat cat sat on the man's black hat."

Important for listening

In most accents, the following words have the vowel /æ/: *ask   dance   castle   bath   fast* But in South East England, speakers change the A sound in words such as these to /ɑː/. (For more about /ɑː/ see Unit 14.)

C
Spelling

		frequently
	/eɪ/	A–E (m<u>a</u>te), AY (say), EY (grey), EI (eight), AI (wait), EA (great)
	/æ/	A but note that if there is an R after the A (and the R does not have a vowel sound after it), A has a different pronunciation, for example *arm*: see Unit 14.

Exercises

2.1 Write words for the things in the picture in the correct part of the table.

/eɪ/	/æ/
cake	apple

2.2 These words all contain the vowel sound /æ/. Make another word with the same consonant sounds, but changing the vowel sound to /eɪ/.

EXAMPLES pan ....*pain*............   plan ....*plane*............

1 at ....   4 tap ....

2 mad ....   5 ran ....

3 man ....   6 hat ....

2.3 Listen and circle the word with a different vowel sound.

A7

EXAMPLE black (want) mad hand

1 sad bag salt tap   5 case lake name care
2 far fat map add   6 space change plate square
3 watch catch match land   7 break great heat weight
4 rain said fail train

Then listen again and check.

2.4 Listen and circle the word you hear. If you find any of these difficult, go to section D4 *Sound pairs* for further practice.

A8

1 Man or men?   Did you see the *man / men*?   (⇒sound pairs 1)
2 Cap or cup?   Have you seen my *cap / cup*?   (⇒sound pairs 2)
3 Hat or heart?   She put her hand on her *hat / heart*. (⇒sound pairs 3)
4 Pain or pen?   I've got a *pain / pen* in my hand.   (⇒sound pairs 4)
5 Hay or hair?   There are bugs in this *hay / hair*.   (⇒sound pairs 5)

> **Follow up:** Record yourself saying the sentences in 2.4, choosing one of the two words. Make a note of which words you say. Then listen to your recording in about two weeks. Is it clear which words you said?

Now go to Unit 22

3 Back, pack
The consonant sounds /b/ and /p/

When you say the alphabet, the letters B and P have the sounds /biː/ and /piː/. In words, they have the consonant sounds /b/ and /p/.

- Look at the mouth diagram to see how to make these sounds:

A9a
- Listen to the sounds /b/ and /p/.
The mouth is in the same position for both sounds, however in the sound /b/ there is voice from the throat, In /p/, there is no voice from the throat. Instead, there is a small explosion of air when the lips open.

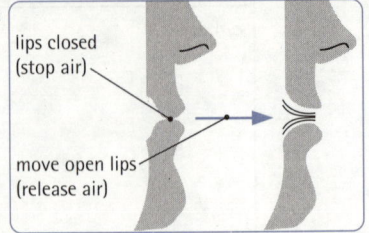

lips closed (stop air)

move open lips (release air)

B

A9b
- Now listen to the sound /b/ on its own.

A9c
- Listen to the target sound /b/ in the words below and compare it with the words on each side.

target /b/

vest	**best**	vest
cups	**cubs**	cups
covered	**cupboard**	covered

A9d
- Listen and repeat these examples of the target sound.

buy   bird   bread
rubber   about   able
job   web   globe

"Bernie brought a big breakfast back to bed."

C

A10a
- Listen to the sound /p/ on its own.

A10b
- Listen to the target sound /p/ in the words below and compare it with the words on each side.

target /p/

full	**pull**	full
cubs	**cups**	cubs
coffee	**copy**	coffee

A10c
- Listen and repeat these examples of the target sound.

park   please   price
open   apple   spring
tape   help   jump

"Pat put purple paint in the pool."

D
Spelling

	frequently	notes
/b/	B (*job*) BB (*rubber*)	B is sometimes silent (*comb*).
/p/	P (*open*) PP (*apple*)	PH pronounced /f/ (*phone*). P is sometimes silent (*psychology*).

Exercises

3.1 First read this conversation to the end, and then write the letter 'b' or 'p' in each gap.
(A11) Listen and check your answers.

SID: Where are the ...P...ears?

JOE: ....ears?!!! Did you say ....ears?

SID: No, ...ears, you know, fruit!

JOE: Oh, I see, ...ears with a P! They're in the ....ack.

SID: What, in the ....ack of the truck?

JOE: No, in the ....ack, you know, with a P!

SID: Oh, I see, ...ack with a P! Would you like one?

JOE: No, I'll have a ....each, please.

SID: A beach?!!!

> **Follow up:** Play the recording again, pausing it after each of Sid's lines.
> *You* say Joe's lines before listening to him saying them.

3.2 The word *ape* contains the two sounds /eɪ/ and /p/. If you reverse the sounds, you get the word
pay /peɪ/. Reverse the sounds in these words and write the new word.

EXAMPLE   tops   ....*spot*....

1 peach   ....

2 cab   ....

3 lip   ....

4 step   ....

5 keeps   ....

3.3 Listen. In one word in each group, the 'b' or 'p' is not pronounced. Circle the word.
(A12)

EXAMPLE   double (doubt) Dublin

1 lamb   label   lab
2 crab   robbed   climb
3 cup   cupboard   copy
4 photo   potato   paper

5 recipe   repeat   receipt
6 possibly   psychology   special
7 Cambridge   combine   combing

3.4 Listen and tick (✔) the sentence you hear, A or B. If you find any of these difficult, go to
(A13) Section D4 *Sound pairs* for further practice.

	A	B	
1	There's a bear in that tree.	There's a pear in that tree.	(⇒sound pair 28)
2	He had the beach to himself.	He had the peach to himself.	(⇒sound pair 28)
3	They burned it.	They've earned it.	(⇒sound pair 29)
4	Say 'boil'.	Save oil.	(⇒sound pair 29)
5	This is a nicer pear.	This is a nice affair.	(⇒sound pair 30)
6	Would you like a copy?	Would you like a coffee?	(⇒sound pair 30)

> **Follow up:** Record yourself saying the sentences in 3.4, choosing
> sentence A or B. Make a note of which you say. Then listen to your
> recording in about two weeks. Is it clear which sentences you said?

Now go to Unit 23

4 Rice, rise
The consonant sounds /s/ and /z/

When you say the alphabet, the letters C and S are pronounced /siː/ and /es/. Notice they both have the consonant sound /s/. But S is also often pronounced as the consonant sound /z/.

A14a • Listen to the sounds /s/ and /z/. Look at the mouth diagram to see how to make these consonant sounds. Notice that in the sound /s/, there is no voice from the throat. It sounds like the noise of a snake. In the sound /z/, there is voice from the throat. It sounds like the noise of a bee.

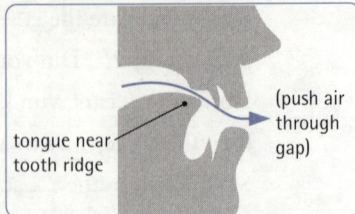

tongue near tooth ridge

(push air through gap)

A14b • Now listen to the sound /s/ on its own.

A14c • Listen to the target sound /s/ in the words below and compare it with the words on each side.

target /s/

zoo	Sue	zoo
rise	rice	rise
shave	save	shave
thing	sing	thing

A14d • Listen and repeat these examples of the target sound.

sad   city   science   scream
glasses   concert   lost
bus   place   class

"It's six or seven years since Sydney's sister sang that song."

A15a • Listen to the sound /z/ on its own.

A15b • Listen to the target sound /z/ in the words below and compare it with the words on each side.

target /z/

Sue	zoo	Sue
place	plays	place
breathe	breeze	breathe
beige	bays	beige

A15c • Listen and repeat these examples of the target sound.

zoo   zero
lazy   easy   scissors   exact
size   wise   times

"Zebras in zoos are like dolphins in pools."

Spelling

	frequently	sometimes	notes
/s/	S (*sad*), SS (*class*) C (*place*)	SC (*science*)	X can spell /ks/ (*mix*). S is not always pronounced /s/ (*sugar, rise, plays*).
/z/	Z (*zero*), S (*nose*)	ZZ (*buzz*) SS (*scissors*)	X spells /gz/ (*exact*). -SE at the end of a word is usually pronounced /z/ (*rise*).

⚠ Pronunciation may be connected to grammar: use /juːs/ = noun   use /juːz/ = verb
close /kləʊs/ = adjective   close /kləʊz/ = verb   house /haʊs/ = noun   house /haʊz/ = verb

Exercises

4.1   Find a way from Start to Finish. You may *not* pass a square if the word contains the sound /z/. You can move horizontally (↔) or vertically (↕) only.

START

spots	squares	prize	since	six	sports
streets	wise	sells	sits	exact	escapes
rice	rise	sense	science	lose	lost
oasis	desert	smokes	songs	crisps	box
place	face	snacks	seas	voice	boxes
plays	phase	nose	smiles	focus	concert

FINISH

4.2
A16   Complete this conversation using words from the box. Then listen and check.

> eyes   ice   niece   knees

SID: Alice's ...... *niece* ...... is nice.

JOE: *Are* nice, Sid. Plural. Her .... *are* nice.

SID: I'm not talking about her .... , I'm talking about her .... !

JOE: Oh, I see, ... with a C.

SID: That's right. She has nice ....

JOE: How can .... be nice? It's too cold.

SID: Not .... , you fool! .... : E-Y-E-S!

> **Follow up:** Play the recording again, pausing it after each of Sid's lines. *You* say Joe's lines before listening to him saying them.

4.3
A17   Listen to the sentences. Look at the words in *italics*. Underline the words in *italics* which contain the sound /s/ and circle the ones which contain the sound /z/. Then listen again and repeat.

EXAMPLE   You can have my tent. It's no <u>use</u> to me. I never ⓤse it.

1 I'm not going to *advise* you. You never take my *advice*.
2 Your tooth is *loose*. You'll *lose* it if you're not careful.
3 The shop's very *close* to home, and it doesn't *close* till late.
4 I can't *excuse* people who drop litter. There's no *excuse* for it.

4.4
A18   Listen and circle the word you hear. If you find any of these difficult, go to Section D *Sound pairs* for further practice.

1 Price or prize?   I got a good *price / prize* for that painting.   (⇒sound pair 31)
2 He sat or he's at?   I don't know where *he sat / he's at*.   (⇒sound pair 31)
3 Suit or shoot?   They didn't *suit / shoot* him.   (⇒sound pair 32)
4 Saved or shaved?   I've *saved / shaved* a lot in the past few days.   (⇒sound pair 32)
5 Sink or think?   We didn't *sink / think*.   (⇒sound pair 33)
6 Closed or clothed?   They were *closed / clothed* for the cold weather.   (⇒sound pair 33)

> Now go to Unit 24 ▶

5

Down town
The consonant sounds /d/ and /t/

A A19a • Listen to the sounds /d/ and /t/. Look at the mouth diagram to see how to make these consonant sounds. Notice that in the sound /d/ there is voice from the throat. In /t/, there is no voice from the throat. Instead, there is a small explosion of air out of the mouth when the tongue moves away from the ridge behind the teeth.

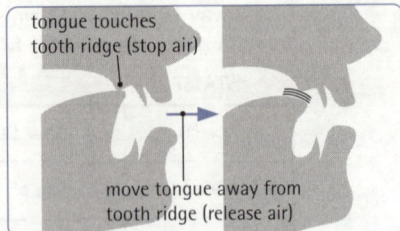

tongue touches
tooth ridge (stop air)

move tongue away from
tooth ridge (release air)

B A19b • Now listen to the sound /d/ on its own.

A19c • Listen to the target sound /d/ in the words below and compare it with the words on each side.

target /d/

town	**down**	town
they	**day**	they
page	**paid**	page
wrote	**road**	wrote

A19d • Listen and repeat these examples of the target sound.
dog   **d**ead   **d**ream
a**dd**ress   a**d**vice   su**dd**en
thir**d**   foo**d**   min**d**

"David's daughter didn't dance but David's dad did."

C A20a • Listen to the sound /t/ on its own.

A20b • Listen to the target sound /t/ in the words below and compare it with the words on each side.

target /t/

die	**tie**	die
hard	**heart**	hard
three	**tree**	three
each	**eat**	each

A20c • Listen and repeat these examples of the target sound.
talk   **Th**omas   **t**rain   **tw**elve
bu**tt**er   un**t**il   ha**t**ed
nigh**t**   work**ed**   wes**t**

"Betty bought a tub of butter."

BUTTER

Important for listening
• In many accents, including American accents, the letter T is pronounced like a /d/ when it is between two vowel sounds. So in America, *writer* /raɪtə/ sounds like *rider* /raɪdə/.
• In some accents, for example in some parts of London, the T between two vowel sounds is made not with the tongue but by stopping the air at the back of the throat to make a short silence. So in these accents, *butter* is pronounced *bu' er*. In fast speech, many speakers drop the /d/ or /t/ when they come between two other consonant sounds. So *facts* /fækts/ sounds like *fax* /fæks/.

D

Spelling

	frequently	sometimes	rarely	notes
/d/	D (*dog*), DD (*address*)			
/t/	T (*tie*) TT (*butter*)	(E)D past tense ending	TH (*Thomas*)	T can be silent (*listen*).

Exercises

5.1
(A21)
Complete these rhymes with words from the box. Then listen and check. The second time you listen to the rhymes pause after each line and repeat it.

rude	said	~~late~~	head	fight	polite	food	wait

There was a young lady called Kate,
Who always got out of bed ....*late*........
The first thing she ....
When she lifted her ....
Was 'I thought it was better to ....,'

There was a young waiter called Dwight,
Who didn't like being ....
If you asked him for ....,
He was terribly ....
And invited you out for a ....

5.2
(A22a)
Listen to and repeat these pairs of words. Then put them into the sentences below and listen and repeat the sentences.

build / built	wide / white	~~weighed / weight~~	heard / hurt
	down / town	dry / try	send / sent

(A22b)
EXAMPLE
Last year, Tom ......*weighed*...... more than Sam, but now they both have the same ......*weight*...... .

1 It wasn't .... in a day; it takes ages to .... a cathedral like that.

2 When you're out in the mountains, you have to .... to stay ....

3 He .... it to the wrong address, so he had to .... another copy.

4 It .... my ears when I .... that noise.

5 The .... sofa is too .... to go through that door.

6 We went .... the hill and into the ....

5.3
Circle the word which does *not* have the sound /t/. You can use a dictionary.

EXAMPLE   asked (castle) letter   first

1 eight   Thames   whistle   walked
2 Thomas   needed   time   liked
3 listen   winter   eaten   after

4 ended   wished   left   hoped
5 whiter   greater   soften   written

5.4
(A23)
Listen and circle the word you hear. If you find any of these difficult, go to Section D4 *Sound pairs* for further practice.

1 Wider or whiter?   Choose Dentocream for a *wider / whiter* smile!   (⇒sound pair 34)
2 Dry or try?   You have to *dry / try* it out.   (⇒sound pair 34)
3 Breeding or breathing?   These animals aren't *breeding / breathing*!   (⇒sound pair 35)
4 Thought or taught?   She *thought / taught* for a long time.   (⇒sound pair 35)
5 Aid or age?   For us, *aid / age* is not important.   (⇒sound pair 36)
6 What or watch?   *What / Watch* a game!   (⇒sound pair 36)

Now go to Unit 25

6 Meet, met
The vowel sounds /iː/ and /e/

When you say the letters of the alphabet, E has the long vowel sound /iː/. You hear this sound in the word *meet*. But the letter E can also be pronounced as the short vowel sound /e/, as in the word *met*.

A

A24a • Listen to the sound /iː/. Look at the mouth diagram to see how to make this long vowel sound.

A24b • Listen to the target sound /iː/ in the words below and compare it with the words on each side.

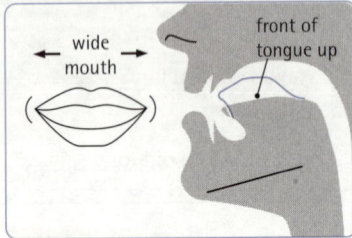

wide mouth | front of tongue up

target /iː/

met	meat	mate
list	least	last
bay	bee	beer
bit	beat	bet

A24c • Listen and repeat these examples of the target sound.

key	keys	keeps
pea	peas	piece
scene	seas	seat

"Steve keeps the cheese in the freezer."

> **Important for listening**
>
> When there is an /iː/ sound before the letter R at the end of a word, many speakers add the vowel /ə/ and do not pronounce the /ɪ/. Compare the vowels in these words: *knee – near*, *pea – pier*, *he – hear*. Many dictionaries give this vowel before R as /ɪə/.

B

A25a • Listen to the sound /e/. Look at the mouth diagram to see how to make this short vowel sound.

A25b • Listen to the target sound /e/ in the words below and compare it with the words on each side.

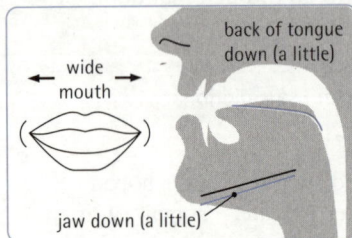

wide mouth | back of tongue down (a little)

target /e/

man	men	mean
heard	head	had
mate	met	meat
sit	set	sat

jaw down (a little)

A25c • Listen and repeat these examples of the target sound.

test	death	red
friend	said	many
check	shelf	leg

"It's best to rest, said the vet to the pet."

C

Spelling

	frequently	sometimes	notes
/iː/	EE (*feet*), EA (*eat*) E-E (*scene*)	E (*me*) IE (*piece*)	Many other vowel sounds are spelt EA, though /iː/ is the most common.
/e/	E (*men*)	EA (*death*), IE (*friend*) A (*many*), AI (*said*)	If E is followed by R, the vowel is not /e/, but /ɜː(r)/ for example in *serve*. (See Unit 19.)

Exercises

6.1
A26
Listen to the letters of the alphabet. If the letter has the sound /iː/, write ee under it. If it has the sound /e/, write e under it. If the letter does not have /iː/ or /e/, don't write anything.

A	B	C	D	E	F	G	H	I	J	K	L	M
	ee	*ee*										

N	O	P	Q	R	S	T	U	V	W	X	Y	Z

6.2 Change the vowel sound from /e/ to /iː/ in these words. Write the new words.

EXAMPLE   met   .... *meat* ....

1 check   ....

2 red   ....

3 bet   ....

4 men   ....

5 fell   ....

6 sweat   ....

7 well   ....

8 set   ....

9 fed   ....

10 led   ....

6.3 Find a way from Start to Finish. You may pass a square only if the word in it has the sound /iː/. You can move horizontally (↔) or vertically (↕) only.

START

leave	earth	health	reach	teach	meat
dream	dead	cream	jeans	steak	cheat
east	bread	tea	death	heat	peak
beach	break	peace	search	leaf	meant
seat	please	team	early	beat	bean
head	bear	wear	dreamt	sweat	clean

FINISH

6.4
A27
Listen and circle the word you hear. If you find any of these difficult, go to Section D4 *Sound pairs* for further practice.

1 Men or man?   Did you see the *men / man*?   (⇒sound pair 1)
2 Pen or pain?   I've got a *pen / pain* in my hand.   (⇒sound pair 4)
3 Bear or beer?   That's a strong *bear / beer*.   (⇒sound pair 8)
4 Live or leave?   I want to *live / leave*.   (⇒sound pair 10)
5 Bed or bird?   Did you see the *bed / bird*?   (⇒sound pair 12)
6 Left or lift?   You should take the *left / lift*.   (⇒sound pair 13)

Follow up: Record yourself saying the sentences in 6.4, choosing one of the two words. Make a note of which words you say. Then listen to your recording in about two weeks. Is it clear which words you said?

Now go to Unit 26 ▶

7 Carrot, cabbage
Unstressed vowels /ə/ and /ɪ/

A

(A28)

In words with two or more syllables, at least one syllable is weak (does not have stress).
- Listen to these words which have two syllables, and the second syllable is weak.

carrot   cabbage

In weak syllables, native speakers of English very often use the weak vowel sounds /ə/ and /ɪ/.
- Listen again to the two words above: the O in *carrot* is pronounced /ə/ and the A in *cabbage* is pronounced /ɪ/.

B

(A29)

- Look at the mouth diagram to see how to make the sound /ə/.
- Listen to these examples and repeat them. The weak vowels in the unstressed syllables **in bold** are pronounced /ə/.

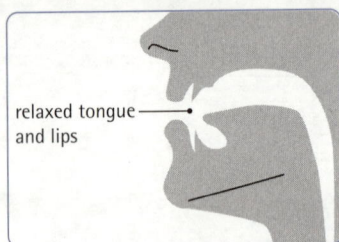

relaxed tongue and lips

weak A:	a**w**ay	banana	woman	sugar
weak E:	garden	paper	under	
weak O:	police	doctor	correct	
weak U:	support	figure	colour	

"I ate an apple and a banana in a cinema in Canada."

Important for listening
- In words like *paper, sugar, colour*, the final R is not pronounced in many accents, so *vista* /'vɪstə/ rhymes with *sister* /'sɪstə/, for example.
- Many speakers of English (especially non-native speakers) do not change vowels in weak syllables to /ə/.

C

(A30)

- Look at the mouth diagram to see how to make the sound /ɪ/.
- Listen to these examples and repeat them. The weak vowels in the unstressed syllables **in black** are pronounced /ɪ/.

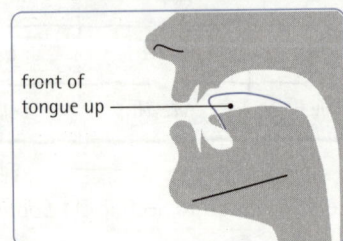

front of tongue up

weak A:	orange	cabbage		
weak E:	dances	wanted	begin	women
weak I:	music	walking		
weak U:	lettuce	minute		

"Alex's lettuces tasted like cabbages."

D

Spelling

Notice in the examples above that nearly any vowel spelling may be pronounced as a weak vowel.

⚠️ **Note:** Often, whole words are pronounced as weak syllables, with a weak vowel. For example: half **an** hour, going **to** work, Jim **was** late. See Unit 33.

Exercises

7.1 Listen to the poem. Circle the words which rhyme.
A31

> Mr Porter loves his pasta.
> No one else can eat it faster.
> Mr Porter's sister Rita,
> Buys the pasta by the metre.
> Mr Porter's older daughter,
> Boils it all in tubs of water.

7.2 Listen. In each sentence or phrase there are two vowels which are **not** /ə/. Circle them.
A32

EXAMPLE   an ⓐpple and a banⓐna

1 from Canada to China
2 The parrot was asleep.
3 The cinema was open.
4 the photographer's assistant
5 a question and an answer
6 a woman and her husband
7 a pasta salad

7.3 Write the words in the correct part of the table. Then listen and check.
A33

~~orange~~	~~woman~~	return	collect	market	begin	visit	asleep
salad	teaches	needed	letter	sofa	peaches	quarter	women

vowel in weak syllable = /ə/	vowel in weak syllable = /ɪ/
woman	orange

7.4 Listen and circle the word you hear.
A34

1 Woman or women?   What time did the *woman / women* arrive?
2 Dress or address?   Where's Kate's *dress / address*?
3 Manager's or manages?   The team *manager's / manages* well.
4 Teacher's or teaches?   The German *teacher's / teaches* English.
5 Weight's or waiter's?   The *weight's / waiter's* heavy.
6 Dancer's or dances?   The woman *dancer's / dances* fast.
7 Officer's or office's?   The *officer's / office's* here.
8 Away or way?   Take that *away / way*.
9 Driver or drive?   What a nice *driver / drive*!
10 Racer's or races?   The *racer's / races* finished.

Follow up: Record yourself saying the sentences in 7.4, choosing one of the two words. Make a note of which words you say. Then listen to your recording in about two weeks. Is it clear which words you said?

Now go to Unit 27

8 Few, view
The consonant sounds /f/ and /v/

A A35a • Listen to the two sounds /f/ and /v/. Look at the mouth diagram to see how to make these consonant sounds. Notice that in the sound /f/, there is no voice from the throat, and when you say this sound, you can feel the air on your hand when you put it in front of your mouth. In /v/, there is voice from the throat.

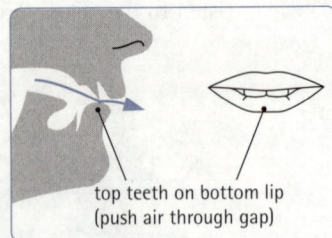

top teeth on bottom lip
(push air through gap)

B A35b • Now listen to the sound /f/ on its own.

A35c • Listen to the target sound /f/ in the words below and compare it with the words on each side.

target /f/

view	few	view
leave	leaf	leave
three	free	three
copy	coffee	copy

"Frank found four frogs laughing on the floor."

A35d • Listen and repeat these examples of the target sound.

photo   fly   freeze
offer   selfish   gift
knife   stuff   laugh

C A36a • Listen to the sound /v/ on its own.

A36b • Listen to the target sound /v/ in the words below and compare it with the words on each side.

target /v/

ferry	very	ferry
best	vest	best
wet	vet	wet
than	van	than

A36c • Listen and repeat these examples of the target sound.

visa   vote   voice
river   wives   loved
wave   twelve   of

"Vera drove to Venice in a van."

D ## Spelling

	frequently	sometimes	notes
/f/	F (*fell*) FF (*offer*) PH (*photo*) GH (*laugh*)		The vowel is shorter before /f/ than /v/, for example in *leaf* and *leave*. If you have difficulty making the difference, exaggerate the length of the vowel in *leave*.
/v/	V (*never*)	F (*of*)	

Exercises

8.1 How many /f/ and /v/ sounds are there when you say these numbers? Write the number.

EXAMPLE 55 ..4..

1 512 ....   2 745 ....   3 5 ....   4 11.75 ....   5 7,474 ....

8.2 Complete this conversation using words from the box. Then listen and check.

(A37)

> fan   van   wife's   wives

SID: My ...*wife's*... left me.

JOE: Your .... left you? How many .... did you have, Sid?

SID: One wife. And now she has left me.

JOE: Oh, I see, ... with an F, not .... with a V!

SID: That's right! Yes, she took the .... and drove off.

JOE: What did she want the .... for?

SID: I said ...., you know, a kind of vehicle.

JOE: Oh, I see: .... with a V, not .... with an F!

> **Follow up:** Play the recording again, pausing after each of *Sid's* lines. *You* say Joe's lines before listening to him saying them.

8.3 Find 12 words beginning or ending with /f/ or /v/. The words are written horizontally (→) or vertically (↓). Note that the last letter is not always F or V. Use all the letters.

D	C	L	A	U	G	H	I
R	O	W	S	A	V	E	F
I	U	I	L	F	I	V	E
V	G	F	I	H	A	V	E
E	H	E	V	G	O	L	F
O	F	F	E	S	A	F	E

8.4 Listen and circle the word you hear. If you find any of these difficult, go to Section D4 *Sound pairs* for further practice.

(A38)

1 Thief's or thieves'?   These are the *thief's* / *thieves'* fingerprints.   (⇒sound pair 37)
2 Few or view?   She's painted a *few* / *view*.   (⇒sound pair 37)
3 Copy or coffee?   Do you want a *copy* / *coffee*?   (⇒sound pair 30)
4 Boat or vote?   What are you going to do with your *boat* / *vote*?   (⇒sound pair 29)
5 Worse or verse?   I don't know which is *worse* / *verse*.   (⇒sound pair 38)
6 Free or three?   We got *free* / *three* tickets!   (⇒sound pair 39)

> **Follow up:** Record yourself saying the sentences in 8.4, choosing one of the two words. Make a note of which words you say. Then listen to your recording in about two weeks. Is it clear which words you said?

> Now go to Unit 28

9 Gate, Kate
The consonant sounds /g/ and /k/

A A39a
- Listen to the two sounds /g/ and /k/. Look at the mouth diagram to see how to make these sounds. Notice that in the sound /g/, there is voice from the throat. In /k/, there is no voice from the throat. When you say this sound, you can feel the air on your hand when you put it in front of your mouth.

back of tongue touches top of mouth (stop air)

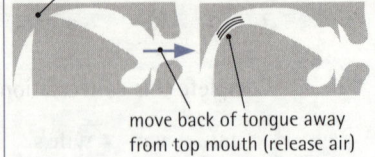

move back of tongue away from top mouth (release air)

B A39b
- Now listen to the sound /g/ on its own.

A39c
- Listen to the target sound /g/ in the words below and compare it with the words on each side.

target /g/

Kate	**gate**	Kate
back	**bag**	back
wood	**good**	wood
loch*	**log**	loch

* This is the Scottish word for *lake*: the final consonant sound does not exist in English.

A39d
- Listen and repeat these examples of the target sound.

ghost   guess   green
bigger   ago   angry
dog   egg   league

"Grandma gave the guests eggs and frog's legs."

C A40a
- Listen to the sound /k/ on its own.

A40b
- Listen to the target sound /k/ in the words below and compare it with the words on each side.

target /k/

gap	**cap**	gap
dogs	**docks**	dogs
missed	**mixed**	missed
water	**quarter**	water

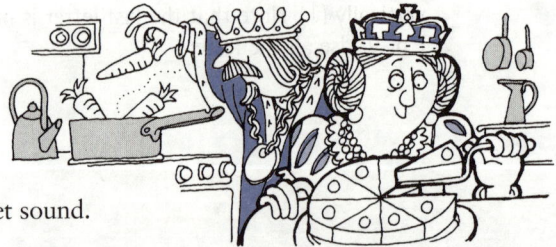

A40c
- Listen and repeat these examples of the target sound.

keep   club   quick
school   soccer   taxi
milk   comic   ache

"The king cooked the carrots and the queen cut the cake."

D Spelling

	frequently	sometimes	notes
/g/	G (*go*) GG (*bigger*)	GH (*ghost*) GU (*guest*)	G can be silent (*sign, foreign*). The vowel sound is a bit longer before /g/ than before /k/ in pairs like *bag* and *back*.

	beginning	middle	end	notes
/k/	C (*can*) K (*king*)	CC (*soccer*) CK (*locker*)	K (*milk*) CK (*black*) C (*comic*) CH (*ache*)	QU spells the sound /kw/, e.g. *quick* /kwɪk/. X spells the sound /ks/, e.g. (*six*) /sɪks/. In some words beginning with K, the K is silent, e.g. *know, knife*.

Exercises

9.1 Add the sound /g/ or /k/ to the beginning of these words and write the new words. Remember: think of *sounds*, not spelling. For example, if you add /k/ to the beginning of water /wɔːtə/, you get quarter /kwɔːtə/. The sound is similar but the spelling is completely different!

EXAMPLE   eight ....*gate*............

1 up ....   5 old ....   8 all ....

2 aim ....   6 lime ....   9 rate ....

3 ache ....   7 air ....   10 ill ....

4 round ....

9.2 Complete the second line to rhyme with the first line, using a word from the box.
(A41) Then listen and repeat.

> rocks   cake   ache   ~~locker~~   key   bigger   queue   kitchen   six   ask

EXAMPLE   He dressed for soccer, And closed his ......*locker*...... .

1 Kelly Collins couldn't figure,   4 I saw a fox,
  How to make the plants grow ....   Behind those ....

2 I'd like five bricks,   5 Clara saw a friend she knew,
  No, make it ....!   Standing quietly in the ....

3 Mr Quinn ate so much steak,
  He came home with a stomach ....

9.3 Complete this conversation using words from the box. Then listen and check.   > lock   log   Loch
(A42)
SID: Hey, there's the monster!

JOE: That's just a ....

SID: Yes, it's .... Ness.

JOE: No, not .... I mean .... ,
      you know, from a tree!

SID: I've never seen a tree with a ....

JOE: No, not a .... that you open with a key; a .... with a G!

> **Follow up:** Play the recording again, pausing it after each of Sid's lines.
> *You* say Joe's lines before listening to him saying them.

9.4 Listen and circle the word you hear. If you find any of these difficult, go to Section D4 *Sound pairs*
(A43) for further practice.

1 Ghost or coast?   Did you see the *ghost / coast*?   (⇒sound pair 40)
2 Glasses or classes?   I don't need *glasses / classes*.   (⇒sound pair 40)
3 Bag or back?   My *bag*'s / *back*'s wet.   (⇒sound pair 40)
4 Goat or coat?   She's lost her *goat / coat*.   (⇒sound pair 40)

> **Follow up:** Record yourself saying the sentences in 9.4, choosing one of
> the two words. Make a note of which words you say. Then listen to your
> recording in about two weeks. Is it clear which words you said?   > Now go to Unit 29

10 Hear, we're, year
The sounds /h/, /w/ and /j/

The sounds /h/, /w/ and /j/ only happen before a vowel sound.

A
🎧 A44a • Listen to the sound /h/. Look at the mouth diagram to see how to make this sound.

🎧 A44b • Listen to the target sound /h/ in the words below and compare it with the words on each side.

🎧 A44c • Then listen and repeat the examples of the target sound.

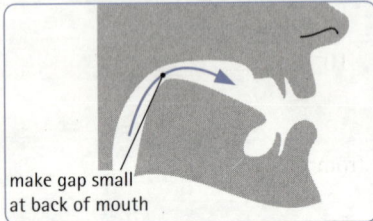

target /h/

old	hold	old
art	heart	art
force	horse	force
sheet	heat	sheet

make gap small at back of mouth

Examples

hair   head   who
ahead   perhaps   behave

"Harry had a habit of helping hitch-hikers."

Important for listening   Some speakers, e.g. in London, do not pronounce the H, so *hair* /heə/ sounds the same as *air* /eə/.

B
🎧 A45a • Listen to the sound /w/. Look at the mouth diagram to see how to make this sound.

🎧 A45b • Listen to the target sound /w/ in the words below and compare it with the words on each side.

🎧 A45c • Then listen and repeat the examples of the target sound.

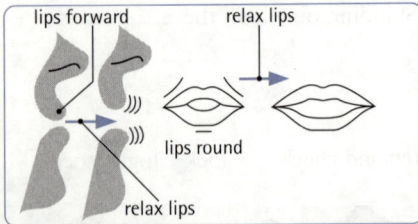

lips forward   relax lips
lips round
relax lips

target /w/

vest	west	vest
of air	aware	of air
good	would	good
Gwyn	win	Gwyn

Examples

wage   what   one
language   quick   square

"Wendy went away twice a week."

C
🎧 A46a • Listen to the sound /j/. Look at the mouth diagram to see how to make this sound.

🎧 A46b • Listen to the target sound /j/ in the words below and compare it with the words on each side.

🎧 A46c • Then listen and repeat the examples of the target sound.

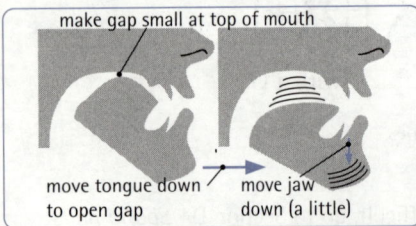

make gap small at top of mouth

target /j/

joke	yolk	joke
jaw	your	jaw
fool	fuel	fool
pleasure	player	pleasure

move tongue down to open gap   move jaw down (a little)

Examples

year   used   euro
few   cure   view

"We didn't use euros in Europe a few years ago."

Important for listening   In American, the /j/ is dropped from words like *new, student, tune,* so for example *newspaper* /ˈnjuːspeɪpə/ sounds like *noose paper* /ˈnuːspeɪpə/.

D
Spelling

	frequently	rarely	notes
/h/	H (*hill*)	WH (*who*)	H is often silent (*hour, honest*).
/w/	W (*will*), WH (*when*)	O (*one, once*)	The letters QU usually spell /kw/ (*quite*).
/j/	Y (*you*), I (*view*), E (*few*), U (*cute*)		

28

Exercises

10.1   Add one of these sounds to the start of these words to make other words: /h/, /j/, /w/. Think of *sounds*, not spelling!

EXAMPLE   air .... *hair, where* ....

1 earth	6 eyes	11 I'll ....
2 ear	7 all	12 eat ....
3 or	8 aid	13 ache ....
4 in	9 ill	14 eye ....
5 eight	10 art	15 old ....

10.2   In these groups of words, three of the words begin with the same consonant sound and one of the words begins with a different sound. Circle the one with the different sound. You can use a dictionary.

EXAMPLE   (hour) half home high

1 union   used   under   university
2 water   whale   whole   window
3 when   who   where   which
4 year   euro   uniform   untie
5 how   honest   healthy   happy
6 one   write   world   waste

10.3   Each sentence contains four or five examples of one of these sounds: /h/, /w/, /j/. Write the phonemic letter under the sounds in the sentences.

EXAMPLE   A fusion of Cuban and European music. /j/
              j   j   j   j

1 Your uniform used to be yellow. /j/

2 Haley's horse hurried ahead. /h/

3 This is a quiz with twenty quick questions. /w/

4 We went to work at quarter to twelve. /w/

5 New York University student's union. /j/

6 The hen hid behind the hen house. /h/

7 Which language would you like to work in? /w/

10.4   Listen and circle the word you hear. If you find any of these difficult, go to Section D4 *Sound pairs*
(A47)   for further practice.

1 Art or heart?   This is the *art / heart* of the country.   (⇒sound pair 41)
2 Hearing or earring?   She's lost her *hearing / earring*.   (⇒sound pair 41)
3 West or vest?   The *west / vest* is very warm.   (⇒sound pair 38)
4 Aware or of air?   They weren't made *aware / of air*.   (⇒sound pair 38)
5 Use or juice?   What's the *use / juice*?   (⇒sound pair 42)
6 Heat or sheet?   I can't sleep in this *heat / sheet*.   (⇒sound pair 43)

> **Follow up:** Record yourself saying the sentences in 10.4, choosing one of the two words. Make a note of which words you say. Then listen to your recording in about two weeks. Is it clear which words you said?

Now go to Unit 30

Wine, win
The vowel sounds /aɪ/ and /ɪ/

When you say the letters of the alphabet, I has the long vowel sound /aɪ/. You hear this sound in the word *wine*. But the letter I is also pronounced as the short vowel sound /ɪ/, as in the word *win*.

A

A48a • Listen to the sound /aɪ/. Look at the mouth diagram to see how to make this long vowel sound.

A48b • Listen to the target sound /aɪ/ in the words below and compare it with the words on each side.

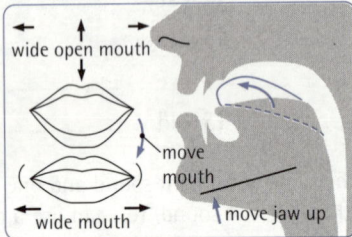

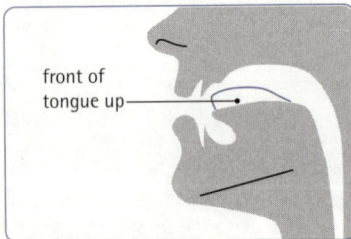

wide open mouth
move mouth
wide mouth
move jaw up

target /aɪ/

mate	might	meet
bay	buy	boy
tip	type	tape
quit	quite	quiet

A48c • Listen and repeat these examples of the target sound.
why   wide   wife
buy   buys   bike
fly   flies   flight

"Nile crocodiles have the widest smiles."

Important for listening

When the long I is before R or L, many speakers put the vowel /ə/ between them. So, for example, *hire* sounds like *higher*. Here are some more examples: *fire tyre child while smile style file wild*.

B

A49a • Listen to the sound /ɪ/. Look at the mouth diagram to see how to make this short vowel sound.

A49b • Listen to the target sound /ɪ/ in the words below and compare it with the words on each side.

front of tongue up

target /ɪ/

peak	pick	pack
wheel	will	while
set	sit	sat
feet	fit	fat

A49c • Listen and repeat these examples of the target sound.
king   kid   kit
pink   pig   pick
fill   fish   fit

"Tim bit a bit of Kitty's biscuit."

C

Spelling

	frequently	sometimes	notes
/aɪ/	I-E (*smile*), IE (*die*) Y (*cry*)	IGH (*high*), UY (*buy*)	These spellings are *not always* pronounced /aɪ/ (*fridge, city, friend*).
/ɪ/	I (*win*)	Y (*gym*)	The sound /ɪ/ is also a weak vowel (see Unit 7), and can have various spellings in an unstressed syllable (*need<u>e</u>d, cit<u>ie</u>s, vill<u>a</u>ge*). If there is an R after the letter I (and the R does not have a vowel after it), I has a different pronunciation. (See Unit 19.)

Exercises

11.1 Make words with these beginnings and endings and write them in the correct part of the table.

beginnings:	wi	li	mi	ni	fi	ti	si	qui		
endings:	ght	fe	t	ce	ne	me	le	de	ll	sh	te	n

words with the vowel /aɪ/	words with the vowel /ɪ/
wife	*wit*

11.2 Read the dialogue. Circle the sound /aɪ/ and underline /ɪ/. Count them and write the number at the end of the line.

A: Wh(y) did J̲i̲m h̲i̲t B̲i̲ll?   /aɪ/ = _1_   /ɪ/ = _4_
B: Well, Jim's a guy who likes a fight.   /aɪ/ = ...   /ɪ/ = ...
A: But Bill's twice his size.   /aɪ/ = ...   /ɪ/ = ...
B: Yeah, that's why Jim got a black eye and a thick lip.   /aɪ/ = ...   /ɪ/ = ...
A: And Bill's got a big smile.   /aɪ/ = ...   /ɪ/ = ...
B: That's right!   /aɪ/ = ...   /ɪ/ = ...

🎧 A50   **Follow up:** On the recording you will hear A's lines. You say B's lines.

11.3 The word *knife* contains the three sounds /n/, /aɪ/ and /f/. If you reverse the sounds, you get the word *fine* /faɪn/. Reverse the sounds in these words.

EXAMPLE   sign   ....*nice*.......

1 might   ....   5 pitch   ....
2 lick   ....   6 tick   ....
3 lip   ....   7 dice   ....
4 kiss   ....   8 lights   ....

11.4
🎧 A51   Listen and circle the word you hear. If you find any of these difficult, go to Section D4 *Sound pairs* for further practice.

1 Live or leave?   I don't want to *live / leave* here.   (⇒sound pair 10)
2 Fill or feel?   Can you *fill / feel* it?   (⇒sound pair 10)
3 Litter or letter?   Who dropped the *litter / letter*?   (⇒sound pair 13)
4 Lift or left?   You should take the *lift / left*.   (⇒sound pair 13)

Follow up: Record yourself saying the sentences in 11.4, choosing one of the two words. Make a note of which words you say. Then listen to your recording in about two weeks. Is it clear which words you said?

Now go to Unit 31 ▶

Sheep, jeep, cheap
The consonant sounds /ʃ/, /dʒ/ and /tʃ/

A

A52a • Listen to the sound /ʃ/. Look at the mouth diagram to see how to make this consonant sound. Notice that there is no voice from the throat, and you can feel the air on your hand when you put it in front of your mouth. If you add voice from the throat, you get the sound /ʒ/, as in *television*, but this sound is not common in English.

A52b • Listen to the target sound /ʃ/ in the words below and compare it with the words on each side.

A52c • Then listen and repeat the examples.

target /ʃ/

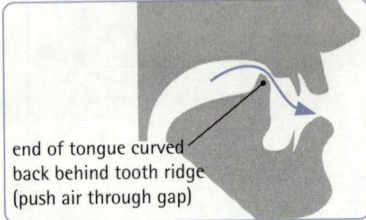

sort	**short**	sort
suit	**shoot**	suit
catch	**cash**	catch
choose	**shoes**	choose

end of tongue curved back behind tooth ridge (push air through gap)

Examples
should   shirt   sugar
fashion   nation   ocean
wish   push   English

"Sharon shouldn't wash her shoes in the shower!"

B

A53a • Listen to the sounds /dʒ/ and /tʃ/. Look at the mouth diagram in C below to see how to make these consonant sounds. With /tʃ/ there is no voice from the throat, with /dʒ/ there is. Notice that you can make the sound /ʃ/ into a continuous sound, but you cannot do this with /tʃ/ and /dʒ/.

C

A53b • Now listen to the sound /dʒ/ on its own.

A53c • Listen to the target sound /dʒ/ in the words below and compare it with the words on each side.

A53d • Then listen and repeat the examples.

tongue moves behind tooth ridge (release air)

target /dʒ/

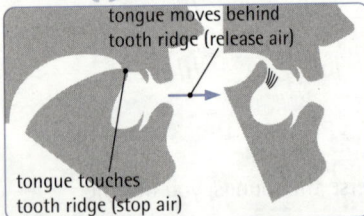

cheap	**jeep**	cheap
tune	**June**	tune
use	**juice**	use
draw	**jaw**	draw

tongue touches tooth ridge (stop air)

Examples
job   general   June
danger   agenda   object
edge   age   village

"Ginger spilt orange juice on George's jacket."

D

A54a • Listen to the sound /tʃ/ on its own.

A54b • Listen to the target sound /tʃ/ in the words below and compare it with the words on each side.

A54c • Then listen and repeat the examples.

target /tʃ/

jeep	**cheap**	jeep
share	**chair**	share
trips	**chips**	trips
what's	**watch**	what's

Examples
chair   cheese   chicken
kitchen   future   question
rich   which   March

"Which child put chalk on the teacher's chair?"

E ## Spelling

	beginning	middle	end
/ʃ/	SH (*shoe*), S (*sugar*)	SH (*fashion*), SS (*Russia*) TI (*nation*), C (*ocean*)	SH (*finish*)
/dʒ/	J (*jaw*), G (*general*)	G (*page*), J (*major*)	GE (*rage*), DGE (*ledge*)
/tʃ/	CH (*chair*)	CH (*teacher*), T (*future*)	TCH (*watch*)

Exercises

12.1 Write these nationality words in the correct column.

Belgian Welsh Dutch Russian Chinese German Japanese Polish French Chilean Turkish

contains /dʒ/	contains /ʃ/	contains /tʃ/
Belgian		

12.2 Complete this conversation using words from the box. Then listen and check.

(A55)

ships	chips
Jeep	cheap

SID: It's fish and .... for lunch, Joe!

JOE: ....!? I can't eat ...., they're too big!

SID: I said ...., you know, fried potatoes!

JOE: Oh, I see, ... with a CH, not .... with an SH.

SID: That's right. You're a genius, Joe!

JOE: Was the fish expensive, Sid?

SID: No, it was ....

JOE: ....!? You bought a ....?

SID: No, ..., the opposite of expensive.

JOE: Oh, I see, ... with a CH, not .... with a J!

> **Follow up:** Play the recording again, pausing it after each of Sid's lines. *You* say Joe's lines before listening to him saying them.

12.3 If a word ends with a /dʒ/ or a /tʃ/, and the next word begins with the same sound, you say the sound twice. If you say *Dutch cheese* with only one /tʃ/, it sounds like *Dutch ease*. The speaker made this mistake in these sentences. Write what they meant to say.

EXAMPLE   Does she <u>tea Chinese</u> in the school?   ....*teach Chinese*..........

1 I don't know <u>which air</u> to sit on.   ....

2 Everyone at the <u>match ears</u> when their team scores.   ....

3 I never <u>what chat</u> shows on the TV.   ....

4 The actor on <u>stay joked</u> with the audience.   ....

5 Foxes sometimes come to the farm and <u>cat chickens</u>.   ....

6 Do you want to <u>chain jackets</u> before we go out?   ....

(A56)

> **Follow up:** You will hear both the incorrect and correct pairs of words from the exercise. Repeat, making the difference clear.

12.4 Listen and circle the word you hear. If you find any of these difficult, go to Section D4 *Sound pairs* for further practice.

(A57)

1 Watch or wash?   You'll have to *watch / wash* the baby.   (⟹sound pair 44)
2 Riches or ridges?   You'll find *riches / ridges* like you've never seen!   (⟹sound pair 45)
3 Save or shave?   He didn't *save / shave* at all last year.   (⟹sound pair 32)
4 Use or juice?   What's the *use / juice*?   (⟹sound pair 42)
5 What's or watch?   *What's / Watch* the time! / ?   (⟹sound pair 46)
6 Trees or cheese?   I saw something in the *trees / cheese*!   (⟹sound pair 47)

Now go to Unit 32

13 Flies, fries
The consonant sounds /l/ and /r/

A

🎧 A58a • Listen to the sound /l/. Look at the mouth diagram to see how to make this sound. Notice that you can make it into a long continuous sound, and there is voice from the throat.

🎧 A58b • Listen to the target sound /l/ in the words below and compare it with the words on each side.

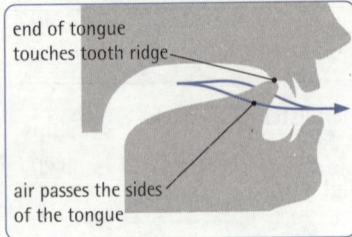

end of tongue touches tooth ridge

air passes the sides of the tongue

target /l/

fries	**flies**	fries
rent	**lent**	rent
correct	**collect**	correct
code	**cold**	code

"Clara's really clever but Lilly's a little silly."

🎧 A58c • Listen and repeat these examples of the target sound.

leave   litre   life
slow   caller   help
fill   final   whistle

B

🎧 A59a • Listen to the sound /r/. Look at the mouth diagram to see how to make this sound. Notice that you can make it into a long continuous sound, and there is voice from the throat. But when you finish the sound, the jaw opens a little and the tongue goes straight again.

🎧 A59b • Listen to the target sound /r/ in the words below and compare it with the words on each side.

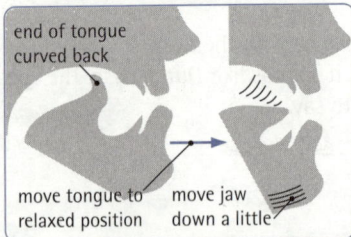

end of tongue curved back

move tongue to relaxed position   move jaw down a little

target /r/

late	**rate**	late
play	**pray**	play
chain	**train**	chain
jaw	**draw**	jaw

"The rabbits raced right around the ring."

🎧 A59c • Listen and repeat these examples of the target sound.

right   wrote   rhyme
carrot   sorry   dress
far away   war and peace

Important for listening

In South East English and many other accents, you only pronounce /r/ if there is a vowel sound after it. So for example, in far /fɑː/ and car /kɑː/, you do not hear it, but in *far away* /fɑːrəweɪ/ and car engine /kɑːrendʒɪn/, you pronounce it because it is followed by a vowel sound. In other accents, including American, the /r/ is pronounced.

⚠ Note: The sound /r/ affects the vowel sound before it: see Units 14 and 19.

C

Spelling

	frequently	sometimes	notes
/l/	L (*leg*), LL (*call*)		L can be silent (*half, calm, talk, could*).
/r/	R (*run*), RR (*carrot*)	WR (*wrong*), RH (*rhyme*)	

Exercises

13.1 Add the sound /l/ or /r/ to the beginning of these words and write the new words. Remember: think of *sounds*, not spelling. For example, if you add /l/ to the beginning of *ache* /eɪk/, you get lake /leɪk/. The sound is similar but the spelling is completely different. There may be more than one possibility. Then say the pairs of words.

EXAMPLE ache   *lake (or rake)*   3 air ....   6 eye ....

1 eight ....   4 earn ....   7 egg ....

2 owes ....   5 end ....   8 each ....

13.2 Think of a computer which people speak into and it writes what they say. Here, the person speaking didn't make the difference clear between R and L. The underlined words are wrong. Correct them.

late   *arrive*
I worked <u>rate</u> that day and I didn't <u>alive</u> home until 10 o'clock. I was very wet because of the <u>lane</u>. Then, to my <u>supplies</u>, my key didn't fit in the <u>rock</u>. So I looked closely at my keys and saw that they were the <u>long</u> ones. I had left my house keys at work. So I got back on my motorbike and <u>load</u> back to the office to <u>correct</u> them. I got home really tired, so I went to bed, <u>led</u> for half an hour, switched off the <u>right</u> and went to sleep.

(A60) **Follow up:** Listen to the correct text. Then read it out yourself, making sure that you pronounce the corrected words clearly. Record yourself if you can.

13.3 Circle the word in which the letters L or R are silent. (Imagine the accent is from South East England, so the R is silent if there is no vowel sound after it.)

EXAMPLE cold (calm) collect film

1 court   correct   curry   dairy   4 shoulder   should   sailor   slow
2 follow   fold   folk   file   5 artist   arrow   arrive   around
3 hurry   hairy   hungry   hair

13.4 Listen and circle the word you hear. If you find any of these difficult, go to Section D4 *Sound pairs*
(A61) for further practice.

1 Surprise or supplies?   The *surprise / supplies* came later.   (⇒sound pair 50)
2 Collect or correct?   I'll *correct / collect* it tomorrow.   (⇒sound pair 50)
3 Flight or fright?   We had a great *flight / fright*.   (⇒sound pair 50)
4 Trees or cheese?   I saw something in the *trees / cheese*!   (⇒sound pair 47)
5 Jaw or drawer?   She broke her lower *jaw / drawer*.   (⇒sound pair 47)

Follow up: Record yourself saying the sentences in 13.4, choosing one of the two words. Make a note of which words you say. Then listen to your recording in about two weeks. Is it clear which words you said?

Now go to Unit 33

14 Car, care
The vowel sounds /ɑː(r)/ and /eə(r)/

In many accents in England, the letter R is not pronounced after a vowel. In other places, the R *is* pronounced, for example in most parts of North America. But in both cases, the letter R makes the vowel before it sound different. If the vowel is A, we usually get the vowel sounds in *car* /ɑː/ or *care* /eə/.

A

A62a • Listen to the sound /ɑː/. Look at the mouth diagram to see how to make this long vowel sound.

A62b • Listen to the target sound /ɑː/ in the words below and compare it with the words on each side.

A62c • Then listen and repeat the examples of the target sound.

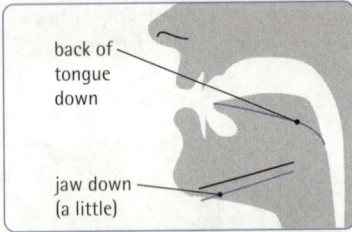

target /ɑː/

fur	far	four
bore	bar	bear
hurt	heart	hate
much	march	match

back of tongue down

jaw down (a little)

Examples
calm   card   cart
star   starve   start
harm   halve   half

"It's hard to park a car in a dark car park."

⚠ Note: Sometimes we get the sound /ɑː/ before L too.

A63

Important for listening

• Listen to the sound with R pronounced, as in North America:
  far   bar   heart   march   card   star   start   charm   chart
• In South East England, the letter A followed by S, F, TH, N is often pronounced /ɑː/:
  ask   fast   after   path   bath   dance   aunt
• In North America, the single letter O is pronounced /ɑː/: *God, strong, lock, top.* (See Unit 16.)

B

A64a • Listen to the sound /eə/. Look at the mouth diagram to see how to make this sound.

A64b • Listen to the target sound /eə/ in the words below and compare it with the words on each side.

A64c • Then listen and repeat the examples of the target sound.

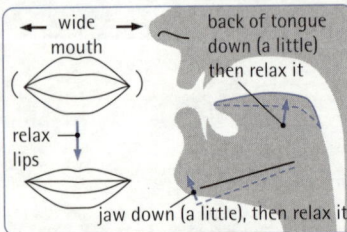

wide mouth

back of tongue down (a little) then relax it

relax lips

jaw down (a little), then relax it

target /eə/

bar	bear	beer
shy	share	sure
dead	dared	died
stars	stairs	stays

Examples
square   squares
where   where's
fair   fairly

"Sarah and Mary share their pears fairly."

A65

Important for listening

Different accents: Listen to the sound with the R pronounced, as in North America:
bear   share   dared   stairs   square   where   cared   fairly

C

Spelling

	frequently	sometimes
/ɑː/	AR (*car*) AL (*half*)	EAR, (*heart*) A (*ask, path, aunt*): South East English accent
/eə/	ARE (*care*), AIR (*fair*) EAR (*bear*), ERE (*where*)	

Exercises

14.1 Make words with these beginnings and endings and write them in the correct part of the table.

beginnings	ba	fa	ra	da	sta	squa	ca	ha	cha
endings	r	re	lf	ir	rd	rt	lm		

words with the vowel /ɑː/	words with the vowel /eə/
bar	bare

14.2 Complete this conversation using the words in the box. Then listen and check.

A66

> cars   cares   stars   stairs

SID: This is a great life, with no worries or ___cares___ !

JOE: It would be nice if we had _____ though, Sid.

SID: I didn't say _____, I said _____!

JOE: Oh, I see. Not _____, as in traffic, but _____ with an ES at the end!

SID: That's right. I've always loved sleeping under the _____.

JOE: But why? There's hardly any space under the _____!

SID: No, not _____, _____! You know, little lights in the sky.

JOE: Oh, _____! I thought you said _____, that people walk up!

> **Follow up:** Play the recording again, pausing the recording after each of Sid's lines. You say Joe's lines before listening to him saying them.

14.3 Listen to these sentences. Is the accent from North America (they pronounce the R after the vowel) or South East England? Write *Am* or *Eng*.

A67

EXAMPLE   He asked her to dance. ___Eng___

1 We started in March. _____
2 It's a fast car. _____
3 My heart's strong. _____
4 Where's the bar? _____
5 It stops and starts. _____
6 A glass of beer. _____
7 Was his hair dark or fair? _____

14.4 Listen and circle the word you hear. If you find any of these difficult, go to Section D4 *Sound pairs* for further practice.

A68

1 Heart or hat?   She put her hand on her *heart / hat*.   (⇒sound pair 3)
2 Nowhere or no way?   There's *nowhere / no way* to go.   (⇒sound pair 5)
3 Fair or far?   It isn't *fair / far*.   (⇒sound pair 6)
4 Part or port?   This is the main *part / port* of Athens.   (⇒sound pair 7)
5 Bear or beer?   That's a strong *bear / beer*.   (⇒sound pair 8)
6 Come or calm?   She told me to *come / calm* down.   (⇒sound pair 9)

Now go to Unit 34

15 Some, sun, sung
The consonant sounds /m/, /n/ and /ŋ/

The consonant sounds /m/, /n/ and /ŋ/ are made by stopping the flow of air out of the mouth so that it goes through the nose instead. The three sounds are different because the air is stopped by different parts of the mouth. You can feel this when you say the words *some, sun, sung*.

A A69a • Listen to the sound /m/. Look at the mouth diagram to see how to make this sound.

⚠ **Note:** Always close your lips for /m/, even at the end of a word when the next word begins with /k/ or /g/, for example: cream cake; warm glow.

A69b • Listen to the target sound /m/ in the words below and compare it with the words on each side.

A69c • Then listen and repeat the examples of the target sound.

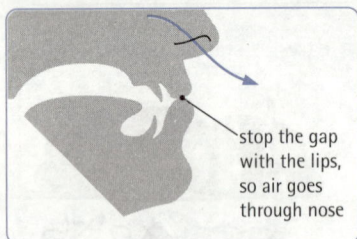

target /m/

nice	**mice**	nice
sun	**some**	sun
swing	**swim**	swing
hang	**ham**	hang

Examples

miss   more   make
smoke   jump   harmed
comb   autumn film

"Mum made me move my models."

B A70a • Listen to the sound /n/. Look at the mouth diagram to see how to make this sound.

A70b • Listen to the target sound /n/ in the words below and compare it with the words on each side.

A70c • Then listen and repeat the examples of the target sound.

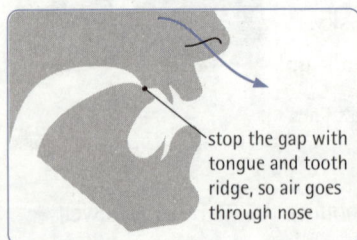

target /n/

might	**night**	might
warm	**warn**	warm
wing	**win**	wing
rang	**ran**	rang

Examples

now   new   know
snow   dinner against
gone   open   listen

"There was no one on the moon on the ninth of June."

C A71a • Listen to the sound /ŋ/. Look at the mouth diagram to see how to make this sound.

⚠ **Note:** Open your mouth but breathe through your nose. If you do this you will find that the air is stopped at the back of the mouth. This is where you stop the air to make the sound /ŋ/.

A71b • Listen to the target sound /ŋ/ in the words below and compare it with the words on each side.

A71c • Then listen and repeat the examples of the target sound.

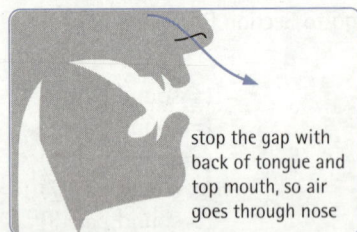

target /ŋ/

some	**sung**	some
Kim	**king**	Kim
thin	**thing**	thin

Examples

sing   singer sink
bang   bank   banks
thing   think   finger

"Young King Kong was stronger than strong."

D Notes on spelling: There may be a silent B or N after /m/ (*comb, autumn*). There may be a silent K before /n/ (*knife*). /n/ changes to /ŋ/ when the next sound after it is /k/ or /g/; the N in *thin* is /n/, but the N in *think* is /ŋ/.

Exercises

15.1 Read this conversation. It contains 19 examples of the sound /m/. How many examples of the sounds
(A72) /n/ and /ŋ/ does it contain? Write your answers. Then listen and check.

> I met a man near the monument this morning. He was a singer and he sang a song for me. I'll always remember that magic moment. Like something out of a dream!

> What, is that the moment, the monument or the man you meant?

15.2 Find a way from Start to Finish. You may pass a square only if the word in it has the sound /ŋ/.
You can move horizontally (↔) or vertically (↕) only.

START

sing	think	thick	strong	wrong	rung
sign	uncle	unless	drug	strange	comb
thanks	angry	signal	drank	English	finger
anxious	angel	single	monkey	money	young
language	tongue	skiing	skin	came	ink
lounge	danger	band	dream	swim	wing

FINISH

15.3 Complete this conversation using words from the box.
(A73) Then listen and check.

worn	warm	thing	thin

SID: Hey, Joe, your coat is very worn.

JOE: No, it isn't .... I always feel cold in this coat.

SID: No, not ....! I said ...., with an N!

JOE: Oh, ... with an N!

SID: Yes, the cloth is ....

JOE: What do you mean "the cloth is .... "?

SID: No, ... with an N at the end, not .... with a G at the end!

15.4 Listen and circle the word you hear. If you find any of these difficult, go to Section D4 *Sound pairs*
(A74) for further practice.

1 Robin or robbing?   My friend likes *Robin Banks* / *robbing banks*.   (⇒sound pair 48)
2 Ran or rang?   Tom *ran* / *rang* yesterday.   (⇒sound pair 48)
3 Swing or swim?   She had a *swing* / *swim* in the garden.   (⇒sound pair 49)
4 Warned or warmed?   The *son warned* / *sun warmed* me.   (⇒sound pair 49)
5 Singing or sinking?   The people were *singing* / *sinking* fast.   (⇒sound pair 48)

> **Follow up:** Record yourself saying the sentences in 15.4, choosing one of the two words or expressions. Make a note of which words you say. Then listen to your recording in about two weeks. Is it clear which words you said?

Now go to Unit 35 ▶

16

Note, not
The vowel sounds /əʊ/ and /ɒ/

When you say the letters of the alphabet, O has the long vowel sound /əʊ/. You hear this sound in the word *note*. But the letter O is also pronounced as the short vowel sound /ɒ/, as in the word *not*.

A

A75a • Listen to the sound /əʊ/. Look at the mouth diagram to see how to make this long vowel sound.

A75b • Listen to the target sound /əʊ/ in the words below and compare it with the words on each side.

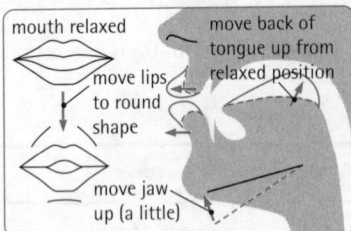

mouth relaxed
move lips to round shape
move back of tongue up from relaxed position
move jaw up (a little)

target /əʊ/

bought	**boat**	boot
blouse	**blows**	blues
cost	**coast**	cast
ball	**bowl**	bull

"Rose knows Joe phones Sophie, but Sophie and Joe don't know Rose knows."

A75c • Listen and repeat these examples of the target sound.

toe   toes   toast
comb   code   coat
roll   rose   rope

B

A76a • Listen to the sound /ɒ/. Look at the mouth diagram to see how to make this short vowel sound.

A76b • Listen to the target sound /ɒ/ in the words below and compare it with the words on each side.

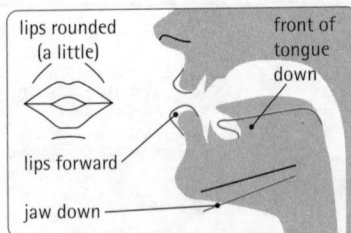

lips rounded (a little)
front of tongue down
lips forward
jaw down

target /ɒ/

won't	**want**	went
luck	**lock**	lack
get	**got**	goat
fund	**fond**	phoned

A76c • Listen and repeat these examples of the target sound.

wrong   rob   rock
gone   God   got
doll   dog   dock

"John wants to watch Walter wash the dog."

Important for listening

In North America, the sound /ɒ/ is replaced by /ɑː/. For this reason, the following words may sound similar if an English speaker says the first word and an American speaker says the second word: *part – pot, heart – hot, shark – shock, barks – box.*

C

Spelling

	frequently	sometimes	notes
/əʊ/	O (*old*), O-E (*stone*) OW (*show*), OA (*coat*) OE (*toe*)		If there is an R after the letter O (and the R does not have a vowel after it), O has a different pronunciation. (See Unit 19.)
/ɒ/	O (*dog*)	A (*wash*)	

Exercises

16.1 Find 14 words in the puzzle (every letter is used once) and write them in the correct part of the table. The words are written horizontally (→) or vertically (↓).

c	s	h	o	p	r	w
o	s	o	n	g	o	h
l	r	s	w	s	c	a
d	o	h	a	n	k	t
b	a	o	n	o	r	w
o	d	w	t	w	o	a
t	j	o	k	e	l	s
h	c	o	a	t	l	h

words with /əʊ/	words with /ɒ/
cold	

16.2 Read the words and circle the one with the different vowel sound. Then listen and check.

(A77) **EXAMPLE** soap hope sold (soup)

1 come gone long want
2 what hot most salt
3 drove love woke hole
4 snow low cow show

5 both cloth clothes road
6 word wash boss cost
7 post lost coast rose

16.3 Listen. You will hear the sentences twice, once in American English (A), once in British English (B). (A78) Write the order A–B or B–A.

EXAMPLE The coffee's hot. ....A–B........

1 The lock's at the top. ....
2 The song's long. ....
3 Stop the clock. ....
4 The dog's gone. ....
5 He's often wrong. ....

16.4 Listen and circle the word you hear. If you find any of these difficult, go to Section D4 *Sound pairs* (A79) for further practice.

1 Cost or coast? What's the *cost / coast* like?   (⇒sound pair 14)
2 Shot or shut? They *shot / shut* the door.   (⇒sound pair 15)
3 Boat or boot? There's water in my *boat / boot*.   (⇒sound pair 16)
4 Woke or walk? I *woke / walk* the dog.   (⇒sound pair 17)
5 Phoned or found? Tim *phoned / found* her.   (⇒sound pair 18)

Follow up: Record yourself saying the sentences in 16.4, choosing one of the two words. Make a note of which words you say. Then listen to your recording in about two weeks. Is it clear which words you said?

Now go to Unit 36

Arthur's mother
The consonant sounds /θ/ and /ð/

A A80a • Listen to the two sounds /θ/ and /ð/. Notice that in /θ/, there is no voice from the throat. Instead, you can feel the air from your mouth on your hand. In the sound /ð/ there is voice from the throat. It is possible to make both sounds long. Look at the mouth diagram to see how to make these consonant sounds.

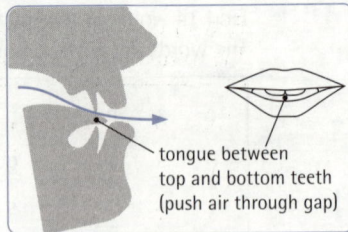

tongue between
top and bottom teeth
(push air through gap)

B A80b • Now listen to the sound /θ/ on its own.

A80c • Listen to the target sound /θ/ in the words below and compare it with the words on each side.

target /θ/

sick	**thick**	sick
boat	**both**	boat
free	**three**	free

A80d • Listen and repeat these examples of the target sound.
thank   **th**ink   **th**ought
heal**th**y   bir**th**day   ma**th**s
ear**th**   leng**th**   four**th**

"Martha Smith's an author and an athlete."

C A81a • Listen to the sound /ð/ on its own.

A81b • Listen to the target sound /ð/ in the words below and compare it with the words on each side.

target /ð/

breed	**breathe**	breed
den	**then**	den
van	**than**	van

A81c • Listen and repeat these examples of the target sound.
these   **th**ough   **th**ey
o**th**er   wea**th**er   clo**th**es
brea**th**e   wi**th**   sunba**th**e

"My father and mother live together with my other brother."

> Important for listening
>
> • Many native speakers of English pronounce TH as /t/, /f/ or /s/ instead of /θ/, and /d/, /v/ or /z/ instead of /ð/. For example, some Irish speakers pronounce *thick* /θɪk/ as *tick* /tɪk/.
> • Some London speakers pronounce *three* /θriː/ as *free* /friː/. Some Nigerian speakers pronounce *then* /ðen/ as *den* /den/.

D
Spelling

	always	notes
/θ/	TH (*three*)	In a few names of places and people, TH is pronounced as /t/ (*Thailand, Thomas*).
/ð/	TH (*then*)	

Exercises

17.1 Find a way from Start to Finish. You may pass a square only if the word in it has the sound /θ/.
You can move horizontally (↔) or vertically (↕) only.

START

north	northern	either	weather	breathe	those
south	bath	bathe	thought	breath	youth
southern	third	their	through	though	thumb
Thailand	cloth	path	fifth	with	worth
month	clothes	these	brother	that	teeth
throw	thing	author	other	they	wealth

FINISH

17.2 Complete this rhyme using words from the box. Then listen and check.

(A82)

earth	Heather	~~brother~~	neither	mothers	brothers
~~another~~	together	birth	either		

Arthur had a ....brother..........

And he didn't want ....another.......... .

And of the brothers, ...

Wanted sisters ....

The last thing on this ....

They wanted was a ....

So Arthur's mother ....

Got them both .... ,

And told them all good ....

Should learn to share their ....

Follow up: Listen to the poem again. Pause the recording after each line and repeat it.

17.3 Think of a computer which people speak into and it writes what they say. This computer wrote these
sentences down wrongly. Correct the underlined mistakes.

EXAMPLE It's <u>free</u> o'clock. ....three..........

1 A <u>bat</u> is more relaxing than a shower. ....

2 The train went <u>true</u> the tunnel. ....

3 Don't walk on the ice; it's very <u>fin</u>. ....

4 You need a <u>sick</u> coat in winter. ....

5 I don't know; I haven't <u>fought</u> about it. ....

6 It's a matter of life and <u>deaf</u>. ....

17.4 Listen and circle the word you hear. If you find any of these difficult, go to Section D4 *Sound pairs*
(A83) for further practice.

1 Youth or use?   There's no *youth / use* talking about that.   (⇒sound pair 33)

2 Thought or taught?   I don't know what she *thought / taught*.   (⇒sound pair 35)

3 Free or three?   *Free / Three* refills with each packet!   (⇒sound pair 39)

4 Closed or clothed?   They weren't fully *closed / clothed*.   (⇒sound pair 33)

5 Breeding or breathing?   They've stopped *breeding / breathing*.   (⇒sound pair 35)

6 These are or visa?   *These are / Visa* problems we can deal with later.   (⇒sound pair 39)

Follow up: Record yourself saying the sentences in 17.4, choosing one
of the two words. Make a note of which words you say. Then listen to
your recording in about two weeks. Is it clear which words you said?

Now go to Unit 37

18 Sun, full, June
The vowel sounds /ʌ/, /ʊ/ and /uː/

When you say the letters of the alphabet, U has the long vowel sound /uː/ (we say it with the consonant /j/ in front of it). You hear the /uː/ sound in the word *June*. But the letter U is also pronounced as the short vowel sounds /ʌ/ or /ʊ/, as in the words *sun* and *full*.

A

A84a • Listen to the sound /ʌ/. Look at the mouth diagram to see how to make this short vowel sound.

A84b • Listen to the target sound /ʌ/ in the words below and compare it with the words on each side.

A84c • Then listen and repeat the examples of the target sound.

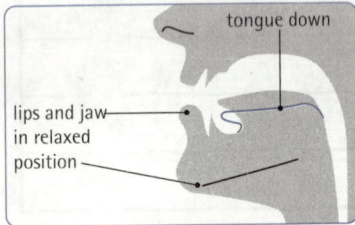

tongue down

lips and jaw in relaxed position

target /ʌ/

shoot	shut	shirt
match	much	March
look	luck	lock

Examples

come   blood   cut
young   does   must

"My mother's brother's my uncle; my uncle's son's my cousin."

> **Important for listening**
>
> In the North of England, speakers may use /ʊ/ in place of /ʌ/, so *luck* /lʌk/ sounds like *look* /lʊk/.

B

A85a • Listen to the sound /ʊ/. Look at the mouth diagram to see how to make this short vowel sound.

A85b • Listen to the target sound /ʊ/ in the words below and compare it with the words on each side.

A85c • Then listen and repeat the examples of the target sound.

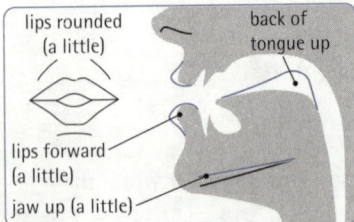

lips rounded (a little)   back of tongue up

lips forward (a little)

jaw up (a little)

target /ʊ/

luck	look	Luke
pool	pull	Paul

Examples

full   good   foot
wolf   would   put

"That cook couldn't cook if he didn't look at a cook book."

C

A86a • Listen to the sound /uː/. Look at the mouth diagram to see how to make this long vowel sound.

A86b • Listen to the target sound /uː/ in the words below and compare it with the words on each side.

A86c • Then listen and repeat the examples of the target sound.

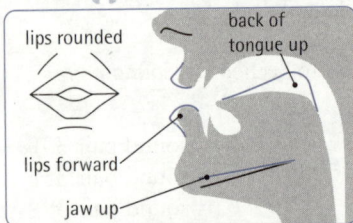

lips rounded   back of tongue up

lips forward

jaw up

target /uː/

full	fool	fall
road	rude	rod
but	boot	boat

Examples

shoe   shoes   shoot
new   lose   soup

"Sue knew too few new tunes on the flute."

> **Important for listening**
>
> Many words which have /j/ before /uː/ in British English don't in American English. Compare: *news* /njuːz/ – *news* /nuːz/, *tune* /tjuːn/ – *tune* /tuːn/.

D

Notes on spelling: If there is an R after the letter U (and the R does not have a vowel after it), U has a different pronunciation. (See Unit 19.)

Exercises

18.1 Listen to this student. Do the underlined words have an /ʌ/ or /uː/ sound? Write them in the correct
(A87) part of the table.

> I <u>studied</u> English at a <u>school</u> in <u>London</u> last
> <u>summer</u>. I was there for <u>two</u> <u>months</u>: May
> and <u>June</u>. England is famous for bad <u>food</u> and
> weather, but I thought the food was good.
> The <u>pub</u> <u>lunches</u> were very nice. But it's <u>true</u>
> about the weather. <u>Too</u> <u>much</u> rain for me!

/ʌ/	/uː/
studied	school

Follow up: Listen again and repeat sentence by sentence.

18.2 Complete these sentences with words from the box. The vowel sound is given. Listen, check and repeat.
(A88)

brother	wood	moon	juice	won	month	June
would	full	~~boot~~	Cup	~~put~~	son	good	

EXAMPLE
Two things you can ......*put*...... /ʊ/ on a foot are a shoe and a ......*boot*...... /uː/.

1 The .... /ʌ/ after .... /uː/ is July.

2 My mother's other .... /ʌ/ is my .... /ʌ/.

3 Brazil .... /ʌ/ the World .... /ʌ/ in 2002.

4 Fruit .... /uː/ is .... /ʊ/ for you.

5 There is a .... /ʊ/ .... /uː/ once a month.

6 You pronounce .... /ʊ/ exactly the same as .... /ʊ/.

18.3 Circle the word with the different vowel sound. You can use a dictionary if you are not sure.

EXAMPLE foot look (blood) push   4 pull full put rule
1 soon book boot room   5 group could would should
2 rude luck run but   6 done move love son
3 shoes does true blue   7 south young couple won

18.4 Listen and circle the word you hear. If you find any of these difficult, go to Section D4 *Sound pairs*
(A89) for further practice.

1 Cut or cat? There's a *cut / cat* on the arm of the sofa.   (⇒sound pair 2)
2 Come or calm? You should try to *come / calm* down.   (⇒sound pair 9)
3 Gun or gone? He's taken his dog and *gun / gone*.   (⇒sound pair 15)
4 Shoes or shows? I've never seen her *shoes / shows* on TV.   (⇒sound pair 16)
5 Pool or pull? It said *'pool' / 'pull'* on the door.   (⇒sound pair 19)
6 Luck or look? It's just her *luck / look*!   (⇒sound pair 20)
7 Shirt or shut? The hairdresser's *shirt / shut*.   (⇒sound pair 21)
8 A gun or again? He shot *a gun / again*.   (⇒sound pair 22)

Follow up: Record yourself saying the sentences in 18.4, choosing one
of the two words. Make a note of which word you say. Then listen to
your recording in about two weeks. Is it clear which words you said?

> Now go to Unit 38 ▶

Shirt, short
The vowel sounds /ɜː(r)/ and /ɔː(r)/

A In many accents in England, the letter R is not pronounced after a vowel. In other places, the R *is* pronounced, for example in North America. But in both cases, the letter R changes the vowel sound before it. If the vowel letter is E, I, O or U, we often get the vowel sounds in *shirt* or *short*.

B A90a • Listen to the sound /ɜː/. Look at the mouth diagram to see how to make this long vowel sound.

A90b • Listen to the target sound /ɜː/ in the words below and compare it with the words on each side.

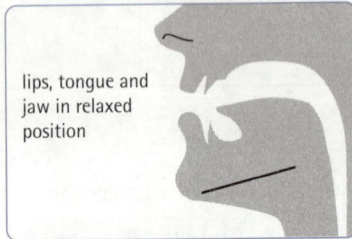

lips, tongue and jaw in relaxed position

target /ɜː/

short	**shirt**	shut
where	**were**	we're
born	**burn**	bone
hard	**heard**	head

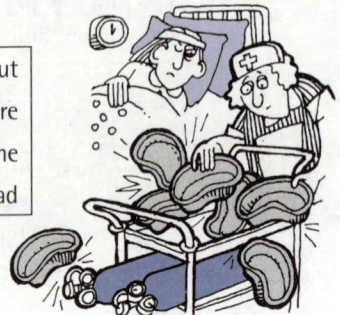

A90c • Listen and repeat these examples of the target language.

were	word	worst
burn	bird	birth
her	heard	hurt

"The girl heard the nurse work."

C A91a • Listen to the sound /ɔː/. Look at the mouth diagram to see how to make this long vowel sound.

A91b • Listen to the target sound /ɔː/ in the words below and compare it with the words on each side.

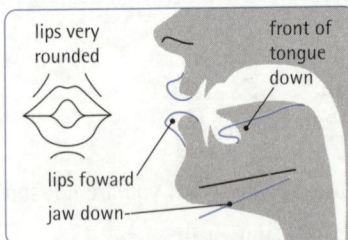

lips very rounded

front of tongue down

lips foward

jaw down

target /ɔː/

shot	**short**	shirt
work	**walk**	woke
far	**four**	fair
boil	**ball**	bowl

A91c • Listen and repeat the examples of the target sound.

bore	bored	bought
call	cause	caught
war	wall	walk

"Laura's daughter bought a horse and called it Laura."

A92

Important for listening

• Listen to the following words with the R pronounced, as in North America:
shirt were heard worst birth hurt born short door four war more

• In words without R, some American speakers pronounce the sound /ɑː/ instead of /ɔː/.
Listen: *ball caught law talk bought.*

D ## Spelling

	I / E / O / U + R	other spellings
/ɜː/	IR (*girl*), ER (*her*), UR (*hurt*)	OR (*word*), EAR (*heard*)
/ɔː/	OR (*form*)	A (*call*), AR (*war*), AU (*cause*), AW (*saw*), AL (*walk*), AUGH (*taught*), OUGH (*thought*), OUR (*four*)

Exercises

19.1 Write these numbers out in full. Which of the two vowel sounds do they contain? Write /ɜː/ or/ɔː/.

EXAMPLE   3rd   ....*third*............ /ɜː/

1 $\frac{1}{4}$ ....

4 1st ....

2 30 ....

5 14 ....

3 4th ....

19.2 Find 14 words in the puzzle (every letter is used once) and write them in the correct part of the table. The words are written horizontally (→) or vertically (↓).

b	b	t	c	o	u	r	s	e
i	a	u	h	w	s	w	a	r
r	l	r	e	o	o	h	g	m
d	l	n	a	r	r	e	i	o
s	a	w	r	d	t	r	r	r
l	a	w	d	a	l	l	e	

words with /ɜː/	words with /ɔː/
bird	

19.3 Listen to these sentences. Is the accent from Britain or America? Write B or A.

(A93)

EXAMPLE   The girl's first birthday. ..A..

1 It's hard work, of course. ....

2 Are you sure? ....

3 Law and order. ....

4 I walk to work. ....

5 I saw the bird fall. ....

6 He was born on Thursday the thirty-first. ....

7 She taught German. ....

8 I learned to surf in Brazil. ....

9 'Caught' and 'court' sound the same in my accent. ....

19.4 Listen and circle the word you hear. If you find any of these difficult, go to Section D4 *Sound pairs* for further practice.

(A94)

1 Four or far?   It isn't *four / far*. (⇒sound pair 7)
2 Worst or west?   It's on the *worst / west* coast. (⇒sound pair 12)
3 Walk or woke?   I *walk / woke* the dog. (⇒sound pair 17)
4 Shut or shirt?   The butcher's *shut / shirt*. (⇒sound pair 21)
5 Port or pot?   There's coffee in the *port / pot*. (⇒sound pair 23)
6 Bird or beard?   He has a black *bird / beard*. (⇒sound pair 24)
7 Her or hair?   Is that *her / hair*? (⇒sound pair 25)
8 Worked or walked?   We *worked / walked* all day. (⇒sound pair 26)

Follow up: Record yourself saying the sentences in 19.4, choosing one of the two words. Make a note of which words you say. Then listen to your recording in about two weeks. Is it clear which words you said?

Now go to Unit 39

20

Toy, town
The vowel sounds /ɔɪ/ and /aʊ/

A

A95a ● Listen to the sound /ɔɪ/. Look at the mouth diagram to see how to make this long vowel sound.

A95b ● Listen to the target sound /ɔɪ/ in the words below and compare it with the words on each side.

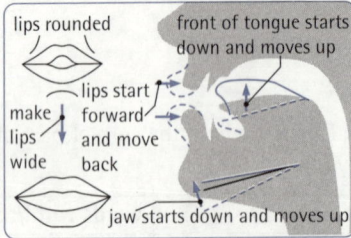

lips rounded   front of tongue starts down and moves up

lips start
make forward
lips and move
wide back

jaw starts down and moves up

target /ɔɪ/

buy	boy	bay
pint	point	paint
all	oil	I'll

"Roy enjoys noisy toys."

A95c ● Listen and repeat these examples of the target sound.

toy   noise   voice
boil   coin   choice
employ   enjoyed

B

A96a ● Listen to the sound /aʊ/. Look at the mouth diagram to see how to make this long vowel sound.

A96b ● Listen to the target sound /aʊ/ in the words below and compare it with the words on each side.

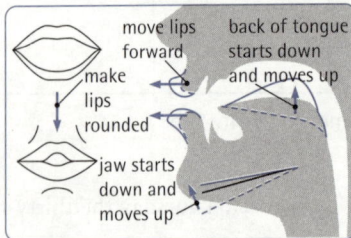

move lips   back of tongue
forward   starts down
make   and moves up
lips
rounded

jaw starts
down and
moves up

target /aʊ/

fond	found	phoned
know	now	new
car	cow	care

"Mrs Brown counted cows coming down the mountain."

A96c ● Listen and repeat these examples of the target sound.

how   houses   house
now   sound   south
town   ground   count

Important for listening

● When the vowel sound /ɔɪ/ is before L, e.g. *oil*, *boil*, soil, many speakers put the vowel /ə/ between them. You may find it easier to say it this way.
● When the vowel sound /aʊ/ is before R or L, many speakers put the vowel /ə/ between them, so *hour* rhymes with *shower*, and *foul* rhymes with *towel*.

A97 ● Listen to these words with the R pronounced, as in North America:
hour, power, shower, flour, flower, tower

C

Spelling

	frequently	notes
/ɔɪ/	OY(*boy*), OI (*coin*)	
/aʊ/	OW (*cow*), OU (*loud*)	Various different vowel sounds are spelt OW or OU.

Exercises

20.1 Put one of the letters *y, i, u* or *w* in each gap to make a word. The word must contain the sound /ɔɪ/ or /aʊ/. Write /ɔɪ/ or /aʊ/ after each word.

EXAMPLE   to_n ...*town* /aʊ/...

1 bo_s	4 po_nt	7 ho__r ....
2 no_se	5 ho_	8 flo_er ....
3 fo_nd	6 bo_l	9 enjo_ ....

20.2 Listen to this text. Find words from it which have an /ɔɪ/ or /aʊ/ sound and write them in the correct part of the table.

(A98)

I enjoy living down town. Well, it's very noisy, of course. The traffic is loud, and the young people often shout when they come out of the clubs. But there are lots of good points too. There's a big choice of shops, and it's easy to get around.

/ɔɪ/ (4 words)	/aʊ/ (6 words)
enjoy	

Follow up: Listen again and repeat, sentence by sentence.

20.3 Find a way from Start to Finish. You may pass a square only if the word in it has the sound /aʊ/. You can move horizontally (↔) or vertically (↕) only.

START

house	sound	group	about	mouth	cow
soup	out	brown	mouse	bought	south
could	couple	grow	low	would	cloud
know	snow	touch	ought	down	count
thought	should	slow	blow	pound	young
soul	country	though	throw	town	round

FINISH

20.4 Listen and circle the words you hear.

(A99)

1 Tie or toy?   He got a *tie* / *toy* for his birthday.
2 Goodbye or Good boy?   '*Goodbye!*' / '*Good boy!*' she said.
3 Phoned or found?   She *phoned* / *found* a friend.
4 Tone or town?   What an ugly *tone* / *town*!

Follow up: Record yourself saying the sentences in 20.4, choosing one of the two words. Make a note of which words you say. Then listen to your recording in about two weeks. Is it clear which words you said?

Now go to Unit 40

21 Eye, my, mine
Introducing syllables

A

We can divide a word into one or more syllables. For example *mum* has one syllable, *mother* has two syllables and *grandmother* has three syllables. A syllable is a group of one or more sounds. The essential part of a syllable is a vowel sound (V). Some syllables are just one vowel sound. For example, these words have one syllable, and the syllable is just one vowel sound:
eye /aɪ/, owe /əʊ/.

A syllable can have consonant sounds (C) before the V, after the V or before *and* after the V. Here are some more examples (they are all words of one syllable).

CV	VC	CVC
go /gəʊ/	if /ɪf/	ten /ten/
my /maɪ/	egg /eg/	nose /nəʊz/
know /nəʊ/	ice /aɪs/	mouth /maʊθ/
weigh /weɪ/	eight /eɪt/	knife /naɪf/

⚠️ Note: There may be *more* than one C before or after the V. (See Units 24, 25.)

B

Remember that letters are *not* the same as sounds. For example, the consonant *letters* W and Y are not consonant *sounds* if they come after the vowel sound in the syllable e.g. *saw*, *say*. They are part of the vowel sound. In some accents, for example South East English, the same is true for the consonant letter R. Here are some more examples. They are words of one syllable and they all have the pattern CV.

how /haʊ/   law /lɔː/   pay /peɪ/   why /waɪ/   car /kaː/   hair /heə/

C

Some people use the word *syllable* to talk about the parts of a written word. But in this book, the word *syllable* is used to talk about the *pronunciation* of words, not the writing. For example, in writing we can divide 'chocolate' into three parts like this: cho-co-late. But when we say the word, we pronounce only two syllables, like this: chocolate /ˈtʃɒk.lət/. (The dot shows where the two syllables are divided.) A number of other words may be pronounced with fewer syllables than in writing. Listen to these examples.

🎧 B1
chocolate /ˈtʃɒk.lət/   different /ˈdɪf.rənt/   interesting /ˈɪn.trəs.tɪŋ/
general /ˈdʒen.rəl/   comfortable /ˈkʌmf.tə.bəl/   secretary /ˈsek.rə.trɪ/

D

The first syllable in these words has the same three sounds, but in the opposite order:
kitchen /ˈkɪtʃ.ɪn/ – chicken /ˈtʃɪk.ɪn/.

If a sentence has similar-sounding syllables like this in it, it may be difficult to say. These sentences are called 'tongue-twisters'. Listen to this example.

🎧 B2   Richard checked the chicken in the kitchen.

⚠️ Note: You can find more about syllables in Units 24 to 27.

Exercises

21.1 Write these words in the correct column.

| aunt | cook | dad | doctor | grandfather | officer |
| passenger | sister | teacher | uncle |

1 syllable	2 syllables	3 syllables
aunt		

21.2 Look at these one-syllable words. Write C where there is a consonant sound. There may be one before V, after V or in both places.

EXAMPLES high   *C* V

  rice   *C* V *C*

1 bought   V

2 eyes   V

3 key   V

4 day   V

5 through   V

6 laugh   V

7 two   V

8 youth   V

9 weigh   V

10 rhyme   V

21.3 The spelling changes if you change the order of sounds in these one-syllable words from CV to VC. Write the missing words.

	CV		VC	
EXAMPLE	/lɔː/ =	*law*	/ɔːl/ =	*all*
1	/deɪ/ =		/eɪd/ = aid	
2	/nəʊ/ =		/əʊn/ = own	
3	/peɪ/ =		/eɪp/ = ape	
4	/tiː/ = tea		/iːt/ =	
5	/meɪ/ = may		/eɪm/ =	
6	/seɪ/ =		/eɪs/ = ace	

21.4 Read the text aloud. Record your voice if you can. Then
B3 listen to the recording. Did you say the same number of syllables in the underlined words as on the recording?

> I went to an <u>interesting</u> <u>restaurant</u> on <u>Wednesday</u>. First I had chicken with a lot of <u>different</u> <u>vegetables</u>. Then I had a piece of <u>chocolate</u> cake. In <u>general</u>, I don't like chocolate, but the cake was <u>lovely</u>.

21.5 Listen to these tongue-twisters. How many syllables
B4 are there in each? Write the number.
Then listen again and repeat.

EXAMPLE She sells sea shells on the sea shore. =   *8 syllables*

1 Walter walked towards the waiter.   =

2 Betty bought a better bit of butter.   =

3 The fat cat sat on the vet's wet hat.   =

> Now go to Unit 41

English Pronunciation in Use   **51**

Saturday September 13th
Introducing word stress

A

If a word has more than one syllable, you give stress to one of the syllables. To give it stress, do one or more of these to the syllable:

- Make it longer. **Saturday**
- Make it louder. **Saturday**
- Make it higher. **Saturday**

We can show stress with circles: each circle is a syllable and the bigger circle shows which syllable has the stress. For example, *Saturday* is Ooo.

B5 Listen to the conversation and listen to the stress patterns of the words in bold type.

A: When do you **begin** your **holiday**?
o O   O o o

B: On the **thirtieth** of **August**.
O o o   O o

A: That's next **Saturday**!
O o o

B: We're leaving in the **afternoon**.
o o O

A: And when are you coming back?

B: Saturday **September** the **thirteenth**.
o O o   o O

A: **Thirtieth**?
O o o

B: No, **thirteenth**!
o O

B

B6 Different words have different stress patterns (patterns of stressed and unstressed syllables). Listen to these two- and three-syllable words.

Oo	**A**pril, **thir**ty, **mor**ning, **Sun**day
oO	Ju**ly**, mid**day**, thir**teen**, to**day**, thir**teenth**
Ooo	**Sat**urday, **thir**tieth, **yes**terday, **hol**iday, **sev**enty

oOo	Sep**tem**ber, to**morr**ow, e**lev**enth
ooO	after**noon**, seven**teen**, twenty-**one**

⚠ Note: The stress pattern of numbers with -*teen* is sometimes different when the word is in a sentence. For example, the normal stress pattern of *nineteen* is oO, but when it is followed by a noun, e.g. *the nineteen nineties*, *nineteen people*, the pattern is Oo.

⚠ Note: *January* and *February* may be pronounced with the stress patterns Ooo or Oooo.

C

Stress patterns can help you hear the difference between similar words, for example, numbers ending in -*teen* or -*ty*. Listen to these examples.

B7
oO	Oo
thirteen	thirty
fourteen	forty
sixteen	sixty
eighteen	eighty
nineteen	ninety

⚠ Note: You can find more about word stress in Units 28 to 31.

Exercises

22.1 Write the full words in the correct column, according to their stress pattern.

~~Mon~~	Tues	Thu	Sat	today	tomorrow	Apr	Jul	Aug	Sept	Oct
Nov	holiday	2nd	11th	13	30	13th	30th	17	70	afternoon

Oo	oO	Ooo	oOo	ooO
Monday				

22.2 Write one word from 22.1 in each sentence below. The word must have the stress pattern shown. Then say the sentences.

1 I'm going to have a party on .... (Ooo).

2 My grandfather is .... (Ooo) years old.

3 I often sleep for an hour in the .... (ooO).

4 My birthday is on the .... (oOo) of March.

5 In Europe, the weather is warm in .... (oO).

6 I left school when I was .... (ooO).

7 Goodnight. See you .... (oOo).

8 How long is your summer .... (Ooo)?

22.3 Find a way from Start to Finish. You may pass a square only if the word has the stress pattern Ooo. You can move horizontally (↔) or vertically (↕) only.

START

eightieth	twentieth	thirtieth	September
twenty-one	thousand	yesterday	October
November	sixtieth	seventy	eleventh
second	fortieth	thirteen	seventeen
vacation	holiday	tomorrow	afternoon
December	Saturday	ninetieth	fiftieth

FINISH

22.4 Listen and circle the number you hear.

1 100 dollars! It only cost *17 / 70* last year!
2 He was the *14th / 40th* President of my country.
3 The maximum number of people is *15 / 50*.

4 She was born in *1916 / 1960*.
5 He was *13 / 30* on his last birthday.
6 She'll be *18 / 80* in March.

Now go to Unit 42

23 Remember, he told her
Introducing sentence stress

A B9 Individual words have a stress pattern, that is a pattern of strong and weak syllables. Sentences also have a stress pattern, and this is *sentence stress*. Sometimes a word and a sentence have the same stress pattern. Listen to these examples.

O o o		o O o		o o O	
word	sentence	word	sentence	word	sentence
photograph	**Answer** me!	Sep**tem**ber	Ex**cuse** me.	after**noon**	Do you **smoke?**
Canada	**Doesn't** he?	to**morrow**	I **think** so.	Japa**nese**	One of **these?**
cabbages	**Copy** it!	re**mem**ber	He **told** her.	Portu**guese**	He's a**rrived.**

B B10 Short sentences and phrases in English have some typical stress patterns. Listen to the examples.

OoO   What's the **time?**   **Yes**, of **course!**   **Thanks** a **lot!**
OoOo   See you **later!**   **Pleased** to **meet** you!   **Can't** you **hear** me?
oOoO   A **piece** of **cake.**   The **shop** was **closed.**   It's **time** to **go.**
OooO   **What** do you **do?**   **Where** do you **live?**   **Give** me a **call.**
ooOo   Are you **coming?**   Do you **like** it?   Is he **happy?**

⚠ Note: For more examples, see Section D5: *Sentence stress phrasebook.*

C There is normally a space between stressed syllables in a sentence. Unstressed syllables can be put in that space. The space stays more or less the same length whether one or more unstressed syllables are pushed into it. So for example, these three sentences take about the same length of time to say. Listen.

B11 OOO   **Don't tell Mike.**
OoOoOo   **Go** and **speak** to **Mary.**
OooOooOoo   **Hurry** and **give** it to **Jon**athan.

D Stress patterns can help you hear the difference between similar sentences. For example, verbs with the negative ending -*n't* are always stressed. This helps us to hear the difference between *can* and *can't* in the following two sentences, because the two sentences have different stress patterns.

ooO   He can **talk.**   oOO   He **can't talk.**

⚠ Note: You can find more about sentence stress in Units 32 to 40.

Exercises

23.1
B12
Listen and <u>underline</u> the sentence which does *not* have the same stress pattern as the word at the beginning of the line.

EXAMPLE

	Ooo	cinema	<u>Wasn't it?</u>	Hasn't she?	<u>Don't you?</u>
1	oOo	tomato	Close the door.	He told me.	I like it.
2	ooO	afternoon	Does he drive?	Were you cold?	What happened?
3	oOo	December	It's open.	They arrived.	They listened.

23.2
B13
Write these sentences in the correct column. Then listen, check and repeat.

~~The bus was late.~~	Come and look.	Close the window.	What do you want?
The water's cold.	Give me a call.	What did she say?	Phone and tell me.
Nice to see you.	Where's the car?	It's cold and wet.	What's the time?

OooO	oOoo	OoO	OoOo
	The bus was late.		

23.3
B14
Combine phrases from the boxes A, B and C to make three sentences or phrases with these patterns: OOO   OoOoOo   OooOooOoo. Then listen, check and repeat.

EXAMPLE

A	B	C
Half a	bottle of	beer
One	glass of	orange juice
Give me a	cold	water

OOO — One cold beer.
OoOoOo — Half a glass of water.
OooOooOoo — Give me a bottle of orange juice.

A	B	C
Doesn't	Jennifer	listen
Can't you make	Pete	talk to you
Can't	Oscar	drive

OOO — _____
OoOoOo — _____
OooOooOoo — _____

23.4
B15
Listen and tick the sentence you hear, A or B.

	A	B
1	I can swim.	I can't swim.
2	Are you coming?	Aren't you coming?
3	We were tired.	We weren't tired.
4	She can help you.	She can't help you.
5	Can you see?	Can't you see?
6	They were talking.	They weren't talking.

Now go to Unit 43

24 Oh, no snow!
Consonants at the start of syllables

A

Some one-syllable words are just a single vowel sound (V), for example *oh* and *eye*. If we add one or more consonant sounds (C) to the beginnings of these words, they are still only one syllable. Look at these examples.

V		CV		CCV	
oh	/əʊ/	no	/nəʊ/	snow	/snəʊ/
oh	/əʊ/	low	/ləʊ/	slow	/sləʊ/
eye	/aɪ/	lie	/laɪ/	fly	/flaɪ/
air	/eə/	where	/weə/	swear	/sweə/
or	/ɔː/	law	/lɔː/	floor	/flɔː/

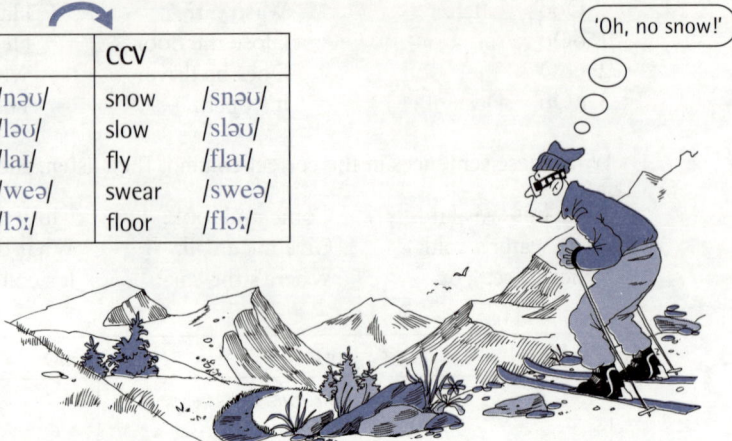

'Oh, no snow!'

B

When there are two Cs at the start of a syllable:
- if the first C is /s/, the second C can be any of these: /f/, /k/, /l/, /m/, /p/, /t/, /w/, /j/.
- if the first C is any sound other than /s/, the second C can only be one of these: /l/, /r/, /w/, /j/.

When there are three Cs at the start of a syllable:
- the first C is always /s/.

You may find some of these syllables with more than one C at the beginning difficult to say. Listen to these examples.

B16 /s/ + C: spell stairs sleep small snack swim
C + /l/, /r/, /w/ or /j/: blue fly dress ground quick swim view tune
/s/ + CC: spring strange square scream

C

When there are two or more Cs at the beginning of a syllable, many learners add a V before the first C or between the Cs. Be careful!

- If you add a V before the first C, you may get a different word. For example, if you add a vowel before *sleep*, it may become *asleep*.
- If you add a V between the Cs, you may get a different word. For example, if you add a vowel between /s/ and /p/ in *sport*, it becomes *support*.

Listen to the difference.

B17

	+ extra syllable
sleep	asleep
dress	address
street	a street
sport	support
That ski.	That's a key.
That smile.	That's a mile.
What snake?	What's an ache?

Exercises

24.1 Add one C to the start of each word to make a new word in the pictures. Be careful: think of *sounds*, not spelling!

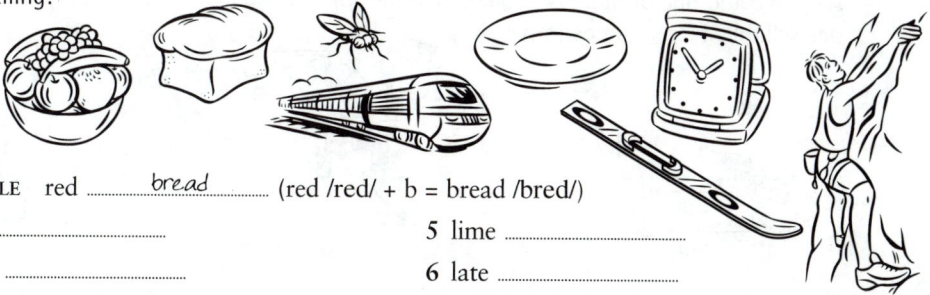

EXAMPLE red ....*bread*........ (red /red/ + b = bread /bred/)

1 lie ....

2 lock ....

3 rain ....

4 key ....

5 lime ....

6 late ....

7 route ....

24.2 Add one of the sounds from the box *after* the consonant at the start of these words to make other words. Think of *sounds*, not spelling!

/k/	/l/	/r/	/p/	/t/

EXAMPLE die ....*dry*........

1 back ....

2 fight ....

3 fat ....

4 go ....

5 pain ....

6 pay ....

7 two ....

8 say ....

9 sin ....

10 send ....

24.3 Listen and circle the word you hear.

B18

1 The *glass* / *gas* is green.
2 I don't want to *play* / *pay*.
3 It was a terrible *fight* / *fright*!
4 The *tooth* / *truth* is out!

5 The dirt came off in the *steam* / *stream*.
6 She didn't want to *stay* / *say*.
7 The *pain* / *plane* went down.
8 I can't *sell* / *smell* anything.

24.4 Listen and tick the sentence or phrase you hear, A or B.

B19

	A	B
1	that slow bus	That's a low bus.
2	an ice-cream	a nicer cream
3	that spot	That's a pot.
4	that street	That's a treat.
5	She loves the States.	She loves the estates.
6	small stream	a smaller stream
7	slow speech	a slower speech
8	straight street	a straighter street

Follow up: Record yourself saying the phrases and sentences in 24.4, choosing A or B each time. Make a note of which sentence or phrase you say. Then listen to your recording in about two weeks. Is it clear which you said?

Now go to Unit 44

25

Go – goal – gold
Consonants at the end of syllables

A

Some one-syllable words have no consonant sound (C) after the vowel sound (V), for example *go*. If we add one or more consonant sounds (C) to the end of these words, they are still only one syllable. Here is an example.

Go!   *Goal!*   *Gold!*

B

Sometimes, if you do not pronounce the last C of a word, you in fact say another word. For example, if you do not pronounce the final /k/ in *think* /θɪŋk/ you get *thing* /θɪŋ/. Listen to the words below. The words on the left sound the same as the words on the right without the final C, so you can see that it is important to pronounce the final consonants.

VCC	VC
belt /belt/	bell /bel/
change /tʃeɪndʒ/	chain /tʃeɪn/
range /reɪndʒ/	rain /reɪn/
help /help/	hell /hel/
film /fɪlm/	fill /fɪl/
tenth /tenθ/	ten /ten/
learnt /lɜːnt/	learn /lɜːn/
wolf /wʊlf/	wool /wʊl/
hold /həʊld/	hole /həʊl/

C

Some learners of English find it difficult to pronounce two Cs together at the end of a syllable. If you have this problem, you may find it easier if you put a word beginning with a V after it and imagine that the last C of the first word is in fact the beginning of the second word. For example, if you find it difficult to say the /nt/ at the end of *weren't*, imagine the /t/ at the start of the next word:

They weren't able to do it.   *They weren' → table to do it.*

⚠ **Note:** We often get the consonant pair /nt/ at the end of negative contractions, e.g. *isn't.* (See Unit 35.)

⚠ **Note:** There are often two or more Cs at the end of verbs in the past tense. For example *walked* is pronounced /wɔːkt/ so it has the pattern CVCC. Similarly with *-es* endings, *likes* is pronounced /laɪks/ (CVCC).

D

Some learners of English add a vowel after words ending in two Cs to make it easier to say. But be careful: if you add an extra V after the last C, you may get a different word.

Listen to these examples.

help	helper
sent	centre
cook	cooker
mix	mixer
past	pasta

Exercises

25.1 Remove a consonant sound from the end of each word to make a new word. Be careful: think of *sounds*, not spelling! Look at the example. If you remove the last sound from *went* /went/, you get *when* /wen/.

EXAMPLE   went ....*when*........

1 field   ....   4 build   ....   7 guest   ....

2 change   ....   5 shelf   ....   8 wild   ....

3 six   ....   6 wealth   ....

25.2 Read the conversation and underline the words which end with two consonant sounds.

A: OK, <u>first</u> question. <u>What's</u> the <u>eighth</u> <u>month</u> in the year?
B: It's August.
A: Correct! Second question. What's the highest mountain on Earth?
B: Mount Everest.
A: Correct again! Mount Everest! Next question.
   Which city is furthest east in Europe: Athens, Brussels or Budapest?
B: Is it Budapest, or perhaps Brussels?
A: No, it isn't. It's Athens. OK, last question. What's the biggest land animal in the world?
B: The elephant.
A: Very good! Three out of four correct, that's seventy-five percent!

Now read the conversation aloud. Pronounce the underlined words carefully.

25.3 Think of a computer which people speak into and it writes what they say. This computer wrote these sentences down wrongly. The mistakes are <u>underlined</u> and one of the correct words is given at the end in (brackets). Write the correct sentences.

EXAMPLE   She <u>dozen turn</u> much. (earn)   ......*She doesn't earn much.*......

1 I <u>thing cold</u> cars are better. (think)   ....

2 The <u>bang caught</u> to be open by now. (ought)   ....

3 I <u>thing call</u> the time. (all)   ....

4 These big cars <u>whole date</u> people. (hold)   ....

5 Did he <u>fill mother</u> kinds of movies too? (other)   ....

6 Three people have <u>sick size</u>. (eyes)   ....

7 If you took aspirins, your head <u>wooden take</u>. (ache)   ....

25.4 Listen and circle the word you hear.
(B22)

1 They took their *cook / cooker* with them.   5 Is that your *guess / guest*?
2 She was a great *help / helper*!   6 They *burn / burnt* the food.
3 He *did an / didn't* exercise.   7 It's all in the *past / pasta* now.
4 They *learn / learnt* quickly.   8 That *mix / mixer* wasn't very good.

> Now go to Unit 45

26 Paul's calls, Max's faxes
Syllables: plural and other –s endings

A

The noun *call* /kɔːl/ is one syllable and the plural *calls* /kɔːlz/ is also only one syllable. Usually the -s ending is just a consonant sound (C), not another syllable. It is pronounced /s/ or /z/.

When we add -s to make the third person singular present, it is the same. For example, the verb *know* /nəʊ/ is one syllable and the third person form *knows* /nəʊz/ is also only one syllable.

When we add -'s to make the possessive it is also the same. For example *Paul* and *Paul's* are both just one syllable.

B23 Listen to the examples of -s endings in these rhymes.
Claire's chairs.
Bob's jobs.
Di's pies.
Rose knows.
Pat's hats.

B

Sometimes, plural, third person and possessive endings *are* another syllable. For example, *fax* /fæks/ is one syllable, but *faxes* /fæk.sɪz/ is two syllables.

B24 The plural and other endings *are* another syllable when the original word ends in one of the sounds below. Listen to the examples and rhymes.

/s/	Chris's kisses, the nurse's purses, Max's faxes
/ʃ/	Trish's wishes
/z/	Rose's roses
/tʃ/	The witch's watches
/dʒ/	George's fridges

⚠ **Note:** When the -s ending is another syllable, it is pronounced /ɪz/.

C

Important for listening

With -s endings, we sometimes get a lot of consonant sounds together at the end of syllables, for example, *facts* /fækts/. Many speakers of English make it simpler and do not pronounce one of the Cs. For example, they may pronounce *facts* like *fax* /fæks/. Here are some more examples.

B25
She never se**nds** birthday cards. (sounds like: She never /senz/ birthday cards)
The lif**t's** broken. (sounds like: The /lifs/ broken)
It tas**tes** funny. (sounds like: It /teɪs/ funny)
That's what he expe**cts**. (sound like: That's what he /ɪkˈspeks/)

D

Try to make sure you pronounce the -s ending. It is very important to the meaning. Listen to the examples and notice how the -s ending changes the meaning.

noun	verb
Jane's nose	Jane knows
Nick's weights	Nick waits

B26

singular	plural
My friend spends a lot.	My friends spend a lot.
Our guest came late.	Our guests came late.

Exercises

26.1 Match the beginnings and ends of these phrases so that they rhyme. Then listen and repeat.

(B27)

1 Ms Fox's	a fridges
2 My niece's	b boxes
3 The witch's	c pieces
4 Mr Bridge's	d phones
5 Mr Jones	e kisses
6 Chris's	f plans
7 Anne's	g switches

26.2 Write the third person forms of the verbs from the box in the correct part of the table below. Then listen, check and repeat.

(B28)

~~watch~~   ~~sing~~   go   get   dance   kiss   come   wash   see   close   push   pull

1 syllable	O	sings
2 syllables	Oo	watches

26.3 These speakers are not pronouncing all the consonants at the ends of some words. What are they saying? Write the sentence.

1

....
(sounds like: /hænz/ up)

2

....
(sounds like: There are many different /kaɪnz/ of whale)

3

....
(sounds like: My favourite /'sʌbdʒeks/ chemistry)

4

....
(sounds like: The /wɪnz/ very strong today)

26.4 Listen and circle the word you hear.

(B29)

1 I saw the *bird / birds* fly away.
2 What time did the *guest / guests* leave?
3 He broke his *arm / arms* in the accident.
4 She sang the *song / songs* her father wrote.
5 Where does she park her *car / cars* at night?

6 I read the *book / books* very quickly.
7 The *bag / bags* fell on the floor.
8 The *shop / shops* will be closed.
9 When will the *class / classes* begin?
10 The *box / boxes* won't be big enough.

Follow up: Record yourself saying the sentences in 26.4, choosing singular or plural. Make a note of which one you said. Then listen to your recording in about two weeks. Is it clear which words you said?

▶ Now go to Unit 46

27

Pete played, Rita rested
Syllables: adding past tense endings

The verb *play* /pleɪ/ has one syllable and the past tense *played* /pleɪd/ also has only one syllable. Usually the *-ed* ending is just a consonant sound (C), not another syllable; the letter E is silent.

So, for example, *smiled* /smaɪld/ rhymes with *child* /tʃaɪld/, even though *child* does not have a letter E before the D. Listen to the rhymes. Notice that *-ed* rhymes with either /t/ or /d/.

B30
He looked round first,
And then reversed.
The car that passed
Was going fast.
It hit the side.
The driver cried.
He never guessed.
He'd pass the test.

B

If the infinitive of the verb ends with the sounds /t/ or /d/, *-ed* or *-d* is a new syllable; the letter E is pronounced as a vowel sound. For example:

hate /heɪt/ = one syllable
hated /ˈheɪtɪd/ = two syllables

Listen and compare the sentences on the left and right below.

B31

O O	OoOo (*-ed* = extra syllable)
Pete played.	Rita rested.
Dan danced.	Colin counted.
Will watched.	Wendy waited.
Liz laughed.	Sheila shouted.
Clare cleaned.	Myra mended.
Steve stopped.	Stacey started.

C

Past tense endings tell you if the sentence is present or past. Listen to the difference.

B32

Present	Past
You never cook a meal.	You never cooked a meal.
I sometimes watch a movie.	I sometimes watched a movie.
We often phone our parents.	We often phoned our parents.

⚠ **Note:** If it is difficult to say the *-ed* ending in words like *cooked*, imagine that the *-ed* is joined to the word after. For example say *cooked all the food* like this: *cook tall the food*.

⚠ **Note:** If the word after the past tense verb begins with a consonant, you may not hear the *-ed*, e.g. *cooked dinner, walked through*.

Exercises

27.1 Match the beginnings and ends of these rhymes.

1 The people queued	a was never found.
2 The thing you missed	b are on the board.
3 The man controlled	c and then she smiled.
4 She saw the child	d to build on sand.
5 The boat that crossed	e was on the list.
6 The man who drowned	f until she coughed.
7 The snow we rolled	g the nation's gold.
8 Her voice was soft	h to buy the food.
9 The points we scored	i was nearly lost.
10 We never planned	j was hard and cold.

27.2 Write the past tense of the verbs from the box in the correct part of the table.
(B33) Then listen, check and repeat.

~~hate~~   ~~walk~~   need   wash   wait   waste   help   taste   phone   dance   end   ask

1 syllable	O	*walked*
–ed = extra syllable	Oo	*hated*

27.3 Complete each sentence with the past tense of a verb from the box. In each sentence, the first sound of the verb is the same as the first sound in the person's name! Then listen, check and repeat.

~~play~~   watch   add   phone   count   mix   cook   start   shout   ~~paint~~

O O O	OoOoOo (–ed = extra syllable)
Paul ....*played*.... games.	Peter ....*painted*.... pictures.
Ken .... lunch.	Karen .... money.
Fred .... friends.	Stella .... singing.
Marge .... drinks.	Alice .... sugar.
Will .... films.	Sheila .... loudly.

(B34) Now listen, check and repeat.

27.4 Listen and circle the verb form you hear, past or present.
(B35)
1 I always *walk / walked* away from fights.
2 I think they *want / wanted* to talk.
3 Me and my friends *laugh / laughed* a lot.
4 On Saturdays, we *dance / danced* all night.
5 I always *hate / hated* Sundays.
6 You never *help / helped* Alice.
7 They *need / needed* more time.
8 They *paint / painted* the walls every few years.

Follow up: Record yourself saying the sentences in 27.4, choosing the present or past tense. Make a note of which tense you say. Then listen to your recording in about two weeks. Is it clear which tense you said?

Now go to Unit 47

28 REcord, reCORD
Stress in two-syllable words

A

Many two-syllable words come from a one-syllable word. For example, the word *artist* comes from the word *art*, and the word *remove* comes from the word *move*. In these two-syllable words, the stress is on the syllable of the original word:

artist = Oo (stress on the first syllable)   re**move** = oO (stress on the second syllable)

Here are some more examples.

nouns and adjectives Oo	verbs oO
art – artist	move – remove
drive – driver	like – dislike
friend – friendly	build – rebuild
fame – famous	come – become

B

Most two-syllable **nouns** and **adjectives** have stress on the first syllable, even if they don't come from an original one-syllable word. For example, 'brother' doesn't come from the original word '~~broth~~', but it still has the stress pattern Oo.

B36 Listen to this sentence: the nouns and adjectives all have the pattern Oo.

The artist's most famous picture shows some women and children in a lovely forest with a purple mountain behind.

⚠ **Note:** However, there are a number of exceptions to this general rule, for example *asleep, mistake, machine, alone*, which have stress on the second syllable.

C

Most two-syllable **verbs** have stress on the second syllable, even if they don't come from an original one-syllable word. For example, 'repeat' doesn't come from the original word '~~peat~~', but it still has the stress pattern (oO).

Listen to this sentence: the verbs all have the pattern oO.

B37 Escape to Scotland, forget about work, just relax and enjoy the scenery!

⚠ **Note:** There are a number of exceptions to this general rule, for example *cancel, copy* and two-syllable verbs ending in *-er* and *-en*, e.g. *answer, enter, offer, listen, happen, open*, which all have stress on the first syllable.

D B38 Some words are both nouns and verbs. For example, *record* is a noun if you put stress on the first syllable, and a verb if you put stress on the second syllable. Listen to these examples. You will hear each word twice, first as a noun and then as a verb.

record   contrast   desert   export   object   present   produce   protest   rebel

⚠ **Note:** There is not always a change of stress in words that are both nouns and verbs. For example *answer, picture, promise, reply, travel, visit* always have stress on the same syllable.

⚠ **Note:** The stress stays in the same place when we make longer words from these two-syllable nouns, adjectives and verbs. For example, in both *happy* (Oo) and *unhappy* (oOo), the stress is on the syllable *happ*, and in both *depart* (oO) and *departure* (oOo), the stress is on the syllable *part*.

Exercises

28.1 Make the word in (brackets) into a verb beginning with 'r' and a noun ending with 'r' and use the
B39 words to fill the gaps. Then say the sentences. Take care to use the correct stress patterns for the
words in the gaps: Oo for the nouns and oO for the verbs. Listen and check.

EXAMPLE
   (build)   I asked the .... *builder* .... to .... *rebuild* .... the wall.

1 (act)   How did you .... when you saw the .... coming in?

2 (write)   The .... decided to .... the whole book.

3 (paint)   The .... tried to .... this part of the picture.

4 (print)   We asked the .... to .... the whole document.

5 (view)   The .... will be able to .... this programme tomorrow.

6 (play)   They had to .... the match after a .... was hurt.

28.2 Listen and circle the word with a different stress pattern from the others.
B40

EXAMPLE   money   (machine)   mountain   message

1 answer   agree   allow   attract   **5** complete   common   careful   crazy
2 middle   minute   mission mistake   **6** pronounce   provide   promise   prefer
3 compare   correct copy   collect   **7** shampoo   shoulder shower   shopping
4 garden   granny   guitar   grammar   **8** reason   remove   receive   review

28.3 Read the sentences and decide what stress pattern the words in **bold** have. Then listen, check
B41 and repeat.

EXAMPLE   I got my first **record** as a **present** when I was eleven.
          record = .. Oo ..   present = ... Oo ....

1 You've **progressed** well this year, but I'd like to see even more **progress**.

   progressed = ... progress = ...

2 We **import** too much petrol and the country's **export** figures are going down.

   import = ... export = ...

3 It started as a student **protest,** but now the army has **rebelled** against the government.

   protest = ... rebelled = ...

4 In the **desert**, there is a big **contrast** between temperatures in the day and at night.

   desert = ... contrast = ...

5 These companies **produce** household **objects** such as fridges and washing machines.

   produce = ... objects = ...

Now go to Unit 48 ▶

29 Second hand, bookshop
Stress in compound words

Compound words are made from two smaller words put together, for example *book* + *shop* = *bookshop*. (They are not always written as one word, for example *shoe shop*.) In most compound words, the stress is on the first part. For example, the word *bookshop* has two syllables and the stress is on the first syllable. Listen to these examples.

B42

Oo	bookshop, bus stop, footpath, airport, shoe shop, road sign, car park, bedroom
Ooo	traffic light, bus station, sunglasses, boarding card, window seat, check-in desk
Oooo	travel agent, art gallery, supermarket, tape recorder, photocopy

⚠️ Note: If the first part of the compound word is an adjective, there may be stress on the second part too, for example OO *double room*.

⚠️ Note: There may be stress on the second part of a compound noun when:
* the object in the second part is made out of the material in the first, for example OO *glass jar*;
* the first part tells us where the second part is, for example OO *car door*.

B

If the compound word is *not* a noun, we often put stress on the second part too. Listen to these examples.

B43

OO	first class, half price, hand made
OOo	bad-tempered, old-fashioned, short-sighted
OoO	overnight, second hand

C

Sometimes a compound word looks the same as
* a normal adjective and noun,
* a normal noun and verb.

But the pronunciation is different. Compare:

Oo compound word	OO adjective and noun
We keep these plants in a **green**house during the winter months.	Mr Olsen lives in a small, **green house** next to the river.
OO compound word	**OO noun and verb**
I saw her **bus** pass.	I saw her **bus pass**.

1

2

Exercises

29.1 Listen. Write the words in **bold** in the correct columns.
B44

> There's a good **shopping centre**. You can find almost **anything** there. There are **bookshops**, **shoe shops**, a **travel agent's**, a **post office**, a **hairdresser's**, a **supermarket**, **everything**… and there are a few **snack bars** if you want a **hamburger** or **something**. Oh, and there's a **sports centre** too, with a **swimming pool** and a **playground** for the kids. But be careful with your **handbag**; I had my **credit card** stolen there once!

Oo	Ooo	Oooo
bookshops	anything	shopping centre

Follow up: Record yourself saying the text. Make sure you put the stress in the correct place.

29.2 Listen. In each sentence, one of the compound words (in **bold**) has stress on the first part (Oo) and the
B45 other has stress on the second part too (OO). Circle the word if there is stress on the second part too.

EXAMPLE   They did the **photocopies** (**overnight.**)

1 I got this **motorbike second hand.**
2 Using a **typewriter** is so **old fashioned.**
3 These **earrings** were **hand made.**
4 I'm **short-sighted**, like my **grandmother.**
5 All the **sunglasses** are **half price.**
6 The **waiting room** is for **first class** only.

29.3 Listen. Which thing is the speaker asking about? Put a tick (✓) next to it and say *Yes, I have* or
B46 *No, I haven't*. Give a true answer!

EXAMPLE   Have you ever seen a ski jump?   a   b
          No, I haven't!

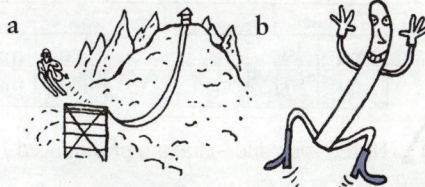

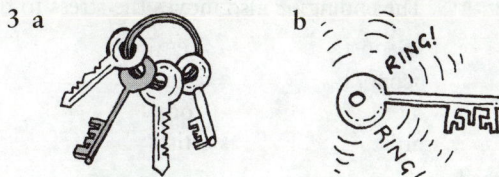

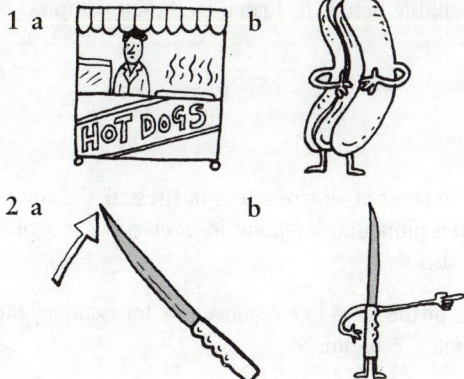

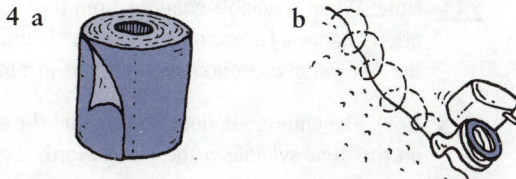

1 a   b   3 a   b ✓

2 a   b   4 a   b

Now go to Unit 49

30 Unforgettable
Stress in longer words 1

A

We can build longer words by adding parts to the beginning or end of shorter words. Usually, this does not change the stress: it stays on the same syllable as in the original word. Look at the example below.

	for	get		
	for	get	ful	
	for	get	ful	ness
	for	gett	a	ble
un	for	gett	a	ble

Here are is a list of beginnings and endings which do not change the stress of the shorter word:

-able (drinkable)
-al (musical)
-er (player)
-ful (helpful)
-hood (childhood)
-ing (boring)

in-/im- (impossible)
-ise (civilise)
-ish (childish)
-less (childless)
-ly (friendly)
-ment (employment)

-ness (happiness)
-ship (friendship)
un- (unhappy)
under- (underpay)

B B47

Some endings *do* change the stress in the shorter word. Look how the ending -ion changes the stress in the word *educate*.

ed	u	cate	
ed	u	ca	tion

When we add the endings -ion or -ian, the stress always moves to the syllable *before* these endings. Here are some more examples.

e	lec	tric	
e	lec	tri	cian

dec	o	rate	
dec	o	ra	tion

mu	sic	
mu	si	cian

co	mmu	ni	cate	
co	mmu	ni	ca	tion

⚠ Note: –*tion* and –*cian* are pronounced /ʃən/.

C B48

The ending -ic also moves the stress to the syllable before it. Listen to these examples.

scientist   scientific
economy   economic
atom   atomic
artist   artistic

⚠ Note: When a syllable changes from unstressed to stressed, or stressed to unstressed, the vowel sound often changes. For example the letter O in *atom* is pronounced /ə/, but in *atomic*, it is pronounced /ɒ/; the A in *atom* is pronounced /æ/, but in *atomic* it is /ə/.

⚠ Note: The ending –*al* does not change the stress of the word (see A above), so, for example, the stress is on the same syllable in these two words: economic   economical.

Exercises

30.1
B49
Use the beginnings and endings in A opposite to make longer words from the words below. Listen and check if you get the same words as on the recording. Then listen again and repeat.

EXAMPLE
child .... *childhood,   childish,   childishness,   childless*

1 believe ....

2 enjoy ....

3 care ....

30.2 Write the words from the box in the correct part of the table according to the stress pattern.

~~population~~	telecommunication	nation	identification	relation
communication	pronunciation	scientific	clinic	romantic
pessimistic	investigation	public	discussion	

Oo	
oOo	
ooOo	population
oooOo	
ooooOo	
oooooOo	

30.3 Combine each word with one of the endings from the box, and give the stress pattern of your new word. You may need to change or add other letters to the first word. Use a dictionary to help you if necessary.

-ion	-ic

EXAMPLE   inform .... *information* .... *ooOo*

1 introduce ....   7 optimist ....

2 base ....   8 celebrate ....

3 economy ....   9 diplomat ....

4 describe ....   10 operate ....

5 romance ....   11 explain ....

6 compete ....   12 decide ....

Now go to Unit 50

Public, publicity
Stress in longer words 2

A B50 There are many longer word endings where the last letter is *-y*. In words with these endings, the stress is placed on the syllable two from the end. Listen to these examples.

pub	lic		
pub	**lic**	i	ty

na	tion	al		
na	tio	**nal**	i	ty

pho	to	graph	
pho	**tog**	raph	y

cli	mate			
cli	ma	**tol**	o	gy

as	tro-		
a	**stron**	o	my

chem	ist	
chem	i	stry

⚠ **Note:** If we add the ending *–ic* to a word, the stress goes on the syllable before *–ic*. (See Unit 30.) Notice the change of stress, for example:
pho**tog**raphy photo**graph**ic.

⚠ **Note:** In words for an expert in the subject, such as *photographer* or *climatologist*, the stress stays on the same syllable as in the word ending in *-y*:
pho**tog**raphy pho**tog**rapher
cli**mat**ology cli**mat**ologist

B Many words for school and university subjects have one of the *-y* endings in this unit or the ending *-ics*. Listen to the names of subjects in this text.

B51 At school, I hated science subjects like **physics**, **chemistry** and **biology**, you know, and ehm… I wasn't very good at **mathematics** and things. I really liked subjects like **history**, **geography**, **economics**. Anyway, when I went to university, I wanted to do **geology**, but I couldn't 'cause I was no good at sciences, so in the end I did **philosophy**!

⚠ **Note:** Many English speakers do not pronounce the second syllable in *history*, so that it sounds like this: /ˈhɪstrɪ/ Oo. The first part of the word *geography* may be pronounced as one or two syllables: /ˈdʒɒɡrəfɪ/ Ooo or /dʒiːˈɒɡrəfɪ/ oOoo. Many speakers do not pronounce the second syllable in *mathematics*, so it sounds like this: /mæθˈmætɪks/ oOo.

C B52 If we combine the various endings in this unit and Unit 30, we can get 'families' of words with moving stress patterns. Listen to these examples.

photograph	pho**tog**raphy	photo**graph**ic	
e**con**omy	eco**nom**ics	eco**nom**ical	
national	natio**nal**ity	**nat**ionalise	nationali**sa**tion
civil	ci**vil**ity	**civ**ilise	civili**sa**tion

Exercises

31.1 Make a word ending in *–ity* from each of these words, and give the stress pattern. Use a dictionary to help you if necessary.

EXAMPLE   author ....*authority*........... ....oOoo...........

1 person ....   5 nation ....

2 universe ....   6 real ....

3 public ....   7 human ....

4 major ....   8 electric ....

31.2 Write the words from the box in the correct column according to their stress pattern.

| economics   economy   physics   chemistry   geography /ˈdʒɒɡrəfɪ/ |
| mathematics /mæθəˈmætɪks/   sociology   history /ˈhɪstrɪ/   geology |
| photography   nation   nationality |

Oo	Ooo	oOoo	ooOoo	oOoo
				economics

31.3 Fill the gaps with a word from the box which has the stress pattern given. Then listen and check.

(B53)

| biology   mathematics   history   geography   sociology   ~~chemistry~~ |

My favourite subjects at school were sciences, especially Ooo ....*chemistry*........... and
oOoo .... I've always been good with numbers, so I was good at
oOo .... I didn't really like the social science subjects like
ooOoo .... and Oo ...., and that's strange because when I
went to university I did Ooo ....

31.4 Write in the word which is missing from the family. Then listen, check and repeat.

(B54)

EXAMPLE   society, ...*sociology*........... (ooOoo), sociological

1 civil, civilise, ... (oooOo)

2 .... (oOoo), biologist, biological

3 personal, ... (ooOoo), personalise

4 legal, legalise, ... (oooOo)

5 .... (Oo), authority, authorise

Now go to Unit 51

32

DON'T LOOK NOW!
Sentences with all the words stressed

In a sentence, we put stress on one syllable of all the most important words. In some situations, emergencies for example, *all* of the words are important. In this case, there is stress on one syllable of all of the words (in some cases, the sentence may have only one word). Listen to the sentence stress in these examples.

B55

O	Help! Quick! Smile!
Oo	Quiet! Sorry!
OO	Look out! Take care! Wake up! Don't move! Come back! Stand still! Sit down!
OoO	Don't forget! Hurry up! Go away! Stay awake! Don't be late!
OOo	Keep quiet! Don't worry!
OOO	Don't look now! Go straight on! Don't turn round!
oOoo	Emergency!

B

In English sentence stress, the following kinds of words are usually stressed. The examples given are from the sentences in A above.

verbs (*help*)
two-part verbs (*look out*)
adjectives (*quick*)
nouns (*emergency*)
negative auxiliary verbs (*don't*)

⚠ Note: Positive auxiliary verbs such as *be* in *Don't be late!* are not usually stressed.

C

Sentences with all the words stressed have a distinctive rhythm. You can hear this well in these chants. Listen.

B56
O O,   O O

Don't move! Take care!
Keep calm!   Stay there!

O O O

Go straight on!
Don't look down!
Go straight on!
Don't turn round!

O O,   O o O

Don't stop!   Carry on!
Run! Run!   Get away!
Quick! Quick! Hurry up!

Exercises

32.1 Match each sentence with a sentence from the box with the same rhythm. Write the sentences in
B57 the correct place. Then listen, check and repeat.

> Don't move!   Run!   Don't worry!   Go straight on!   Go away!   Sorry!

EXAMPLE OoO Don't be late! .... *Go away!* ....

1 Oo Silence! ....

2 OOO Don't look down! ....

3 O Wait! ....

4 OO Get back! ....

5 OOo Keep quiet! ....

32.2 What are they saying? Use the grammar and sentence stress information to guess.

EXAMPLE

oOoo (noun) ...... *Emergency!* ......

3

OoO (two-part verb) ....

1

O (verb) ....

4

OOO (negative auxiliary,
two-part verb) ....

2

OO (two-part verb) ....

5

Oo (adjective) ....

32.3 Listen and complete these chants. Then play the recording and say the chant at the same time.
B58
1 Don't sleep! ...... *Stay* ...... awake!   3 Say please! Don't .... rude!

  Get dressed! Don't .... late!   Sit ....! Eat your food!

2 .... still! Stay there!

  Don't move! .... care!

Now go to Unit 52

33

THAT could be the MAN
Unstressed words

A

All of the sentences below have three syllables with this stress pattern: OoO. The middle word in each sentence is unstressed because it is not as important as the other two words. Listen.

B59

O	o	O
What's	your	name?
Tom	was	right.
Dogs	can	swim.
Close	the	door!
Wait	and	see.
Go	to	bed!

B

These are the kinds of words which are not normally stressed, with example words from the sentences in A above.

pronouns (*your*)
the verb *be* (*was*)
auxiliary verbs (*can*)
articles (*the*)
conjunctions (*and*, *or*)
prepositions (*to*)

⚠ Note: Negative auxiliary verbs (*can't*, *don't*, *hasn't*, etc.) are usually stressed. See Unit 32.

Important for listening

There may be more than one of these unstressed words between two stressed words. In the sentences below, each sentence has the same two stressed words with an increasing number of unstressed words between. Listen. Notice that the length of time between the two stressed words is about the same, however many unstressed words are fitted between.

B60

OO	That man.
OoO	That's the man.
OooO	That was the man.
OoooO	That could be the man.

⚠ Note: Speakers can choose to put stress on words which are normally unstressed. They do this for emphasis or contrast. (See Unit 49.)

Exercises

33.1 Give the stress patterns for these sentences.

EXAMPLE Go to the shops. .... OₒₒO ....

1 Go to school. ....

2 Where was the key? ....

3 Tell John. ....

4 What was in the news? ....

5 What's your name? ....

33.2 Put one of the unstressed words from the box in the middle of each phrase or sentence below. Then say the phrases or sentences with this stress pattern: OoO.

or	my	a	it	can	some	of	are

1 Bring .... here!

2 Mel's .... nurse.

3 Whales .... big.

4 Jane .... drive.

5 Lots .... eggs.

6 Pass .... fail?

7 Have .... bread.

8 Where's .... bike?

33.3
(B61)

Listen. How many unstressed words are there between the stressed words in each sentence? Write 0, 1, 2 or 3.

EXAMPLE Drink ... milk. __3__

1 Eat ... cheese. ....

2 That ... man. ....

3 What ... name? ....

4 What ... for? ....

5 Go ... shops. ....

6 Go ... home. ....

7 Turn ... right. ....

33.4
(B62)

Complete each set of four sentences with the unstressed words given. Each sentence should have one more unstressed word than the sentence before, so that the four sentences have the same pattern as in the example. Then listen, check and repeat.

EXAMPLE unstressed words: *it, some, with*

OO Eat cheese.

OoO Eat __some__ cheese.

OooO Eat __it with__ cheese.

OoooO Eat __it with some__ cheese.

1 unstressed words: *it, of, the, some, with*

OO Drink milk.

OoO Drink .... milk.

OooO Drink .... milk.

OoooO Drink .... milk.

2 unstressed words: *it, the, to*

OO Turn right.

OoO Turn .... right.

OooO Turn .... right.

OoooO Turn .... right.

Now go to Unit 53

34 I'll ASK her (Alaska)
Pronouns and contractions

A

Pronouns in sentences are usually unstressed. Look at this sentence: *I met him*. The first and third words are pronouns. So this sentence has the stress pattern oOo.

B

Important for listening

Listen to these sentences. You will hear each one twice: first in careful speech and then in fast speech. Notice that in fast speech:

* the speaker doesn't pronounce the letter H in *he, her, him, his* unless it is at the beginning of the sentence.
* the vowel sound in the pronouns and *his, her, their, our* is very short.

B63

oOo	oOoO
I met him.	I met his wife.
You know her.	They read my book.
They saw you.	He knows their son.
She phoned me.	We called their friends.
He likes them.	She hates her job.
We found it.	You need our help.

⚠ **Note:** You don't need to copy the fast speech pronunciation. People will understand you if you use careful speech. But you need to be able to understand fast speech.

C

Important for listening

Pronouns are often joined to auxiliary verbs (*is, have, will*, etc.) in contractions. For example, when we speak, we join the *I* and *will* together to form *I'll*. In the sentence *I'll ask her* there are four words but only three syllables. This is because the pronoun and contraction are pronounced as one syllable. This sentence therefore has the stress pattern oOo (the pronouns and contractions *I'll* and *her* are unstressed). In fast speech, it may be pronounced the same as *Alaska*. Listen to these examples.

B64

oOo		
I'll **ask** her.	/æ'læskə/	(like *Alaska*)
I'm **com**ing.	/æm'kʌmɪŋ/	(like *am coming*)
He's **fin**ished.	/hɪz'fɪnɪʃt/	(like *his finished*)
They're **hun**gry.	/ðe'hʌŋgrɪ/	(like *the hungry*)
We've **seen** him.	/wɪv'siːnɪm/	(like *wiv seen im*)
She's **an**gry.	/ʃɪ'zæŋgrɪ/	(like *shiz angry*)

⚠ **Note:** You do not join the pronoun to an auxiliary verb at the end of a sentence. For example, say *Yes, I will*, don't say ~~*Yes, I'll*~~.

⚠ **Note:** You only put stress on pronouns if you want to emphasise or contrast something. It is like underlining with your voice. For example:
You don't need *him*, but *he* needs *you*!
(See Unit 49.)

Exercises

34.1 Add pronouns to these words to make sentences with the pattern oOoO. Do not use the same pronoun twice. Then say your sentences aloud, making the rhythm clear.

EXAMPLE drove/car ....*She drove her car.*........

1 read/book ....   3 drank/milk ....

2 sang/song ....   4 ate/lunch ....

34.2 Listen and write the words you hear in the gaps.

B65

EXAMPLE Can you tell ....*her*........ to call ....*me*........ please?

1 Can you give .... to .... please?

2 Did .... meet .... daughter, Catherine?

3 I don't think .... likes ....

4 What did .... say to .... ?

5 Where did .... buy .... guitar?

6 What's .... mother's name?

7 Where are .... parents from?

8 .... bought presents for .... children.

34.3 Write the sentences below again. Change the people to pronouns, and make the auxiliary verbs (*has/is/are* etc.) into contractions. Then underline the stressed syllables in your sentences. There should be two in each sentence. Then listen, check and repeat.

B66

EXAMPLE Helen has given Robert some money. ....*She's given him some money.*........

1 Robert is buying presents for the children. ....

2 Bonnie and Max are opening their presents. ....

3 Bonnie and Max will thank Robert for the presents. ....

4 Robert will thank Helen for the money. ....

34.4 Think of a computer which people speak into and it writes what they say. This computer wrote the underlined parts of these conversations incorrectly. (You can read what the computer heard in phonemic letters.) Write the correct words.

EXAMPLE
– Do you know Mike?
– Yes. Ametim /æˈmetɪm/ yesterday. ....*I met him*........

1 – Come on kids, do your homework!
   – Wivdunit /wɪvˈdʌnɪt/ already! ....
2 – What's his name?
   – I don't know. Alaskim /æˈlæskɪm/. ....
3 – Goodbye.
   – Goodbye. Alseeya /ælˈsiːjə/ tomorrow! ....
4 – Why isn't Neil here?
   – Hisgonta /hɪzˈɡɒntə/ Paris for the weekend. ....
5 – Have you told Maria yet?
   – No. Altella /ælˈtelə/ tomorrow. ....

Now go to Unit 54

35 She was FIRST
Pronouncing the verb *be*

A

You don't normally put stress on *are* in the middle of a sentence. Listen to this rhyme.

B67a
Roses are red,
Violets are blue,
Flowers are nice,
And so are you!

⚠️ Note: Many speakers pronounce *are* just as the weak vowel sound /ə/, but if the following word begins with a vowel sound, the /r/ is pronounced too, for example *People are angry*. (See Unit 39.)

B

B67b The word *is* (and '*s*) is not usually spoken as a separate syllable; it is usually joined to the syllable before, for example *Snow is/'s white*. But if the word before ends with letters like S, CE, GE and CH, it is a new syllable, for example *Grass is green*. (See Unit 24.) Listen to the examples.

is and '*s* – not a separate syllable	*is* and '*s* – a separate syllable
Snow is white.	Grass is green.
Your hair is dirty.	Your face is dirty.
The road is closed.	The bridge is closed.
The clock is broken.	My watch is broken.

⚠️ Note: After a pronoun, *am*, *is* and *are* are usually written as a contraction ('*m*, '*s*, '*re*). (See Unit 34.)

C

In the middle of a sentence, *was* and *were* are also usually unstressed. Listen to the chant.

B68 She was first.
You were last.
    It was hard.
      She was fast.
You were slow.
She was strong.
    I was tired.
    It was long.

D

The verb *be* is normally unstressed at the start of a sentence too. Listen to this chant.

B69 Am I right? Am I wrong?
Is it short? Is it long?
Are you hot? Are you cold?
Were they young? Were they old?
Is it false? Is it true?
Was it me? Was it you?

> **Important for listening**
>
> Note that the vowel is very weak in fast speech (see Unit 7, which looks at weak vowels).
> am = /əm/; is = /ɪz/; are = /ə/; were = /wə/; was = /wəz/
> You don't need to copy the fast speech pronunciation. People will understand you if you use careful speech. But you need to be able to understand fast speech.

⚠️ Note: The verb *be* is stressed in negative contractions (e.g. *aren't*), and at the end of sentences (e.g. *Yes, I am*). (See Unit 36.)

⚠️ Note: The verb *be* is also stressed for emphasis or contrast, for example:
That can't be John ... Wait a minute ... It is John! (See Unit 49.)

Exercises

35.1

B70

Circle the word *are* if you think the /r/ is pronounced. Then listen, check and repeat.

> There (are) a lot of books in the picture. Some of them are on the desks and some are on the shelves. There are some trees outside the windows. The windows are open. There are some pens on one of the desks.

35.2

B71

Tick (✔) the sentences where *is* is always a separate syllable. Then listen, check and repeat.

EXAMPLE

    a Lunch is ready! ✔   **b** Dinner is ready!

1 a The house is cold.   **b** The room is cold.
2 a The taxi is here.   **b** The bus is here.
3 a The beach is crowded.   **b** The park is crowded.
4 a The steak is good.   **b** The fish is good.
5 a The meaning is clear.   **b** The message is clear.
6 a The smell is awful!   **b** The noise is awful!
7 a Juice is good for you.   **b** Fruit is good for you.

35.3

B72

Listen and circle the verb you hear.

1 People *are* / *were* angry.
2 Alice *is* / *was* here.
3 Your face *is* / *was* dirty.
4 The birds *are* / *were* singing.
5 The books *are* / *were* cheap.

6 The fish *are* / *were* dying.
7 The place *is* / *was* nice.
8 Paris *is* / *was* nice.
9 The children *are* / *were* tired.
10 My friends *are* / *were* coming.

35.4

B73

Listen and fill the gaps with one word.

EXAMPLE That ....*was*........ my favourite.

1 His parents .... rich.
2 The birds .... singing.
3 The beach .... crowded.
4 The children .... at home.
5 He .... going out at the weekend.

6 Her dog .... called Kip.
7 This car .... very expensive.
8 The drinks .... free on this flight.
9 The weather .... terrible.
10 The banks .... closed on Saturday.

Now go to Unit 55 ▶

36

WHAT do you THINK?
Auxiliary verbs

A

OooO is a very common rhythm in questions beginning with *Wh-* words (*when, where, what,* etc.) followed by auxiliary verbs.

Wh- word (stressed)	auxiliary (unstressed)	pronoun (unstressed)	main verb (stressed)
What	do	you	think?
O	o	o	O

B74

Important for listening

Listen to these examples. You will hear each one twice; first in careful speech and then in fast speech. Notice how, in fast speech, the vowel is very weak in the auxiliary *do* and *does*.

> OooO
> **What** do you **think?**
> **Where** do you **live?**
> **What** does she **mean?**
> **Where** does he **work?**
> **What** did he **say?**
> **Why** did you **go?**

B

B75

Important for listening

Other auxiliaries are also usually unstressed in questions. Listen. Note that the speaker does not pronounce the first letters of the auxiliaries *will, have* and *has.*

> **What** will he **do?**   **Where** has she **been?**
> **What** have I **done?**   **What** can you **see?**

C

B76 Auxiliaries *are* stressed in negative contractions and at the end of sentences. Listen to these examples.

Yes, I do.
I don't know.
Yes, I will.
He won't say.
Yes, I have.
I haven't done it.
Yes, I can.
I can't help.

⚠ **Note:** Auxiliaries can also be stressed for emphasis or contrast. For example: *I'm not English, but I am British!* (See Unit 49.)

D

B77

Important for listening

In very fast speech, some speakers pronounce many of these questions with only three syllables. Listen.

OoO		
What do you **want?**	/wɒdjə'wɒnt/	(sounds like: What dya want?)
What does he **do?**	/wɒtsɪ'duː/	(sounds like: What si do?)
Where have you **been?**	/weəvjə'bɪn/	(sounds like: Wherve ya bin?)
Where did he **go?**	/weərdɪ'gəʊ/	(sounds like: Where di go?)

Exercises

36.1 Listen and complete the questions.

B78

EXAMPLE   What ....*did he*.... do?

1 Where _____ live?
2 What _____ say?
3 Where _____ work?
4 What _____ see?
5 Where _____ gone?

6 Who _____ meet?
7 Where _____ sit?
8 When _____ end?
9 Where _____ been?
10 Who _____ asked?

36.2 Write the questions in this conversation and give the stress patterns. Then listen, check and repeat

B79 the questions.

EXAMPLE

A: _____*What do you do?*_____ ? ___Oooo___

B: I'm a doctor.

1 A: _____ ? _____
   B: I live in Kingston, Jamaica.

2 A: _____ ? _____
   B: I work in the University Hospital.

3 A: _____ ? _____
   B: Yes, I'm married. My husband is a teacher.

4 A: _____ ? _____
   B: He teaches History and Geography.

5 A: _____ ? _____
   B: At the Grove Road Secondary School.

6 A: _____ ? _____
   B: I met him when I was on holiday in Florida.

7 A: _____ ? _____
   B: We got married in 1999.

36.3 Think of a computer which people speak into and it writes what they say. This computer wrote the
underlined parts of these questions incorrectly. (You can read what it heard in phonemic letters.)
Correct the writing.

EXAMPLE   What <u>dya</u> /djə/ mean? _____*What do you mean?*_____

1 Who <u>vya</u> /vjə/ told? _____ ?
2 What <u>di</u> /dɪ/ say? _____ ?
3 When <u>dya</u> /djə/ start? _____ ?
4 Where <u>zi</u> /zɪ/ gone? _____ ?
5 How <u>dya</u> /djə/ do? _____ ?

> Now go to Unit 56

37

A PIECE of CHEESE
Pronouncing short words (*a, of, or*)

A

Short words like articles (*a, the*), conjunctions (*and, or*) and prepositions (*to, of*) are usually unstressed. Listen to this chant. Every line has the stress pattern oOoO. They have this rhythm because the first and third words are all unstressed. These words are: *some, and, a, of, for, the, to, or, as*.

B80

Shopping list

Some milk and eggs,
A tin of peas,
A snack for lunch:
Some fruit and cheese.

The loaf of bread,
A jar of jam,
Some juice to drink,
A piece of ham.

Some pears or grapes,
Some beans and rice,
A can of beer
As cold as ice!

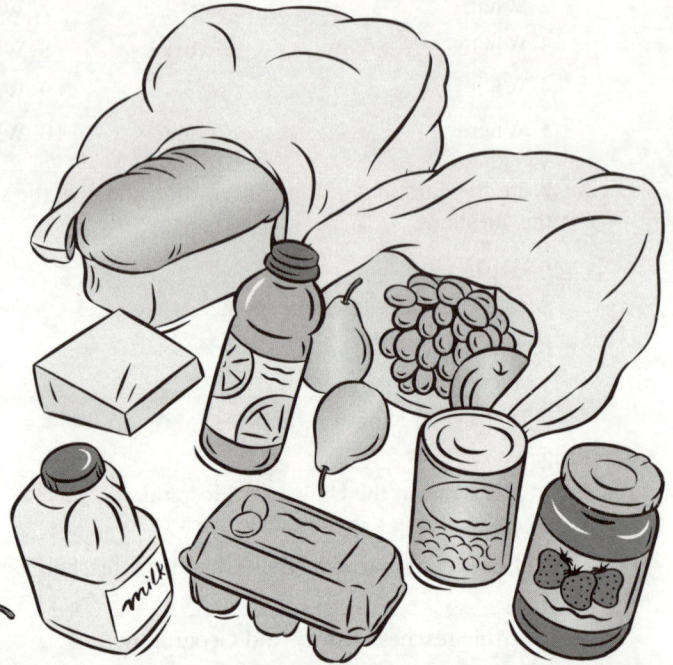

B

Important for listening

Listen again to the chant in A. Notice that the vowels in all the unstressed syllables are pronounced the same. This sound is written as /ə/ in the phonemic alphabet (see Unit 7). Also, in fast speech, the consonant sounds after the vowel in these words may not be pronounced. In this case, *and* sounds like *an*, and *of* sounds like *a*. Listen to these examples.

B81

and sounds like *an*:
an apple and an orange and an onion

of sounds like *a*:
a bit of this and a bit of that

You don't need to copy the fast speech pronunciation. People will understand you if you use careful speech. But you need to be able to understand fast speech.

⚠ **Note:** The consonant sound in *of* is not dropped when the following word begins with a vowel, for example *some of each*.

C

The vowel sound in *to* and *the* is different if the following word begins with a vowel. In this case, *to* changes from /tə/ to /tu/, and *the* changes from /ðə/ to /ði/. Listen to the difference.

B82 We need water to drink and food to eat.
I'll have the fish, and the apple pie for dessert.

Exercises

37.1 What are the things in the picture? Write them in the correct column according to the rhythm (there are two phrases in each column). Use these words: *bowl, bottle, jar, packet, bag, pot, carton, kilo.* Then say the phrases aloud.

oOoO	oOooO	oOooO	oOoooO
		A bowl of soup	

37.2 In these sentences, both of the words in *italics* are possible and they sound similar in fast speech. **B83** Listen and circle the word you hear.

1 I had a salad *as / and* a main course.
2 Give her *an / some* egg if she's hungry.
3 She went to look *at / for* the fruit.
4 He gave me a basket *of / for* bread.
5 Get some pasta *and / or* rice.

6 I like *the / to* cook.
7 She ordered *a / the* soup.
8 Have *some / an* orange juice.
9 He invited me *at / for* lunch.
10 He made this jar *for / of* jam himself.

37.3 Listen and fill the gaps. Then listen, check and repeat. Make sure you keep the same rhythm: oOoO. **B84**

EXAMPLE

_____*a*_____ glass _____*of*_____ milk

1 _____ time _____ lunch
2 _____ egg _____ chips
3 _____ bag _____ nuts
4 _____ drink _____ eat
5 _____ cook _____ rice

6 _____ fast _____ that
7 _____ meal _____ two
8 _____ box _____ food
9 _____ fish _____ meat

37.4 Think of a computer which people speak into and it writes what they say. This computer wrote these sentences incorrectly. Write the correct sentences.

EXAMPLE   We had beans an rice.   _We had beans and rice._

1 We had a nice cup a tea. _____

2 I don't want a go out tonight. _____

3 I need a drinker water. _____

4 We cook to chicken. _____

5 He can't cooker meal. _____

6 Have a nice cream! _____

7 Come in an sit down. _____

Follow up: Practise saying the chant in A on the opposite page.
Tap the table or your foot in time as you say it.

Now go to Unit 57

38 Pets enter, pet centre
Joining words 1

A

Important
for listening

In speech, words are not separated; they join together. Sometimes it is difficult to know where one word finishes and the next word begins. For example, *pets enter* sounds the same as *pet centre* because the consonant /s/ could be at the end of the first word or at the start of the second word. Listen to the examples. The phrases on the left sound the same as the phrases on the right.

B85

pets enter	pet centre
stopped aching	stop taking
ice-cream	I scream
known aim	no name
called Annie	call Danny
clocks tops	clock stops
missed a night	Mr Knight

PET
CENTRE

Note: The spelling may be different in the two phrases which sound the same. For example, the consonant sound /s/ is spelt S in *pets*, but C in *centre*. The consonant sound /t/ is spelt D at the end of *stopped*, but T in *taking*.

Note: The /h/ is often dropped from the beginning of pronouns, so that *thanked him* sounds like *thank Tim*.

B

Important
for listening

Normally, we know from the context what a word is. For example, these two sentences sound the same, but we know the first one is wrong because it has no sense.

It snow good.
It's no good.

C

Important
for listening

In fluent speech, people join words together. When one word ends with a consonant and the next word begins with a vowel, imagine that the consonant is at the beginning of the next word. For example, say the first line of the chant below as if the words were divided like this:
/gɒ tə pə teɪt/.

Listen to the chant and repeat. The rhythm of each line is the same. The symbol ‿ shows where the consonant sound joins to the vowel sound of the next word.

B86

Got‿up‿at‿eight,
Got‿on‿a bus,
Went‿into work,
Worked‿until two,
Went‿out for lunch,
Worked‿until six,
Back‿on the bus,
Switched‿on the box*,
Slept‿in‿a chair.

(*box = television)

NEW @ 1
VHS

English Pronunciation in Use

Exercises

38.1 What two words do you get if you move the consonant from the end of one word to the beginning of the next or vice versa? Complete the table. Remember: think about sound, not spelling!

EXAMPLE

cats eyes   *cat* ....size........

1 .... *able* ⟺ fell table   6 an ocean ⟺ *a* ....

2 known you ⟺ *no* ....   7 *stop* .... ⟺ stopped earning

3 *cooks* .... ⟺ cook steak   8 escaped error ⟺ .... *terror*

4 seen you ⟺ .... *new*   9 .... *cheer* ⟺ meant year

5 *faced* .... ⟺ face told   10 learn chess ⟺ .... 'yes'

38.2 Think of a computer which people speak into and it writes what they say. This computer wrote the sentences below incorrectly. Correct the phrases that are wrong using the phrases in the box.

phoned your	joined us	felt rain	no news is	stopped using
ships take	~~'s no good~~	heard you lie		

EXAMPLE   It ~~snow good~~; I can't fix it.   ....'s no good........

1 Known uses good news, as they say.   ....

2 Have you phone jaw parents this week?   ....

3 I've never her July before.   ....

4 I think I fell train; let's go inside.   ....

5 These ship steak cars across the river.   ....

6 They join does for dinner.   ....

7 We stop choosing the typewriter when we got the computer.   ....

38.3
(B87)
Show where you can join a word ending with a consonant sound to a word starting with a vowel sound using this symbol: ‿ (there are eight in total). Then listen and practise saying the poem.

There   was ‿ an   old   man   called   Greg,

Who   tried   to   break   open   an   egg.

He   kicked   it   around,

But   fell   on   the   ground,

And   found   that   he'd   broken   a   leg.

Now go to Unit 58 ▶

39 After eight, after rate
Joining words 2

A

When we say the spellings of words or names, we normally join them together in one continuous sound. For example, we say ABC like this: /eɪbiːsiː/ (without any pause between the letters). Sometimes we have to add an extra sound to separate vowel sounds. Listen to these examples. The added sound is in small letters.

🎧 B88

URL /juː‿ʷɑː‿ʳel/
AIM /eɪ‿ʲaɪ‿ʲem/
BORN /biː‿ʲəʊ‿ʷɑː‿ʳen/

The same three sounds, /r/, /j/ and /w/, are also added between whole words to separate vowel sounds.

B

> Important for listening

The consonant sound /r/ is used to separate vowel sounds when there is a letter R at the end of the first word. In many accents of English, including Southern British, this final letter R is not pronounced, so the word ends in a vowel sound. For example, the word *after* is pronounced /ɑːftə/. But if the following word begins with a vowel sound, the R is pronounced, in order to separate the two vowels. For example, the R *is* pronounced in *after eight* /ɑːftə‿ʳeɪt/. In this case, the R sounds like it is at the start of the next word, so *after eight* sounds like *after rate*. Listen to the examples.

🎧 B89

R not pronounced	R pronounced	sounds like ...
her card	her ace	her race
under sixteen	under age	under rage
after nine	after eight	after rate
four legs	four eyes	four rise
clear skies	clear air	clear rare

⚠️ **Note:** Sometimes we pronounce an /r/ to separate vowel sounds even if there is no R in the spelling. For example *saw Alice* can be pronounced /sɔː‿ʳælɪs/.

'I saw her race.'
'I saw her ace.'

C

> Important for listening

The sounds /j/ and /w/ can also be pronounced to separate vowel sounds.
- If the first word ends in a vowel sound like /ɪ/ and the next word starts with any vowel sound, we add the sound /j/ (Y).
- If the first word ends in a vowel sound like /uː/ or /ʊ/ and the next word starts with any vowel sound, we add the sound /w/ (W).

Listen to the examples. Notice that /j/ or /w/ is pronounced even when there is no Y or W in the spelling.

🎧 B90

no /j/ or /w/ pronounced	/j/ or /w/ pronounced	sounds like ...
every toe /evri təʊ/	every ear /evri ‿ʲɪə/	every year
he saves /hi seɪvz/	he earns /hi ‿ʲɜːnz/	he yearns
you drank /juː dræŋk/	you ache /juː ‿ʷeɪk/	you wake
you hurt /juː hɜːt/		

Exercises

39.1 Spell out these names. If possible, record yourself. Then listen to the recording and compare it with yours.

(B91)
1 TOM
2 BEN
3 ERIN

4 TANIA
5 ROSIE

39.2 In these pairs, the first and second word are joined with the phonemic letter shown. Read them
(B92) aloud, then say them again, this time reversing the order of the words, so that a different sound joins
the first and second word. You don't have to write anything. Then listen and check.

EXAMPLE two ‿^{w} or three   (three ‿^{j} or two)

1 grey ‿^{j} and blue
2 you ‿^{w} and me
3 where ‿^{r} or why
4 you ‿^{w} or her
5 here ‿^{r} or away

39.3 The word *rise* is 'hidden' in this sentence: *Her eyes are open.* It is the underlined part. This is clear if
we look at the phonemic spelling. The word *rise* is /raɪz/. You can see this underlined in this
phonemic spelling of the sentence: /həraɪzərəʊpən/. The words in the box are 'hidden' in the
sentences below. Find them and <u>underline</u> them, and write the hidden word after the sentence.

| wait | rage | winter | ~~yours~~ | reach | years | why | rise | ride | wake |

EXAMPLE   The boat's useless without the o<u>ars.</u> ....*yours*........

1 Are you into golf? ....

2 He has hair over the ears. ....

3 It's starting to ache. ....

4 I'm not sure I'd agree with you. ....

5 She has a shower each morning. ....

6 It's quarter to eight already. ....

7 Do I owe you anything? ....

8 Her eyes are a strange colour. ....

9 You should know better at your age! ....

(B93) Now listen to the sentences. Can you hear the 'hidden words'?
Try saying the sentences, making sure you pronounce the hidden words.

Now go to unit 59

40

Greet guests, Greek guests
Joining words 3

When one word ends with a consonant sound and the next word begins with a consonant sound, the first consonant sound is often changed. For example, *greet guests* sounds the same as *Greek guests* because the T in *greet* and the K in *Greek* are both pronounced like /g/. This is because of the influence of the /g/ in the following word, *guests*.

The sounds which most frequently change when they are at the end of a word are /d/, /t/ and /n/. They can change so much that the word sounds like another word. Listen to these examples:

I've got a bad cold. (*bad* sounds similar to *bag*)
We had a bad year. (*bad* sounds similar to *badge*)

They shot bears. (*shot* sounds similar to *shop*)
They shot cats. (*shot* sounds similar to *shock*)

What's your son called? (*son* sounds similar to *sung*)
My son made this. (*son* sounds similar to *sum*)

The consonants /d/ and /t/ may disappear completely when the next word starts with a consonant. For example, in the phrases below, the verb may sound as if it is in the present tense.

asked questions   mixed paint   boiled carrots   used power

⚠ Note: We can usually tell what a word is from the context. For example, in the sentence *I sat in the waiting room and dig crosswords*, the word before *crosswords* sounds like *dig* but we know from the context it must be *did*.

Exercises

40.1
B95

The <u>underlined</u> word in each sentence sounds like one of the words in the box. Match them. Then listen and check.

EXAMPLE   torch / talk

| talk / torch | **a** I <u>taught</u> classes this morning. ....*talk*........ . |
| | **b** You <u>taught</u> yourself French. ....*torch*........ |

1

| sum / sung | **a** The <u>sun</u> burnt my neck. .... |
| | **b** The <u>sun</u> came up over the mountains. .... |

2

| beak / beach | **a** I can't <u>beat</u> you at this game. .... |
| | **b** I can <u>beat</u> Carol at tennis. .... |

3

| coke / coach | **a** I can't get this <u>coat</u> clean. .... |
| | **b** Is this the <u>coat</u> you bought? .... |

4

| cheap / cheek | **a** They <u>cheat</u> quite a lot. .... |
| | **b** They <u>cheat</u> people out of their money. .... |

40.2
B96

Think of a computer which people speak into and it writes what they say. This computer wrote these sentences incorrectly. Listen. Guess from the context which word is wrong, circle it and write the correct word.

EXAMPLE   (Watch) your name? ....*What's*........

1 I hate going to museums and arc galleries. ....

2 Have you ever tribe Belgian beer? ....

3 I got ache questions correct out of ten. ....

4 She's a good player and can wing games against most people. ....

5 He copied out the text lime by line. ....

6 It was a bag question; nobody got the answer right. ....

40.3
B97

You will hear sentences with one of the two beginnings given. Listen and complete the correct sentence. Put a – in the other space.

EXAMPLE

He put the soup back in the ....*pan*........ .

He put the suit back in the ....–........ .

1 I got this cut by ....

  I got this cup by ....

2 I'll have to warn my ....

  I'll have to warm my ....

3 Her heart broke when ....

  Her harp broke when ....

4 It's the last turn before ....

  It's the last term before ....

Now go to Unit 60

41

Could you say that again?
Understanding conversation

A C1

Listen to this conversation. What is the cause of the misunderstanding?

> A: I've just got this one bag.
> B: Wow! Do you always travel so light?
> A: Yeah. Can't stand the wait, you know, at the airport …
> B: Yeah, I know. My bag's really heavy. But it's got wheels, so I don't have to carry it.
> A: No, I mean the waiting, you know, waiting for your cases to come out on the belt.

The speakers pronounce all the words clearly but there is a misunderstanding because the words *weight* and *wait* have the same pronunciation. When Speaker B says *heavy*, Speaker A knows he understood *weight*, not *wait*, so she corrects the misunderstanding.

In conversation, we need to know when communication is going wrong, and then correct it.

B C2

When we don't understand what someone says in a foreign language, we often think it is because we don't know the language well. But often it is not our fault. Listen to this man from London. Do you understand what he is saying?

> It leaves at free forty-five this afternoon.

There are many different accents in English. In this accent, *three* sounds like *free*. In this example, you can probably guess from the context that he is saying *three* forty-five. The context often helps us understand what people are saying.

C

We can't always guess from the context. Sometimes we need to ask questions in order to understand. Remember these ways of asking.

1 Sorry, I don't understand.

3 Could you repeat that?

2 How do you pronounce this?

Machynlleth

4 My name's /ʃɪvɔːn/.

How do you spell that?

Exercises

41.1 In each of the sentences below, one of the words is written wrongly. It is written wrongly because
that's what it sounds like in the accent of the speaker. All the accents are different from standard,
British English. Listen and guess from the context which word is written wrongly and correct it.

EXAMPLE   She's a ~~rider~~ of romantic novels. ......*writer*......

1 Read about it in the noose papers. ....

2 She went to hospital 'cause she had art problems. ....

3 We watched TV and den we went to bed. ....

4 I want to tank you for your help. ....

5 They were jailed for robin a bank. ....

6 With a bit of look, we'll win this game. ....

7 Can you old the umbrella while I get my keys out? ....

41.2 Listen to these dialogues and fill in the missing words. Then listen again and say B's lines.

1

A: Can I help you?

B: Yes, I'd like to see... I'm sorry, ...
   do you pronounce this name?

A: O'Shaughnessy. Doctor O'Shaughnessy.

B: Yes, I'd .... to see Doctor
   O'Shaughnessy, please.

2

A: My name's Mark.

B: ...., Mike, you say?

A: No, Mark. M-A-R-K.

B: Oh, I see. You don't .... the R?

A: No, not in my accent.

3

A: My surname's Vaugn.

B: Sorry, could you .... that, please?

A: Vaugn.

B: Vaugn? How do you .... that?

A: V-A-U-G-N.

B: Oh yes, I've seen that name before!

41.3 Listen. Reply to each sentence you hear using one of the expressions below. Number the expressions
in the order you use them.

.... Sorry, could you repeat that, please?

.... Sorry, I don't understand.

....1.... How do you pronounce that?

.... Can you speak more slowly, please?

Now go to Unit 2

42

'Was that the question?' he asked.
Reading aloud: 'pronouncing punctuation'

A C6 Listen to this text. Notice that in speech there are pauses where, in writing, there are punctuation marks.

> I can never guess the weather right. If I wear a warm shirt, the weather's hot. If I wear cool clothes, there's a cold wind. When I don't take my umbrella, it rains. If I take my umbrella, does it rain? Of course not! Then I leave it on the bus! Oh well. We all have our weaknesses, I guess!

⚠ **Note:** Reading aloud is good pronunciation practice. Don't forget to 'pronounce the punctuation'.

B C7 Pauses can change the meaning of what we say. Listen to these pairs of sentences and note the difference in pronunciation.

a It was cold outside. There was snow on the ground.
b It was cold. Outside, there was snow on the ground.

a Was that the question he asked?
b 'Was that the question?' he asked.

a I got up, quickly got dressed, and went downstairs.
b I got up quickly, got dressed, and went downstairs.

C C8 We need to use pauses to give us time to think, and to give the listener time to take in the information. Listen to this address and note that there are pauses where there are line breaks and where there are gaps in the telephone number. Notice also that when the speaker spells her surname and email address, she divides the letters into groups.

> Linda Wharton
> 29 Bolton Road
> Wigan
> Lancashire
> WI16 9FT
> England
> Tel: 090 827 7365
> email: linwar@applegroove.com

⚠ **Note:** Practise saying the spelling of your own name. Decide how you will group the letters, if your name is long.

Exercises

42.1
C9
Read this weather forecast aloud, 'pronouncing the punctuation'. Record yourself if you can. Then listen and compare.

> And for Friday, well, another wintry day in all parts of the region. Temperatures near freezing in many places, and along the coast, the wind will make it feel very cold indeed. Inland, some snow on the hills, and there may be fog in the valleys. If you're out and about driving, watch out for those icy roads! And for the weekend? Well, we're not expecting much change, I'm afraid. And that's all from me. Goodnight.

42.2
C10
The texts below are really two sentences, but the punctuation is missing. The two sentences are divided *before* or *after* the underlined expression. Listen and draw one line / to show where the sentences are divided.

EXAMPLE   They're leaving / soon it'll be quieter.

1 There was nothing inside it was empty.

2 We walked carefully downstairs it was dark.

3 I watched him silently he opened the drawer.

4 The rain didn't stop the next day it just carried on.

5 The weather was hot at the weekend it was 40 degrees.

6 I saw her clearly she was hungry.

7 It was cold last night the roads were icy.

Follow up: Read the sentences above aloud, once with the sentence break *before* the underlined expression, then again with the sentence break *after* it.

42.3
C11
Listen and write the name, address and contact details that you hear.

Name: _____
Address: _____
_____
_____
Postcode: _____
Telephone: _____
email: _____

Follow up: Read out the information you wrote above. Try to put the pauses exactly where they were in the recording you heard. Then listen again and compare.

42.4
Say your own name, address and contact details. Record it if possible.

Now go to Unit 3 ▶

43 A shirt and a tie / a shirt and tie
Grouping words

A C12 Listen to the underlined phrase in these two sentences. Notice that in the first one, the speaker pauses after the word *shirt*, so the words are divided into two groups. The line / shows where they are divided. The second phrase is pronounced all as one group.

I bought <u>a shirt / and a tie</u>.
He was wearing <u>a shirt and tie</u>.

The speakers group the words differently because the first speaker thinks of the shirt and tie as separate things, and the second speaker thinks of them as things that go together in a group.

B C13a Listen to this sentence. Notice that the speaker divides it into groups. In each group, the words are pronounced all joined together like one long word.

I bought a nice new jacket / with a zip down the front / and a lot of pockets.

There is no rule about where to divide words into groups, but it must make sense. If the word groups don't make sense, it is very hard to understand.

C13b Listen to the same sentence again, but this time divided *badly*. Notice how strange it sounds.

I bought a nice new / jacket with a zip down the / front and a lot of pockets. ✗

C C14 Listen to this woman. She is remembering the uniform she had at school. Listen to how she divides her words into groups. This is shown here by the / lines.

... I remember / we had this school uniform / and it was like all dark brown / a dark brown skirt and jacket / and a white blouse / and we had to have black shoes / and the skirt had to be below the knees / and we all hated this uniform / so we tried to change it / things like / you know / use a belt to bring the skirt higher / or ehh ... whatever / and we weren't allowed to have earrings / but we wore them anyway / outside the school / and then took them off / when we walked in ...

⚠ Note: When you are speaking, you often have to pause to think (or breathe!). Put the pause in the break between two groups of words. If you put the pause in the middle of a group of words, it will make you difficult to understand.

Exercises

43.1 Look at the two ways of dividing the sentences below. For each pair of sentences, cross out the one where the grouping does not make sense.

EXAMPLE
a ~~I bought a ticket and got / on the train.~~
b I bought a ticket / and got on the train.

1 a It was a small car / with a red stripe along the side.
   b It was a small car with a red / stripe along the side.

2 a Do you want chicken and chips / or fish and salad?
   b Do you want chicken / and chips or fish and salad?

3 a Derek can wear the most / expensive suit but he never looks smart.
   b Derek can wear the most expensive suit / but he never looks smart.

43.2
C15 Here are some sentences giving advice on what clothes to take on different kinds of trip. Divide the sentences using a line (/) over *one* of the gaps. Choose the gap which makes the best sense. Then listen and check.

EXAMPLE *A hot place which gets cold in the evenings:*
Take shorts .... and T-shirts ...**/**... and long trousers .... and a sweater for the evenings.

1 *A ski resort:*
Take your boots .... and ski suit .... and a dress .... and some nice shoes for the evenings.

2 *A sunny place which sometimes has rain:*
Take a hat .... and sunglasses .... and T-shirts .... and an umbrella in case it rains.

3 *A business trip with a weekend off in the middle:*
Take a smart suit .... and a shirt .... and tie .... and some casual clothes for the weekend.

4 *A sightseeing holiday with a few days on the beach at the end:*
Take your camera .... and some good walking shoes .... and a towel .... and bathing costume for the beach.

43.3
C16 Listen and draw lines (/) showing where the speaker divides the words into groups.

A man wanted to buy his wife a new dress because it was her birthday so he went to a department store and looked around and he was looking for about an hour but he couldn't decide and finally this shop assistant came and asked if he needed help he said he was looking for a dress and the shop assistant asked is it for you sir?

Now go to Unit 4

44 Ehm ...
Showing that you want to continue

A C17 Listen to this short conversation. The lines of six dots (::::) means that the speaker is making the word before the dots longer.

A: What did you think of the music?
B: Well, it was::: interesting.

B needs time to think of the best word to describe the music. She makes the word *was* longer to show A that she is still in the conversation. If she paused for all that time, A might think she was not going to answer.

B We often say noises like *ehm* to keep our speaking turn while we are thinking of what to say or doing something else. In the example below, B says it to keep his speaking turn while he looks at his watch.

A: *What's the time?*
B: *Let's see, it's ehm::: nearly seven.*

⚠️ Note: You can use noises like *ehm* to 'buy time' when you are speaking English and you need time to think of a word. If you are silent, the other person may think you have finished and start talking.

C C18 Listen to this conversation. A and B have started a web site and they are thinking of having some music on it. They are trying to decide what kind of music to have. Both speakers use (::::) often to keep their speaking turns. Notice how they keep their voices on the same level when they say the word before the pause (::::) but their voices go down at the end of their speaking turns (shown with a full stop below).

A: Ehm::::, I don't know, I think it's a bit ehm::: sort of::: well, like the music you get in supermarkets or in ehm::: in hotel lifts and places like that.
B: Yeah, I know what you mean, but ehm::: I mean, if we have something stronger like ehm::: well, you know, blues ::: or modern jazz or whatever, well, somebody'll hate it.
A: Yeah right, so::: maybe we shouldn't have any music.
B: Yeah well::: but ehm::: but I think everyone expects it these days.
A: Absolutely! So let's be different!
B: Well, OK::: or::: or we could have something classical?

⚠️ Note: It is very common for speakers to start their speaking turn by agreeing with what the other person said. Look in the conversation above, for example. At the start of their turns, the speakers use expressions like: *Yeah, I know what you mean   Yeah, right   Absolutely   Well, OK.*

Exercises

44.1
C19

In all of these conversations, B is doing something else at the same time as speaking. Guess which of these things B is doing and write it. Then listen and check.

> doing a mental calculation   looking in a wallet   ~~writing the numbers down~~
> checking in a personal diary   looking in a business appointments book

EXAMPLE   A: My phone number's 067 3786.
               B: Just a moment, so that's::: 0::: 6::: 7::: 3::: 7::: 9:::
               A: No, 8. It's 3786.
               B: Ah, OK, 8::: 6.   *B is* *writing the numbers down.*

1 A: Hi! I have an appointment to see Ms Jones.
  B: Yes, so you must be Mr::: Mr Gleason?   *B is* ....
  A: Yeah, that's right.

2 A: It's just over fifty pounds.
  B: Right, so that's ehm::: about 70 dollars?   *B is* ....

3 A: Let's meet on Thursday.
  B: Let's see, Thursday::: Thursday::: Yes,
    Thursday, that's fine.   *B is* ....

4 A: Can you change this ten for two fives?
  B: I think so, let's see, ehm::: yeah, sure.
    Here you are.   *B is* ....

> **Follow up:** Listen and repeat B's lines (including the long sounds).

44.2
C20

Listen to these sentences. Does the person want to keep the speaking turn (write ●●●) or has he/she finished (write ●)?

EXAMPLE   I like all kinds of music really, you know, ehm::: rock and roll ●●●

1 I don't really have much time to ehm::: to listen to music

2 Yeah, I love Brazilian music, people like Gal Costa

3 She plays quite a lot of instruments, piano, guitar

4 Dad's really into classical music, you know, specially Mozart

5 I started the piano when I was, let's see, ehm::: fifteen

44.3
C21

You will hear a girl telling a story. She uses *ehm* a lot. Write down what she says without the *ehm*s.

> I didn't go to the concert because ....
>
> ....
>
> ....
>
> ....

> Now go to Unit 5

45 Well, anyway ...
Telling a story

C22

A

Important for listening

Two words you will often hear in conversation are *anyway* and *well*. Listen to the conversation below. Notice that *anyway* and *well* are often said in quite a high-pitched voice.

A: I nearly got arrested, you know, the other day.

B: You what ... arrested? What do you mean?

A: **Well**, I'm doing this project on graffiti, you know, at college, and ehm ... so I have to take lots of photos of graffiti and ...

B: Uh huh.

A: So **anyway**, I saw this train with some amazing graffiti on the side, so I went there to ehm ... take a photo of it. The thing is, it was a bit far from the platform ...

B: So what happened?

A: **Well**, I walked along next to the lines, and then these two ehm ... station police came along and said I shouldn't be there, so ehm ... they took me to the office, and then they asked for my ID card, you know, my identity card ...

B: Mmm?

A: **Well**, I didn't have it. I left it at home that day.

B: Oh no!

A: Yeah, so **anyway**, then they didn't know what to do with me, so ehm ... I said, 'Look, I'll leave my camera here and I go home to get my ID card'. In the end, they agreed, so I did that, and they ehm ... wrote my ID number, and then just let me go ...

In the conversation above, A uses *anyway* to show that she is moving on to the next part of the story. In this context, it is usually pronounced in a high voice. Notice that before the word *anyway*, the speaker is not moving the story on, she is just giving some background information. *Anyway* shows she is returning to the story.

In the conversation above, A uses *well* to show that she is responding to B's questions. In this context, it is usually pronounced in a high voice.

B

Important for listening

In the conversation above, notice that the listener, B, is not silent. He asks questions. He also encourages A to continue by making noises like *uh huh* and *mmm*. Listen again, and notice that he makes these noises in a low-pitched voice. He does this to show that he does not want to speak, he wants A to continue speaking.

Exercises

45.1
Listen and answer the questions. Listen for the word *anyway*, because the important information comes *after* it. Before it, the speaker is just giving background information.

EXAMPLE

What did the speaker see on the way home from work? .... *He saw an accident.*

1 What happened to Katy the other day? ....

2 What did the old man do in the bar? ....

3 What is the good news about Clara? ....

45.2
Fill the gaps with the words *well* or *anyway*. Then listen and check.

A: I wonder what happens if you lose your passport.

B: I lost mine once.

A: So what happened?

B: .... (1), I was abroad, just travelling around,

you know, and .... (2), somebody stole my

bag on the last day.

A: So what did you do?

B: .... (3), I reported it to the police, which

took absolutely ages – so many forms to fill in, and

.... (4), they gave me a special travel

document and then when I arrived home …

Follow up: Listen to the conversation again and say B's lines.

Now go to Unit 6

46 I mean, it's sort of like ...
Understanding small talk

A C25

A *Important for listening*

Listen to this conversation. Note that the expressions in black do not really have any meaning; you could easily understand the text without them.

Notice that the speakers say them very fast, often in a low voice: they are 'throw away' words, i.e. you could throw them away and the meaning wouldn't change.

A: Ugh! This coffee is really horrible!
B: Yeah, I know. Machine coffee, I mean, why do we drink the stuff?
A: It's sort of like ... someone puts the contents of an ashtray in water and ehm ... like, heats it up or something, you know ...
B: Yeah, that's what it tastes like, ... and ... I mean, have you tried the ehm ... the tea?
A: Oh yeah, the tea! That's even worse!
B: I mean the plastic cups don't help, do they?
A: No, I know, ... plastic cups! ... We like even had champagne in plastic cups, you know, at what's-her-name's leaving party ...
B: Jenny. Jenny Glen. Yeah, I remember that, last January it was ... I kind of liked Jenny. I wonder what she's doing now ...

B *Important for listening*

Different people often have their own favourite 'throw away' words. For example, in the conversation above, A says *like* and *you know* a lot and B says *I mean* a lot.

⚠ **Note:** When you are listening, you don't need to understand every word. Often, the things people say really fast are just 'throw away' words, and you can ignore them.

C C26

C *Important for listening*

The same expressions which people use as 'throw away' words *do* have meaning in other contexts. In all the sentences on the left below, the expressions in black have meaning. In the sentences on the right, they are 'throw away' words.

Listen and notice the difference in pronunciation: the 'throw away' words are said faster and in a low voice.

Tell me everything you know.	She tells me everything, you know.
'Blue Mountain' is a kind of coffee.	'Blue Mountain' coffee is kind of nice.
We like to go away at weekends.	We like go to the beach or whatever.
I mean the one on the right.	I mean, what's the point of buying one shoe?!

Exercises

46.1
C27
You will hear someone speaking about the weather in Montana (in the USA) with a lot of 'throw away' words. Write what the person says, but miss out the 'throw away' words.

....
....
....
....
....
....
....
....

moustache ———— beard

46.2
C28
You will hear four people speaking. What are their favourite 'throw away' words? Write them after the name.

Speaker 1: Frank .... *I mean* ....

Speaker 2: Debbie ....

Speaker 3: Kimberly ....

Speaker 4: Greg ....

46.3 Underline the 'throw away' words in this text. There are nine more expressions to underline.

> We don't <u>like</u> have coffee breaks, I mean we just like get
> a coffee or tea and sort of like take it back to our desks,
> you know, but it's kind of dangerous 'cause, I mean, people
> sometimes like knock the drink over the computer, you know.

Follow up: Read the text aloud, saying the underlined expressions fast and in a low voice.
Record yourself if possible.

46.4
C29
Listen to these sentences. Is the expression in *italics* 'throw away' (said fast and in a low voice) or not? If it is 'throw away', underline it. Note that the punctuation is not written, so you must decide from the pronunciation.

1 I don't think these are the men *you know*
2 I've taught you everything *you know*
3 Do you know the place *I mean* it's just over there
4 She's not the one *I mean* she's too tall
5 They're *like* wild animals
6 This is *like* Arctic weather

Now go to Unit 7 ➤

Right, OK ...
Understanding instructions

When listening to instructions, listen for the signals *right*, *now* and *OK*, which tell you that you are moving on to the next step. In the conversation below, B is giving A instructions on how to do something on a computer. B uses the words *right*, *now* and *OK* to signal that she is starting a new step in the instructions. Listen and notice that these words (in **black** below) are said in an emphatic voice.

> A: How do you copy bits of text off a document?
> B: **Right**, well first you have to ehm ... select the bit of text you want, you know, just click and drag with the mouse ...
> A: Oh, so it's just click and drag?
> B: Yeah, and the bit of text comes up in a different colour, yeah?
> A: Uh huh, a different colour ...
> B: **Now**, click 'Edit' and choose 'Copy' ...
> A: Edit ... Copy ... OK ...
> B: **OK**, and finally, open your document and click 'Paste'.
> A: Open document ... Paste ... Oh, I see.

The words *right*, *now* and *OK* are used in other contexts, apart from as a signal to the next step. In these other contexts, they are often not pronounced so strongly. Listen and compare the difference.

> Close the box ... that's right. **Right**, now you can close the whole program.
> I think we're on line now. **Now**, type the address in the box at the top.
> **Now** look at the whole page and see if it looks OK. **OK**, now you can print!

Listen again to this line from the conversation in A. Notice that the speaker pronounces *Oh* in a high voice.

> Open document ... Paste ... **Oh**, I see.

The speaker uses the word *Oh* to signal that he has learnt something new.

Exercises

47.1
C32
Listen to the instructions and complete this picture. First you will hear instructions to draw the line and square below. Then you will hear more details to add.

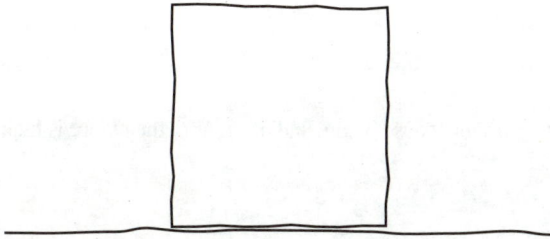

47.2 Listen to the instructions for 47.1 again and write a number each time you hear one of the words *right, now, OK*. Write the numbers at the start of each line below. Then write the instruction after each number.

1 ....Take a piece of paper and a pen...

2 ....Draw a line across the page...

....

....

....

....

....

....

Follow up: Give the instructions, but don't say the numbers, say *right, now* or *OK* instead. Record yourself if possible.

47.3
C33
Listen to these instructions. Is the expression in *italics* a signal to a new step in the instructions (said in a high voice) or not? If it *is* a signal, underline it. Note that the punctuation is not written, so you must decide from the pronunciation.

EXAMPLE   Click on that icon now the program is opening <u>*right*</u> now start a new document

1 Check that everything looks *right* and then send it
2 Click here so you get a new page *OK* and now write the title at the top
3 Make sure you save that *OK* and now close the program
4 You will see the icon on the *right* of your screen
5 Open the program *right* and now start a new document
6 I think it's ready *now* you can switch it on

Now go to Unit 8

'Like father like son' as they say
Quoting speech

C34 Listen to two people having a conversation about a neighbour's son. Notice how they pronounce the quote marks (' ').

A: I said to Terry, I said, 'Can you open the door for me?' and he says, 'Open it yourself!' Can you believe it!
B: I know. That boy's so rude! I said to his father, I said, 'You should do something about that boy', and do you know what he said to me? He said, 'It's none of your business'.
A: Oh, he's just as bad as Terry. 'Like father like son' as they say!

The speakers show the quotes by putting a short pause before and after. Also, their voice is higher on the quotes. Listen to recording C34 again.

'Can you open the door for me?'   'Open it yourself!'
I said,   and he says,

'Like father like son'
              as they say.

C35 Listen and compare these lines. Notice how you can hear the quote marks (' ').

Do you know what he said to me?
'Do you know what?' he said to me.
I said to his father, 'I said you should do something'.
I said to his father, I said, 'You should do something'.

C36 Listen to this story. Notice that we may pronounce quote marks for written words or thoughts, not just speech.

Question one was 'What's the capital of Australia?'
'This is easy,' I thought, so I wrote 'Sydney'. Then when I got home I looked in a book. 'Australia' it said, 'Capital: Canberra'. 'Oh no,' I thought. 'Failed again!'

Canberra • Sydney

Exercises

48.1
C37

Listen. Which do you hear first and which second? Write 1 or 2 after each sentence.

EXAMPLE   a   'You're an idiot, that's what,' she said. _2_

              b   'You're an idiot', that's what she said. _1_

1 a   What she said was good. ....
  b   What she said was 'Good!' ....

2 a   He said, 'Linda was married.' ....
  b   He said Linda was married. ....

3 a   That's the thing she said. ....
  b   'That's the thing,' she said. ....

4 a   He wrote a letter to the president. ....
  b   He wrote 'A letter to the president'. ....

5 a   I don't know what I thought. ....
  b   'I don't know what,' I thought. ....

6 a   She says, 'What she thinks is right.' ....
  b   She says what she thinks is right. ....

7 a   'Who?' wrote Julius Caesar. ....
  b   Who wrote *Julius Caesar*? ....

8 a   Who said 'Martin'? ....
  b   'Who?' said Martin. ....

> **Follow up:** Record yourself saying one of the sentences, **a** or **b**, for each number. Make a note of which one you chose. Then listen to your recording again in about two weeks and try to do this exercise with it.

48.2
C38

This speaker is telling some gossip. Put the quote marks (' ') in the text. (Don't worry about other punctuation or capitals.) Then listen and check your answers. Then try saying it yourself.

> So I say to Claire 'where's David, Claire?' and she says oh, he's staying at home to do his homework, and of course I thought oh no he's not! because I saw him, you see, going into the café with Lorraine and I said hi David! and he went completely red, and Lorraine said we're doing a school project together, and I thought oh yes, I know what kind of project that is!

Now go to Unit 9

49 He <u>will</u> win
Introduction to emphatic stress

A Short sentences have a typical sentence stress, or rhythm. (See Unit 23.) For example:

He won't win! oOO (The sentence has three syllables, and there is stress on the second and third.)

He'll win! oO (The sentence has two syllables and there is stress on the second.)

B But in conversation, speakers can choose to put the stress in any place. This is like <u>underlining</u> words in writing: we do this to put emphasis on words. Here are the same two examples from A again, but this time they are in the context of a short conversation. Notice the way the speakers 'underline' some words.
A: He'll win, you know.
B: He <u>won't</u> win!
A: He <u>will</u> win!

In this example, the speakers do not agree with each other. B 'underlines' <u>won't</u> to show that he is saying the opposite of what A said. Then A 'underlines' <u>will</u> for the same reason. Note that the written form also changes, from *'ll* to *will*.

C C39 To 'underline' a word, a speaker does one or more of these things: **a** makes it louder, **b** makes it longer, **c** makes it higher. Listen to this conversation. It shows the 'underlining' very clearly.

A: He won't win.
B: <u>Who</u> won't?
A: <u>He</u> won't.
B: He <u>will</u> win.
A: He <u>won't</u> win.
B: He <u>will</u>!
A: He <u>won't</u>!
B: I <u>hope</u> he wins.
A: <u>I</u> hope he <u>loses</u>.
B: He <u>won't</u> lose.
A: He <u>will</u> lose.
B: You're <u>wrong</u>!
A: <u>You're</u> wrong!
B: He's <u>won</u>!
A: <u>Who's</u> won?
B: <u>He's</u> won!
A: Oh no!

We emphasise words for example when we want to make a contrast with what the other person says, or correct some wrong information. (Units 50 to 53 give more detail on this.)

106 *English Pronunciation in Use*

Exercises

49.1
C40
Write three different ways to disagree with each of A's sentences, and <u>underline</u> the words you would put emphasis on. Then listen, check and repeat.

EXAMPLE   B: _____ <u>No</u>, I'll win! _____ (opposite subject)

   A: I'll win.   B: _____ <u>You</u> won't win! _____ (negative)

                 B: No, _____ you'll <u>lose</u>! _____ (word with opposite meaning)

1   B: No, _____ (opposite subject)

   A: I finished first.   B: No, you didn't _____ (negative)

                 B: No, you _____ (word with opposite meaning)

2   B: No, _____ (opposite subject)

   A: You're stupid!   B: I'm _____ (negative)

                 B: No, I'm _____ (word with opposite meaning)

49.2
C41
Read this conversation. Guess which words the speakers will 'underline' for emphasis and <u>underline</u> them in the text. You are told which lines have no underlining. Then listen and check.

A: I won't pass. (no underline)
B: You <u>will</u> pass.
A: <u>You'll</u> pass.
B: I don't know. (no underline)
A: You won't fail.
B: I might fail.
A: I will fail.
B: The exam's not hard. (no underline)
A: It's very hard.
B: But not too hard.
A: Too hard for me.
B: But you're very clever! (no underline)
A: You're the clever one.
B: Yes, I suppose you're right. (no underline)

Follow up: Listen to the conversation again and repeat B's lines. Remember to 'pronounce the underlining'.

Now go to Unit 10

50

Schwartz ... <u>Pedro</u> Schwartz
Emphasising added details

A C42 Listen to the way the speaker 'underlines' certain words in this text.

My name's <u>Schwartz</u> ... <u>Pedro</u> Schwartz.
I'm from <u>Chile</u> ... the <u>South</u> of Chile.
I live in <u>Puerto Montt</u> ... well, <u>near</u> Puerto Montt.
Actually, I live on an <u>island</u> ... an island called <u>Chiloé</u>.
My grandparents were <u>German</u> ... well, <u>Swiss</u>-German, in fact.

In the first line, both phrases contain the name *Schwartz*. In the first phrase, the speaker 'underlines' this word because it is new information. But in the second phrase, he doesn't, because now it is old information. The new information in the second phrase is *Pedro*, so the speaker 'underlines' this.

NEW   OLD

My name's <u>Schwartz</u> ... <u>Pedro</u> Schwartz.

NEW

There is a similar pattern in each of the other examples above.

B C43 Above, the same speaker gives information and then adds new details. But in a conversation, one speaker can give information and *the other* can add new details. In both cases, the speaker 'underlines' the added detail. Listen to this example.

A: I hear you've got a boat.
B: A <u>small</u> boat, yes.
A: And a big house.
B: Well, it's <u>quite</u> big, I suppose.
A: And you live in Hollywood.
B: Well, <u>near</u> Hollywood, yes.
A: So you must be rich then?
B: Well, <u>quite</u> rich I guess.

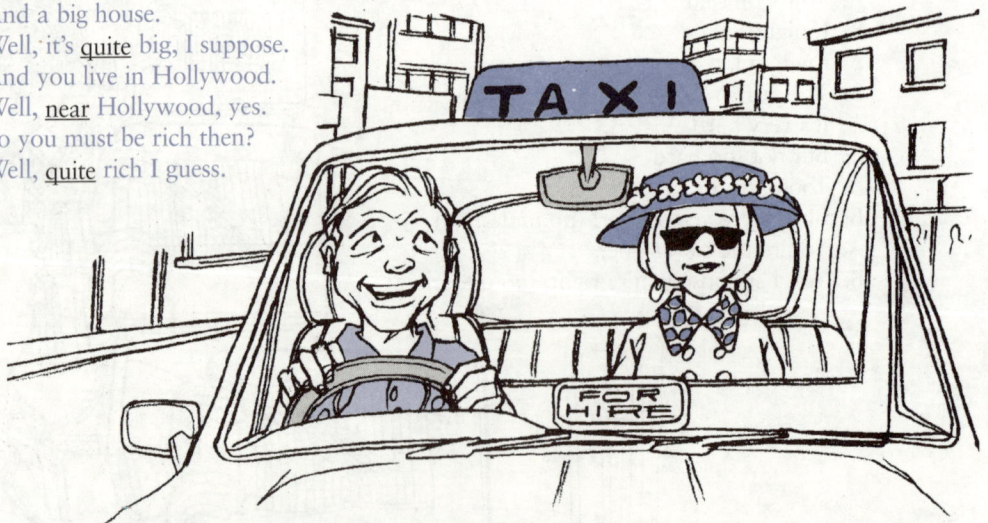

C C44 Listen to these two short conversations. A's question shows that she doesn't know anything about where B comes from. C's question shows that she knows he comes from India, so when B says *South India*, he 'underlines' *South* because this is added information.

A: Where are you from?
B: South India.

C: Which part of India are you from?
B: <u>South</u> India.

Exercises

50.1 Use the words from the box to add details to the sentences below. <u>Underline</u> the added detail. Say your sentences out loud.

~~car~~	plastic	James	French	very	central

EXAMPLE
It's a radio ...   *a <u>car</u> radio*

1 It's cold ...   _____   4 It's in Asia ...   _____

2 It's a bag ...   _____   5 He's a composer ...   _____

3 My name's Bond ...   _____

50.2 Listen and <u>underline</u> the words which B 'underlines' with her voice.
C45

A: It's very quiet.
B: <u>Too</u> quiet.
A: I think something's wrong.
B: Very wrong.
A: I don't like it.
B: I don't like it at all.
A: Let's get out of here.
B: Let's get out fast!

Follow up: Listen again and repeat B's lines.

50.3 The answers to the pairs of questions **a** and **b** below are the same, but the speaker puts stress on a
C46 different word in each answer. For example, in the answer to Example a, the speaker puts stress on the word 'Vettori' but in b, she puts stress on the word 'Clara'. Read the other questions and <u>underline</u> the words the speaker will put stress on. Then listen and check.

EXAMPLE a What's your name?
    Clara <u>Vettori</u>.

b What's your full name, Ms Vettori?
    <u>Clara</u> Vettori.

1 **a** Do you live in Milan?
    Near Milan, yes.

1 **b** Do you live near Milan?
    Near Milan, yes.

2 **a** What do you do?
    I'm a graphic designer.

2 **b** What kind of designer are you?
    I'm a graphic designer.

3 **a** Do you have your own home?
    Yes, a very nice flat.

3 **b** Do you have a nice flat?
    Yes, a very nice flat.

4 **a** What do you do in the evenings?
    Well, I'm learning French.

4 **b** Do you speak French?
    Well, I'm learning French.

5 **a** Do you know London?
    Yes, I lived there for a year.

5 **b** You lived in London, didn't you?
    Yes, I lived there for a year.

6 **a** Do you have any brothers or sisters?
    Yes, two brothers.

6 **b** You have some brothers, don't you?
    Yes, two brothers.

7 **a** What kind of music do you like?
    I like jazz and classical.

7 **b** Which do you prefer, jazz or classical?
    I like jazz and classical.

Follow up: Play the recording again and repeat the answers.

Now go to Unit 11 ▶

51 I think you're in <u>my</u> seat
Emphasising important words

A C47 Listen to this conversation. Notice that the speakers 'underline' the words which are most important in their argument.

A: Excuse me, I think you're in <u>my</u> seat.
B: Sorry, but it says <u>7A</u> on my boarding card.
A: Oh, er … right … I asked for a <u>window</u> seat, you see …
B: Yeah, so did <u>I</u>. What's <u>your</u> seat number?
A: Let's see … Oh, it's <u>8A</u>.
B: So I guess you're in the seat <u>behind</u> me.
A: Oh yes. Sorry about that.

B C48 Listen to this conversation. Notice how the speaker 'underlines' a different word in her second request. In the first request, what is important is *what* the passenger must do. In the second request, it is *when* he should do it.

A: I'm sorry, but you must switch that <u>off</u>, sir.
B: OK, just a minute.
A: Switch it off <u>now</u>, please!

C C49 The word which is more important depends on the context. Listen to these sentences. Notice that the speaker 'underlines' different words in the different contexts.

Sentence	*Context*
Could I have a glass of <u>water</u> <u>too</u>, please?	A passenger asked the stewardess for a tomato juice and wants water too.
Could <u>I</u> have a glass of water <u>too</u>, please?	A passenger asked for water and now the next passenger is asking for the same.
You have to check in at <u>five</u>.	A travel agent is telling a customer the check-in time.
You have to <u>check in</u> at five.	You are talking to your friend who is worried because she thinks her flight is at five and she could miss it.

Exercises

51.1
C50

In each of these conversations, A has to repeat the request, but 'underlining' a different word. Which word? Underline one word in the third line of each conversation. Then listen and check.

EXAMPLE A: Can I have a donut?

B: What do we say, Benny?

A: Can I have a donut, <u>please</u>?

1 A: A black coffee, please.

B: Sorry, do you want milk with your coffee?

A: No, a black coffee please.

2 A: What's your nationality?

B: Well, my wife's an American citizen.

A: Yes, but what's your nationality, sir?

3 A: What time is it?

B: Well, the clocks changed last night …

A: So what time is it then?

> **Follow up:** Listen again and repeat A's lines.

51.2
C51

The sentences in the contexts **a** and **b** below are the same, but with different pronunciation. You will hear each sentence twice, once for context **a** and once for context **b**. Listen and decide which you hear first, context **a** or context **b**. Write 1 and 2 in the boxes.

EXAMPLE

a I <u>think</u> that's my bag. [2]
She's not completely sure that it's her bag.

b I think that's <u>my</u> bag. [1]
Another person is picking up her bag.

1 a Is that your <u>phone</u>? ☐
He can hear an electronic sound from someone's pocket.

1 b Is that <u>your</u> phone? ☐
He can see somebody's mobile phone on the seat.

2 a Is your seat <u>29</u> F? ☐
She is not sure she heard the number correctly.

2 b Is your seat 29 <u>F</u>? ☐
She is not sure she heard the letter correctly.

3 a Is there a bank in <u>this</u> terminal? ☐
He knows there is a bank in the other terminal but not if there is one in this terminal.

3 b Is there a <u>bank</u> in this terminal? ☐
He is looking for a bank.

4 a Where's the women's <u>toilet</u>? ☐
She is looking for the toilet.

4 b Where's the <u>women's</u> toilet? ☐
She can see the men's toilet, but not the women's.

> **Follow up:** Record yourself saying the sentence for context **a** or **b**. Make a note of which one you choose. Then use your recording to do the exercise again in about two weeks.

Now go to Unit 12

52 Chips or salad?
Emphasising contrasting alternatives

A C52 When we present alternatives, we 'underline' the contrast between them. Listen to this example. Notice the way the speaker 'underlines' the alternatives.

A: I'd like a hamburger, please.
B: Do you want a <u>super</u> burger or a <u>regular</u> burger?
A: What's the difference?
B: Well, the <u>super</u> comes with <u>chips</u> and the <u>regular</u> comes <u>without</u> chips.

B C53 The same sentence can be pronounced differently, depending on the sentence that came before it. Listen to these examples. Notice how B 'underlines' in a different place depending on what A said.

A: You can pay by credit card.   B: I haven't <u>got</u> a credit card.
A: Why are you paying in cash?   B: I haven't got a <u>credit card</u>.

A: Shall we sit inside or outside?   B: Let's sit <u>out</u>side.
A: Where shall we sit?   B: Let's sit out<u>side</u>.

⚠ **Note:** In the second example above, it is not a different word which is underlined; it is a different part of the same word *outside*.

C C54 The word we choose to 'underline' can change the meaning of our sentence. Listen to these sentences pronounced in two different ways and see the different meanings in the pictures.

Do you want the <u>hamburger</u> with chips, or <u>salad</u>?

Do you want the hamburger with <u>chips</u> or <u>salad</u>?

Would you like <u>chicken</u> with vegetables, or Russian <u>salad</u>?

Would you like chicken with <u>vegetables</u> or Russian <u>salad</u>?

⚠ **Note:** In writing, the pause may be indicated by a comma.

Exercises

52.1
C55

Read the short conversations. Which words do you think B will 'underline'? <u>Underline</u> them in the texts below. Then listen and check.

1 A: I'd like a salad, please.
B: A mixed salad or a Greek salad?
A: What's the difference?
B: Well, a mixed salad has tuna and a Greek salad has cheese.

2 A: I'd like to stay two nights, please.
B: Do you want full board or half board?
A: What's the difference?
B: Full board includes all meals and half board includes just breakfast and dinner.

3 A: We'd like a room for two, please.
B: Would you like a standard or deluxe?
A: What's the difference?
B: Standard has a mountain view and deluxe has a sea view.

Follow up: Play the recording again and repeat B's lines.

52.2
C56

Listen. You will hear only the answers. Which do you hear first, **a** or **b**? Write 1 and 2 in the boxes.

EXAMPLE

a – Would you like a starter?
– I'll have a mixed <u>salad</u>, please. ☐ 1

b – What kind of salad would you like?
– I'll have a <u>mixed</u> salad, please. ☐ 2

1 a – What time do you close?
– We're closing <u>now</u>, sorry. ☐

1 b – A table for two please.
– We're <u>closing</u> now, sorry. ☐

2 a – Would you like anything to drink?
– I'd like red <u>wine</u>, please. ☐

2 b – Would you like red or white?
– I'd like <u>red</u> wine, please. ☐

52.3
C57

Listen. Which choice is the waiter offering first: picture **a** or **b**? Write a – b or b – a.

1 Would you like peaches or strawberries with cream?
a    b

2 Would you like tea with lemon or milk?
a    b

3 Would you like sausage or bacon and eggs?
a    b

Now go to Unit 13

53 Fifty? No, fifteen!
Emphasising corrections

A C58 When we hear an error and we correct it, we 'underline' the correct information.
Listen to this conversation. Notice how Sid 'underlines' the words which Joe has heard
incorrectly.

SID: Let's meet up tonight.
JOE: OK. When and where?
SID: How about the Blues Café?
JOE: The Mews Café? Don't like that place …
SID: No, the <u>Blues</u> Café. In Rawton Street.
JOE: Where's Lawton Street?
SID: Not Lawton Street, <u>Rawton</u> Street, you know …
JOE: Ah yes, OK. What time?
SID: How about nine fifteen.
JOE: Five fifteen? That's too early.
SID: No, <u>nine</u> fifteen. What's wrong with your ears today?!

B C59 If only a part of a word or phrase is not heard correctly, we 'underline' only that part when we
correct. Listen to these examples.

A: My nephew's fifteen.
B: Thirteen?
A: No, <u>fif</u>teen!

A: You must be more careful!
B: Careless?
A: No, care<u>ful</u>!

A: Her room is really untidy.
B: Tidy?
A: No, <u>un</u>tidy!

A: I saw a blackbird in the garden.
B: A blackboard?
A: No, a black<u>bird</u>!

A: The Amazon's the longest river in the world.
B: Oh, I thought the <u>Nile</u> was the longest river.

C In the first four examples you heard, the mistake was that B did not hear correctly. But we can
also use extra stress when correcting other kinds of mistakes, for example, if the information is
wrong, as in the last example you heard.

Exercises

53.1 Read this phone conversation. Notice the words which are 'underlined' by A and decide whether B
C60   says phrase **a** or phrase **b**. Circle the correct answer. Then listen and check.

>   A: Hello Joe, I'm coming to visit next month.
> **EXAMPLE** B: You're coming   a *this month?*   b *next week?*
>   A: No, <u>next</u> month. Can you meet me? I'll be on the evening plane.

1 B: On the   a *morning plane?*   b *evening train?*
     A: No no. On the evening <u>plane</u>. On Sunday the third.
2 B: On   a *Sunday the first?*   b *Monday the third?*
     A: No no, <u>Sunday</u> the third. At nine fifteen.
3 B: At   a *five fifteen?*   b *nine fifty?*
     A: No no, nine <u>fifteen</u>. You'll know it's me. I'll have a blue jacket.
4 B: A   a *new jacket?*   b *blue packet?*
     A: No no, a <u>blue</u> jacket. See you there. Bye.

> **Follow up:** Record yourself saying A's lines and use your recording to do the exercise again in about
> two weeks.

53.2 Read these short conversations. Which syllable do you think the speaker will stress in the third line?
<u>Underline</u> it.

> **EXAMPLE** A: I disagree with you.
>   B: You agree?
>   A: No, I <u>disa</u>gree!

1 A: He's in the bathroom.
     B: In the bedroom?
     A: No, the bathroom!

2 A: My father's retired.
     B: Why is he tired?
     A: No, he's retired!

3 A: I bought a bookshelf.
     B: A bookshop?
     A: No, a bookshelf!

4 A: But that's impossible!
     B: You think it's possible?
     A: No, I said impossible!

5 A: The kitchen's downstairs.
     B: Upstairs?
     A: No, downstairs!

C61   **Follow up:** Listen. You will hear the first two lines and then a pause before the third line.
       Say the third line with the stress you underlined. Then listen and check if you were right.

Now go to Unit 14

54 Look who's talking!
Introducing tones

Some idiomatic expressions have a fixed melody, or tone, in English. For example, in *Look who's talking*, the voice goes down at the end. The syllable *talk–* is higher than the syllable *–ing*. In *You'll be lucky*, the voice goes up at the end. The syllable *luck–* is lower than the syllable *–y*. Listen.

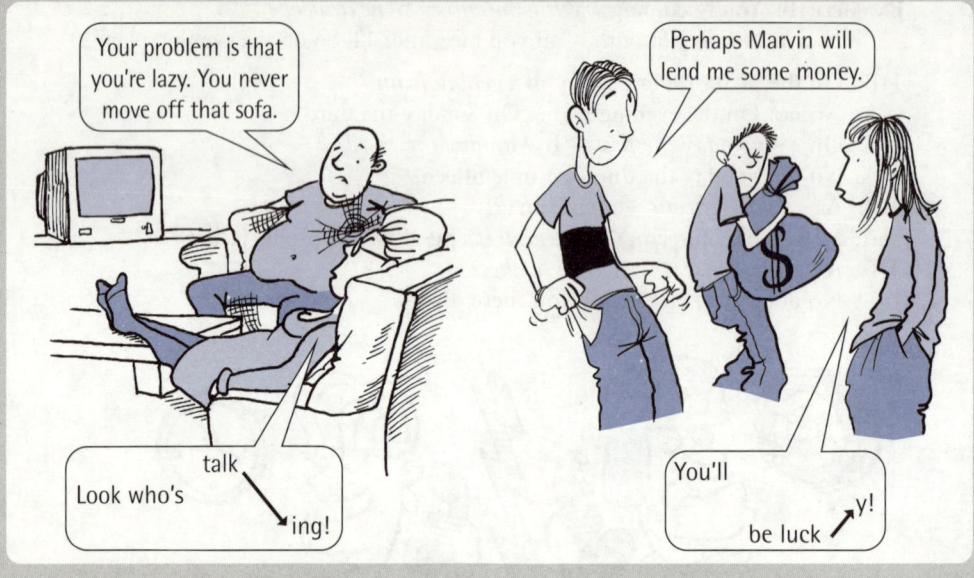

Your problem is that you're lazy. You never move off that sofa.

Perhaps Marvin will lend me some money.

Look who's talk ing!

You'll be luck y!

But normally we can choose to make our voice go up or down at the end. For example, in the conversation below, Sid says 'bear' with his voice going down. Joe repeats the word with his voice going up. Listen and notice the way their voices go up or down at the end.

SID: Shh!
JOE: What?
SID: Bear!
JOE: Bear?
SID: Bear!
JOE: Where?
SID: There!
JOE: Far?
SID: No!
JOE: Near?
SID: Yeah!
JOE: Run?
SID: Run!

Listen again and say Joe's lines.

⚠ Note: The choice of tone (voice going up or down) has meaning. We will look at the meaning in Units 55 to 60.

⚠ Note: The meanings of the idiomatic expressions in this unit are explained in the Answer Key on page 186.

Exercises

54.1 Listen to these short conversations. All of the replies are idiomatic expressions. Listen.
C64 Does the voice go up or down on the last word? Draw a line in the box: ⟋ or ⟍

1

2

3

4

> **Follow up:** Listen again and repeat.

54.2 The responses to the pairs of sentences **a** and **b** below are the same, but the speaker uses a different
C65 tone. For example, in the response to Example **a**, the voice goes down, but in the response to Example **b**,
the voice goes up. Listen and draw a line in the box to show if the voice goes up or down.

EXAMPLE
  a Let's go away for the weekend.   – Where? ⟍
  b Let's go to Llantisiliogogogoch.   – Where? ⟋

1 a I know who stole your glasses.   – Who?
  b It was Mickey Mumpkin.   – Who?

2 a I've got some bad news for you.   – What?
  b I'm afraid your house has burnt down.   – What!

3 a Excuse me, can you help us?   – Yes?
  b Can you take a photo of us with this camera?   – Yes.

4 a We're going for a picnic if you want to come.   – When?
  b At midnight tonight.   – When?

54.3 You will hear just the responses from 54.2. Listen and decide if it is the response to **a** or **b**.
C66 EXAMPLE *b*   1 ....   2 ....   3 ....   4 ....

Now go to Unit 15

Here? Yes, here!
Asking and checking tones

A

A C67

Important for listening

Questions can be pronounced with the voice going up at the end or going down at the end. You can hear the difference in this conversation. Two people are fixing a place to meet. Listen to the way A pronounces his three questions.

A: Where?   (A's voice goes **down** at the end.)
B: Here.
A: Where?   (A's voice goes **up** at the end.)
B: Here.
A: Here?   (A's voice goes **up** at the end.)
B: Yes, here.

A's first question is an 'open' question. The answer could be any place; he has no idea. A's questions 2 and 3 are 'check' questions. He thinks he knows the answer and he just wants to check. The voice usually goes down at the end of 'open' questions and up at the end of 'check' questions.

B C68

Important for listening

Here is another example. A is asking directions to B's house. Notice how both of them use 'check' questions (in **black**) to make sure they understand each other. Listen.

A: Help! We're lost!
B: Where are you?
A: I don't know. There's a supermarket and a river.
B: Oh, I think I know where you are ... **Can you see a bridge**?
A: Yes.
B: OK, well go across the bridge and turn right.
A: **Turn right**?
B: Uh huh. Now, **can you see some trees on the left**?
A: Yes.
B: Turn left after the trees.
A: What, **in front of the bar**?
B: Yes, in front of the bar. You'll see my house on the left.
A: **It's opposite the farm**?
B: That's it. Well done, you're here!

⚠ **Note:** In the sentence *It's opposite the farm?* we know the speaker is asking a question from the context. Also, the voice going up at the end makes it sound like a question.

Exercises

55.1 Read these short conversations and tick (✓) the questions. Then listen and check.

C69

1 A: When?
    B: Tomorrow.
    A: When?
    B: Tomorrow.
    A: Tomorrow?
    B: Yes, tomorrow.

2 A: Which way?
    B: Left.
    A: What?
    B: Left.
    A: In front of the shop?
    B: Yes.

Follow up: Listen and repeat A's lines.

55.2 Listen. You will hear one half of a conversation on a mobile phone. You can tell which way the

C70 speaker is going from the check questions. Draw the route on the map.

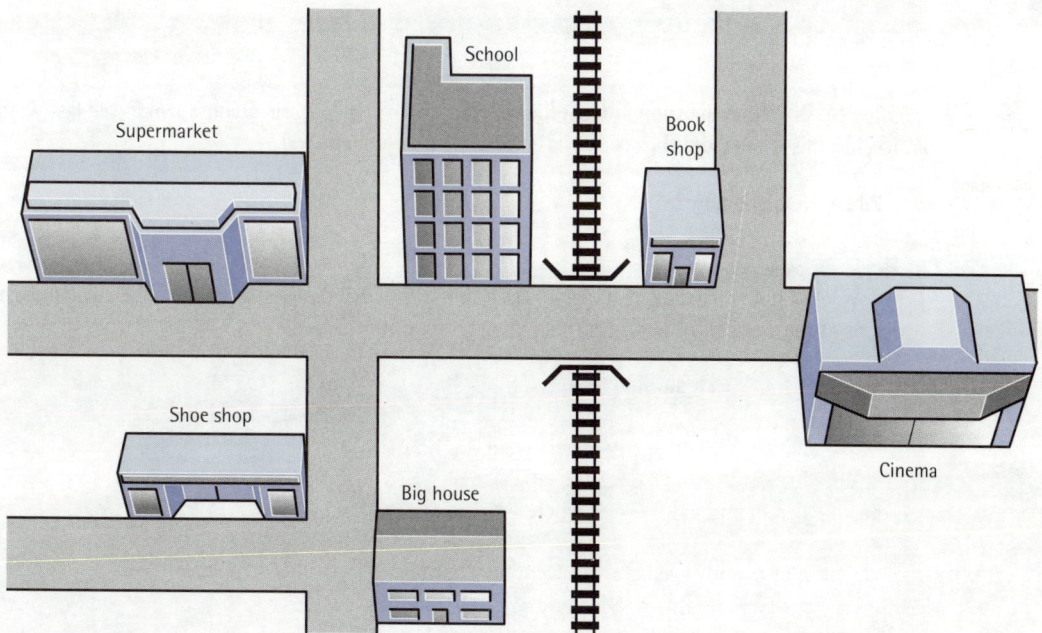

55.3 Listen to the phrases or sentences. Do they sound like questions? Write (?) after the questions and (.)

C71 after the ones that are **not** questions.

EXAMPLE
Go straight across (.)

1 Right at the lights (   )
2 Next to the supermarket (   )
3 It's this one (   )
4 It's opposite the school (   )

5 It's a long way (   )
6 Under the bridge (   )
7 Take the next left (   )

Now go to Unit 16

56 Where were you born?
Tones in asking for information

A C72

Important for listening

We pronounce an 'open' question differently from a 'check' question. An 'open' question is where we ask for information we didn't have before, and the voice usually goes down at the end. A 'check' question is where we make sure that the information we have is correct. The voice usually goes up at the end. Listen to the examples in this conversation.

A: What's your **name**?
B: Sonia.
A: And where were you **born**?
B: Surinam.
A: Is that in South **America**?
B: Yes, that's right.
A: And how long have you lived **here**?
B: Five years.
A: I see. Are you **married**?
B: No, I'm not.
A: And what do you **do**?
B: I'm a boxer.
A: You're a **boxer**?

B C73

Important for listening

Listen to A's second question in recording C72 again. The voice starts going down in the last word only, because this is the word the speaker is emphasising, or 'underlining'.

Where were you <u>born</u>?

But we may 'underline' any of the words (see Units 49 to 53). Listen. Notice that the voice movement begins at the word with the underlining and continues to the end.

So your parents were born in Uruguay. And where were <u>you</u> born?

Oh, so you weren't born here? Where <u>were</u> you born?

So you were born in 1969? And <u>where</u> were you born?

I know your parents live here, but were they <u>born</u> here?

I know you were born here, but were your <u>parents</u> born here?

My mother and father were born here. Were <u>your</u> parents born here?

⚠ **Note:** In check questions the voice sometimes goes down before it goes up at the end. This is shown in the lines in the boxes.

Exercises

56.1 Listen to the questions below. Are they open or check? Draw a down or an up line in the boxes.
C74

EXAMPLE

Are you a student? ⟋

1 Have you been to America? ▨   5 Can you drive? ▨
2 What do you study? ▨   6 Where's he going? ▨
3 What time is it? ▨   7 Do you like it? ▨
4 Are you over eighteen? ▨

56.2 Listen. After each sentence below, there is a question. Which word in the question does the speaker
C75 'underline' with his voice? Underline the word. Then draw the voice movement line, starting in the
box below the underlined word. The voice goes down in all of them.

EXAMPLE

I'm from Canada.   Where are you from?

1 So you're from Cuba.   Where in Cuba?

2 From Havana? Interesting.   And what's your name?

3 So you don't live in Cuba now?   Where do you live?

4 You're a student?   What do you study?

5 So you won't finish this year?   When will you finish?

Follow up: Listen again and repeat.

56.3 Look at the questions in black below. Underline the word you think the speaker will emphasise. Then
C76 listen and check.

EXAMPLE

   a So your sister's a teacher? Where does she <u>work</u>?
   b Oh, so she doesn't work here? Where <u>does</u> she work?

1 a So you're married? Do you have any children?
   b I have two daughters. Do you have any children?
2 a So French is your second language? What's your first language?
   b My first language is Urdu. What's your first language?
3 a So you work Mondays to Saturdays? What do you do on Sundays?
   b So your favourite day is Sunday? What do you do on Sundays?
4 a I know how he did it, but ... why did he do it?
   b *She* was going to do it, so ... why did he do it?
5 a My glasses aren't here, so ... where are my glasses?
   b Here are your glasses, but ... where are my glasses?

Now go to Unit 17 ▶

57

We're closed tomorrow
Tones in new and old information

A C77

In conversation, we often refer back to something we said before. This is 'old' information, and the voice normally goes up at the end. We also tell the listener things we haven't mentioned before. This is 'new' information, and the voice normally goes down at the end.

Listen. In conversation 1 below, the voice goes up at the end, because the last word 'tomorrow' has already been mentioned. In conversation 2, the voice goes down, because the last word 'tomorrow' has not been mentioned.

1 A: I'll come in tomorrow.
  B: We're closed tomorrow. ⬈
2 A: When are you closed?
  B: We're closed tomorrow. ⬊

C78 Listen to this example. They are talking about buying a television. Notice how the voice goes up on the words **in black**. This is because these are words which have been mentioned before, so they are old information.

A: Let's get the Viewmaster. It's really nice.
B: But the Megavision is **nicer**.
A: But the Viewmaster has a guarantee.
B: They both have a **guarantee**.
A: Anyway, the Megavision is too expensive.
B: I know it's **expensive**, but it's better quality.
A: They're both good **quality**.
B: The Megavision has access to the internet.
A: We have access to the **internet** on the computer.

B

When we are referring to something before in the conversation, we don't have to repeat exactly the same words. In this conversation, the voice goes up on 'from there' because in this context it means 'Cairo', so it is something which has been mentioned before.

A: I'm from Cairo.
B: Really? My wife's from there.

Exercises

57.1
C79

Read the short conversations. Do you think the voice goes up or down at the end? Draw lines in the boxes. Then listen, check and repeat.

EXAMPLES

A: This one's nice.

B: I know it's nice, but it's expensive. ◣

A: This one's big.

B: I know it's big, but the other one's bigger. ◢

1 A: This one's slow.

　B: I know it's slow, but it's strong. ▨

3 A: This one's good.

　B: I know it's good, but the other one's better. ▨

2 A: This one's ugly.

　B: I know it's ugly, but it's comfortable. ▨

4 A: This one's fast.

　B: I know it's fast, but it's dangerous. ▨

57.2
C80

The responses to the pairs of sentences **a** and **b** below are the same, but the speaker uses a different tone in each response. For example, in the response to Example a, the voice goes *up* at the end of the sentence, but in the response to Example b, the voice goes *down*. Draw lines to show if you think the voice will go up or down. Then listen and check.

EXAMPLE

　a – The train's cheap.
　　– The bus was cheaper. ◢

　b – Why did you take the bus?
　　– The bus was cheaper. ◣

1 a – Was the movie good?
　　– The book was better. ▨

1 **b** – Why did you read the book?
　　– The book was better. ▨

2 a – What time's lunch?
　　– Lunch is at two. ▨

2 **b** – Let's go swimming at two.
　　– Lunch is at two. ▨

3 a – I'd like a leather one.
　　– They're all leather. ▨

3 **b** – Why are they so expensive?
　　– They're all leather. ▨

4 a – Let's go tomorrow.
　　– It's closed tomorrow. ▨

4 **b** – When is it closed?
　　– It's closed tomorrow. ▨

5 a – Where's menswear?
　　– Menswear is upstairs. ▨

5 **b** – What's upstairs?
　　– Menswear is upstairs. ▨

6 a – The fish is expensive.
　　– The steak's more expensive. ▨

6 **b** – Why didn't you have steak?
　　– The steak's more expensive. ▨

7 a – What happens if one of them breaks?
　　– They all have a guarantee. ▨

7 **b** – This one has a guarantee.
　　– They all have a guarantee. ▨

Now go to Unit 18 ▶

58

Oh, really?
Continuing or finishing tones

A C81

Important for listening

When we are telling someone a piece of news, we often check that they know the background to the story first. When we do this, the voice goes up at the end. Then, when we finally tell the news, the voice goes down at the end. This shows that we have finished the story.

Listen and compare A's first question in these two conversations. In 1, he is checking that B knows about Max's grandfather's death, so the voice goes up. In 2, he is telling B the news that Max's grandfather died, so the voice goes down.

> 1 A: You know Max's grandfather died? ⟋
>   B: Yes. ⟋
>   A: Well, he's left all his money to charity. ⟍
> 2 A: You know Max's grandfather died? ⟍
>   B: Oh. ⟍
>   A: Yeah, terrible, isn't it? ⟍

B C82

Important for listening

Listeners also signal if they expect the story to continue or not. In conversation 1 above, B's voice goes up at the end when she says *Yes*. This shows that she expects A to continue. In conversation 2, B's voice goes down at the end when she says *Oh*. This shows that she knows A has finished telling her the news. There are more examples in the conversation below. Listen.

> A: You know Angela?
> B: Yes. ⟋
> A: And you know her brother David?
> B: Uh huh. ⟋
> A: Well, you know he lives in Southside?
> B: Mmm ... ⟋
> A: Well, somebody broke into his house last night!
> B: Oh, really!? ⟍

⚠ **Note:** In B's last line, her voice goes down, but it starts from very high. This shows that she did not expect this news; she is surprised.

C C83

Important for listening

If we are saying a list of things, our voice goes down at the end of the last thing to show we have finished. On the other things, the voice goes up to show the list is *not* finished. Listen to the continuation of the conversation from B above, and notice A's pronunciation of the list of things stolen.

> B: Did they steal anything?
> A: Yes, they took his computer, television,
>   video, CD player and all his CDs.
> B: Oh, that's terrible!

Exercises

58.1
C84
Listen to these sentences. If they are said as news (◥), write *Oh*. If they are said as check questions (◢), write *Yes*.

EXAMPLES You know Bradford won? ...... *Oh* ......
         You know Sylvia's had a baby? ...... *Yes* ......

1 You know I'm a photographer? ....
2 You know Danny's got flu? ....
3 You know she's gone? ....

4 You know he broke his arm? ....
5 You know the war's finished? ....
6 You know the meeting is cancelled? ....

58.2
C85
You will hear a story. The speaker on the recording will ask questions to check that you know some background information, which is in the text below. Say *Yes*, *Uh huh* or *Mmm* ... with your voice going up at the end. Then, when finally you hear the news, respond with one of these sentences:

How fantastic!
That's great!
Oh, that's terrible!
Brilliant!

> *Background information*
>
> You and the speaker on the recording have a friend called Colin. Colin has a sister called Linda. Linda is an actress in the movies. She was making a movie in Australia recently.

58.3
C86
Read these conversations. Write (!) after *really* if you think B would be surprised at A's news, and just write (.) if you think B would not be surprised. Then listen and check. You know if B is surprised because the voice starts very high.

EXAMPLE
A: There's a lot of water in the sea.
B: Oh, really ......

1 A: My husband is an astronaut.
  B: Oh, really ......
2 A: My bike has two wheels.
  B: Oh, really ......

3 A: My grandmother is 130.
  B: Oh, really ......
4 A: There's a programme on TV tonight.
  B: Oh, really ......

58.4
What did you do yesterday? Answer this question by giving a list of your actions. Make sure your voice goes up at the end of each action until the last one, then your voice goes down. Record yourself if possible.

EXAMPLE
Well, I got up, had breakfast, went to work ... and finally, I went to bed.

Now go to Unit 19

59 It's fun, isn't it?
Agreeing and disagreeing tones

A C87

Important for listening

When we agree with the other person, our voice often goes down at the end. We tell the other person our opinion, confident they will not be upset.

Listen to this conversation. Notice that the voices go down at the end of each line.

> A: Football's so boring, isn't it?
> B: Yeah, I know. I hate it.
> A: I mean, it's just 22 people running after a ball.
> B: Yeah, how can that be interesting?
> A: No, golf's much more fun, isn't it?

⚠️ **Note:** The expression *isn't it?* is called a question tag. When we use question tags to tell someone our opinion, the voice goes down at the end.

B C88

Important for listening

But when we disagree, our voice often goes up at the end, so our opinion sounds unfinished and less strong, because we do not want to upset the other person.

Listen to the rest of the conversation from A. Notice how the voices go up at the end of each line.

> B: Well ...
> A: You like golf, don't you?
> B: It's alright I suppose ...
> A: You don't sound very sure.
> B: Well, I guess I'm not really a sporting person, you know.

⚠️ **Note:** The expression *don't you?* is a question tag. When we use question tags to check information, the voice goes up at the end.

C C89

Important for listening

We can say the same sentence, but change the meaning by changing how we say it.

Listen to these two examples. The speaker in 1 is telling his opinion clearly. The speaker in 2 is leaving something unsaid. You feel he is going to continue with *but*...

> 1 I think they're good.   (That is my opinion.)
> 2 I think they're good ... (They're not too bad, *but* there's a reason why I don't like them.)

D C90

Important for listening

We can also change the meaning of a question tag by changing how we say it. Listen to these conversations.

> A: It's too hot, isn't it? (opinion)
> B: Yeah, let's open the window!

> A: We sometimes have snow in Morocco.
> B: But it's too hot, isn't it? (check question)
> A: No, not in the mountains.

Exercises

59.1
C91

Listen. Are these the speakers' real opinions, or can you 'hear' a *but*? Write a (.) or (, but...) after each line.

EXAMPLE   I like tennis ....*but*...

1 It's nice ....
2 We're quite good ....
3 Yes, it is ....
4 I don't know ....
5 Yes ....

6 He does ....
7 She likes you ....
8 They're friendly ....
9 Not bad ....

> **Follow up:** Record yourself saying these sentences. Use your recording to do this exercise again in about two weeks.

59.2
C92

Listen to the four short conversations about the things in the pictures. Are the speakers agreeing or disagreeing? Write *agreeing* or *disagreeing* under each picture.

EXAMPLE   1   2   3

................*agreeing*................   ....

59.3
C93

Complete each sentence with an ending from the box. Then decide if they are opinions or check questions and draw lines in the boxes. Then listen and check.

> is it?   isn't it?   is she?   isn't he?   are you?   aren't they?   was it?
> wasn't he?   don't you?   doesn't it?   have you?

EXAMPLE   You aren't hungry, ...*are you?*...... ▱

1 How's your headache? It isn't getting worse, ...

2 Those flowers are lovely, ...

3 You haven't seen my glasses anywhere, ...

4 Torsen's a great player, ...

5 I'm not sure. He was from Brazil, ...

6 I can't quite remember. You need 40 points to win, ...

7 Tennis is so boring, ...

8 She isn't a very good swimmer, ...

9 I'm not sure. It starts at nine, ...

10 It wasn't a very interesting game, ...

> Now go to Unit 20 ▶

60 It was brilliant!
High tones

A C94

Important for listening

Listen to these three people saying *thank you*. Notice that the woman who forgot her bag makes her voice go very high. This shows that she really means what she is saying. The other two people do not really mean it, and so their voices do not go high.

⚠️ Note: Sometimes the ticket collector's voice goes up at the end when he says *thank you*, which makes it sound like a routine habit: he doesn't really mean it. And of course the woman in picture 3 doesn't really mean *thank you*. She means the opposite!

B C95

Important for listening

When we give an opinion about something with a very strong adjective like *excellent*, our voice usually goes high to show our strong feeling. If we use weaker adjectives like *nice*, our voice does not usually go high. Listen and compare the voices of the man and woman telling their friend about their holiday.

Liz:	So, how was your trip?
Claire:	Oh, it was quite nice.
Paul:	What do you mean, nice? It was brilliant!
Liz:	Good hotel?
Claire:	Quite pleasant, yes.
Paul:	Pleasant? It was excellent! Superb!
Liz:	How about the food?
Claire:	It was OK.
Paul:	OK? It was absolutely delicious!
Liz:	And the scenery?
Claire:	Quite pretty.
Paul:	It was amazing! Beautiful!

C C96

Important for listening

People often say a strong adjective like *brilliant* with a flat voice, to mean the opposite. For example, you could say *brilliant* with a flat voice after something bad happens. Listen and compare the pronunciation of this word in these two conversations. In the first one, the person really means it, and in the second she doesn't.

1 A: We've won a holiday for two in Jamaica!
 B: Brilliant! ⌒

2 A: Our flight has been cancelled!
 B: Brilliant! →

⚠️ Note: If you use strong adjectives, make your voice go high or people may think you do not mean it!

Exercises

60.1
C97
Listen. What do Sue and Jim think about the people they are speaking about? Write the names in the correct column.

people they like	people they don't like
	Jeremy

SUE: Jeremy is going to stay at the same hotel as us.
JIM: Oh great!
JIM: Anne's invited us to a party.
SUE: Fantastic!
JIM: Kathleen's coming to stay with us for a few days.
SUE: That'll be fun!
SUE: Gail and Tim want to come on holiday with us.
JIM: That'll be nice!

60.2
C98
You will hear Claire (from part B on the opposite page) giving her opinion about these things on their holiday. Imagine you are Paul. Listen and say stronger opinions. There are gaps on the recording for you to speak. Don't forget to make your voice high.

EXAMPLE:
You hear Claire say *The beach was quite nice.* You say *Nice? It was absolutely fantastic!*

60.3
C99
The responses to the pairs of sentences **a** and **b** below are the same, but the speaker pronounces them differently. For example, in the response to Example **a**, the voice is flat, but in the response to Example **b**, the voice goes high. Draw lines to show if you think the voice will be flat or go high. Then listen and check.

EXAMPLE
a – We had to stay in a five-star hotel.
  – How awful for you! ⟶

b – We had to spend two days in the airport.
  – How awful for you! ⌒

1 a – Forget the beach; it's raining again!
  – Brilliant!

1 b – They say we don't have to pay; it's free.
  – Brilliant!

2 a – I got an A in the exam!
  – Well done!

2 b – I've crashed the car again!
  – Well done!

3 a – I can count to three in German.
  – Amazing!

3 b – I learnt how to fly a plane while we were on holiday.
  – Amazing!

4 a – We could pick fresh fruit off the trees in the garden.
  – Delicious!

4 b – We had a tiny bit of cheese on a dry, old piece of bread.
  – Delicious!

5 a – Frank says he'll take us to the airport.
  – Excellent!

5 b – The car's broken down and there are no taxis.
  – Excellent!

Introduction to phonemic symbols
The phonemic alphabet

/æ/ apple	/e/ egg	/ɪ/ insect	/ɒ/ orange	/ʌ/ umbrella	/ʊ/ book
/ɑː/ arm	/ɜː/ earth	/iː/ eagle	/ɔː/ organ	/uː/ two	
/eə/ aeroplane	/ɪə/ ear	/aɪ/ eye	/eɪ/ eight	/ɔɪ/ coin	
/əʊ/ oval	/aʊ/ owl	/ə/ banana			

/b/ bird	/tʃ/ chair	/d/ dog	/f/ fish	/g/ girl	/h/ heart
/dʒ/ jar	/k/ key	/l/ leaf	/m/ monkey	/n/ nine	/ŋ/ ring
/p/ pear	/r/ rose	/s/ sofa	/ʃ/ sheep	/ʒ/ television	/t/ table
/ð/ mother	/θ/ thirteen	/v/ volcano	/w/ web	/j/ yacht	/z/ zebra

Exercises

Phonemic spellings which are the same as normal spellings

D1.1 In each of these groups of words, one word is exactly the same as in normal letters. Underline it. Then write the others in normal letters.

EXAMPLE *Furniture:* /'teɪbəl   <u>bed</u>   'səʊfə   tʃeə/
table   sofa   chair

1 *For writing:* /'pensəl   'peɪpə   pen   'nəʊtbʊk/

2 *In the office:* /desk   fæks   kəm'pju:tə   'telɪfəʊn/

3 *Body parts:* /nek   hed   hænd   leg/

4 *Farm animals:* /hen   pɪg   ʃi:p   caʊ/

5 *Colours:* /gri:n   blu: red   blæk/

6 *Verbs:* /get   teɪk   gɪv   gəʊ/

7 *Numbers:* /'sevən   ten   θri: faɪv/

Phonemic spellings which are very different from normal spellings

D1.2 Some phonemic spellings are surprisingly different from normal spellings. For example, in phonemic spelling, quick is /kwɪk/. Can you find all the words in this wordsearch? The words are horizontal → or vertical ↓ . Use all the letters.

tʃ	eə	ɪ	ŋ	g	l	ɪ	ʃ
m	k	w	e	s	tʃ	ə	n
ɪ	k	n	j	u:	z	b	s
k	w	k	əʊ	s	f	r	ɪ
s	ɪ	w	ʃ	k	j	i:	k
t	k	aɪ	ə	u:	u:	ð	s
e	dʒ	t	n	l	tʃ	z	θ
dʒ	u:	s	ʃ	u:	ə	ð	əʊ

breathes   ocean
chair   question
edge   ~~quick~~
English   quite
future   school
juice   shoe
mixed   sixth
news   though

Phonemic symbols for vowels

D1.3 Complete these phonemic crosswords. The words in normal spelling are next to the crosswords. You need to write one of these consonant symbols in each empty square. You can use the symbols more than once.

/b d f g h k l m n p r t v w z/

1 Long vowel crossword

rain ~~bike~~ warm boot
late leave five room
woke born bean phone

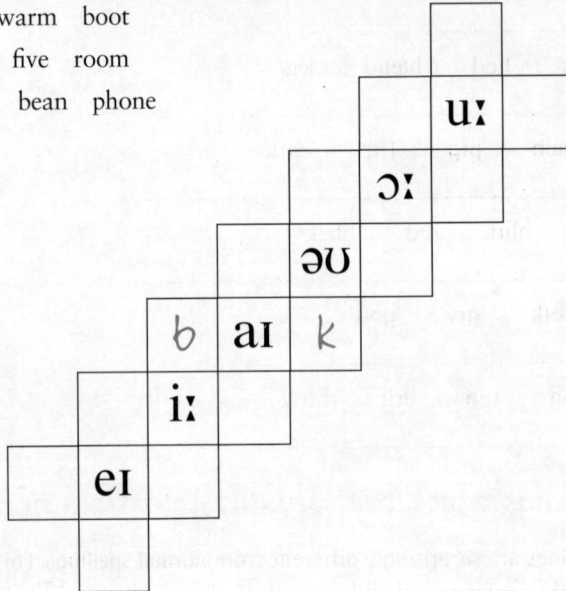

2 Short vowel crossword

hat put ~~fit~~ lip gone
fun pet pack get look
cot cup

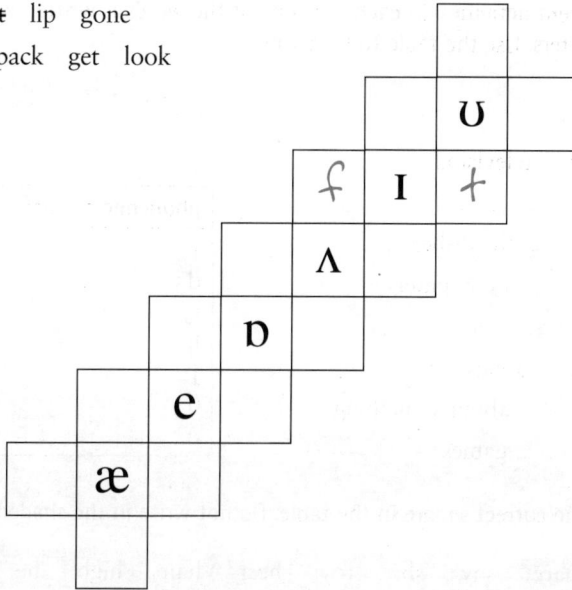

3 Vowels before R crossword

port hairs bears ~~beers~~
heard card beard heart
hers court

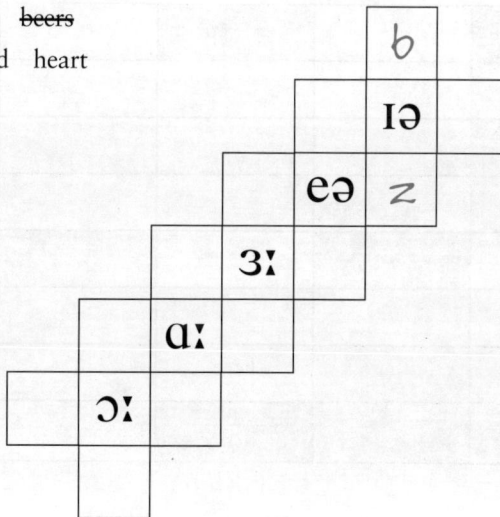

Phonemic consonants which are different from normal consonants

D1.4 Here is a list of different activities. In each one, one of the words is written with phonemic symbols. Write it in normal letters. Use the table to help you.

EXAMPLE

/wɒtʃɪŋ/ ......*watching*...... television

phonemic symbol	usual spelling
ʃ	SH
dʒ	G or J
tʃ	CH
ŋ	NG
j	Y or U
θ	TH
ð	TH

1 ski /dʒʌmpɪŋ/ ....

2 /wɒʃɪŋ/ .... the dishes

3 /juːzɪŋ/ .... a computer

4 sun /beɪðɪŋ/ ....

5 /sɪŋɪŋ/ .... songs

6 /θɪŋkɪŋ/ .... about something

7 /pleɪjɪŋ/ .... games

D1.5 Put these words in the correct square in the table. Do not write in the shaded squares.

~~boy~~	~~here~~	share	shy	she	toy	beer	hair	high	he	bore
pier	bear	buy	be	pour	tea	tie	pair	deer	pea	we	die
pie	dare	door	fear	four	wear	why	fair	wore	tear		

	ɔɪ	ɔː	ɪə	eə	aɪ	iː
w	▓		▓			
f	▓				▓	▓
d	▓					▓
p	▓					
t		▓		▓		
b	*boy*					
h	▓		*here*			
ʃ	▓	▓	▓			

D1.6 Find phonemic spellings for thirteen different foods in the wordsearch.
The words are horizontal → or vertical ↓ . Use all the letters.

h	æ	m	b	ɜː	g	ə	s
p	r	f	b	r	e	d	t
æ	aɪ	ɪ	tʃ	ɪ	p	s	r
s	s	ʃ	m	iː	t	ɒ	ɔː
t	k	æ	r	ə	t	r	b
ə	ʌ	n	j	ə	n	ɪ	r
t	ə	m	ɑː	t	əʊ	n	ɪ
b	ə	n	ɑː	n	ə	dʒ	z

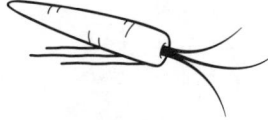

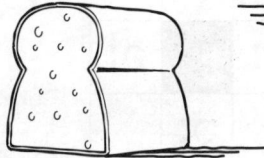

D1.7 Find phonemic spellings for thirteen jobs in the wordsearch. The words are horizontal → or vertical ↓ .
Use all the letters.

k	d	ɒ	k	t	ə	n
ʊ	d	r	aɪ	v	ə	ɜː
k	p	eɪ	n	t	ə	s
m	ə	k	æ	n	ɪ	k
f	e	n	dʒ	ə	n	ɪə
ɑː	v	r	aɪ	t	ə	g
m	e	s	ɪ	ŋ	ə	ɑː
ə	t	w	eɪ	t	ə	d

D1.8 Here is a word square making the words
can, *cap*, *not* and *pot*.

c	a	n
a	■	o
p	o	t

Here is a phonemic word square making the words
beach, *bean*, *cheese* and *knees*.

b	iː	tʃ
iː	■	iː
n	iː	z

Now complete these word squares to make the four words underneath each one.

1

	aɪ	
aɪ	■	aɪ
	aɪ	

rhyme might tight write

2

	ɔː	
ɔː	■	ɔː
	ɔː	

laws cause tall talk

3

	ɒ	
ɒ	■	ɒ
	ɒ	

shop wash what top

4

	ʌ	
ʌ	■	ʌ
	ʌ	

cut come touch much

5

	æ	
æ	■	æ
	æ	

back tap cap bat

6

	ʊ	
ʊ	■	ʊ
	ʊ	

could bush should book

7

	eɪ	
eɪ	■	eɪ
	eɪ	

pain page jail nail

8

	e	
e	■	e
	e	

yes sell tell yet

9

	əʊ	
əʊ	■	əʊ
	əʊ	

wrote roll loan tone

Pronunciation test

Section A   Letters and sounds

A1   Circle the word with a different vowel sound.

EXAMPLE   hot   (hold)   gone   swan

1 black	want	mad	hand		5 foot	look	blood	push
2 case	lake	name	care		6 rude	luck	run	but
3 soap	hope	sold	soup		7 leave	beach	bread	clean
4 what	hot	most	salt					

My score = _____/7

A2   Circle the word if one of the consonant letters is not pronounced.

EXAMPLE   camp   crisp   (climb)   cost

1 lamb	label	cable	cab		5 old	pile	half	help
2 recipe	repeat	receipt	rope		6 cold	calm	colour	film
3 listen	winter	eaten	after		7 hurry	hairy	hungry	here
4 hour	hate	home	hill					

My score = _____/7

A3   Add the consonant sound to the word to make another word.

EXAMPLE   /g/ + eight = ...*gate*....

1 /k/ + aim = ...

2 /k/ + ache = ...

3 /l/ + eight = ...

4 /r/ + owes = ...

5 /w/ + eight = ...

6 /s/ + eyes = ...

7 /h/ + eye = ...

8 /b/ + air = ...

9 /b/ + earn = ...

My score = _____/9 × 2 = _____/18

A4   Listen and circle the word you hear.

D1

1 Have you got a *pan / pin / pen* I could borrow?

2 We should clean the *cut / cat / cot* first.

3 You won't be able to *fill / feel / fail* this.

4 I think that's the *west / worst / waist*.

5 The *cot / coat / court*'s too small.

6 I don't think it's *far / fur / fair*, you know.

7 What time did the *woman / women* arrive?

8 The *officer's / office's* here.

9 I used to have a *bet / vet / pet*.

10 I got a good *price / prize* for it.

11 They didn't *suit / shoot* him.

12 I think it's in the *code / coat / coach*.

13 That's a *fine / wine / vine* colour.

14 His *back / bag* was broken.

15 You can smell it in the *air / hair*.

16 You'll have to *watch / wash* the baby.

17 They're *singing / sinking*.

18 I'll *collect / correct / connect* it tomorrow.

My score = _____/18

Total score for Section A = _____/50

Section B   Syllables, words and sentences

B1 Listen and circle the word you hear.

(D2)

1 The *glass / gas* is green.
2 The *tooth / truth* is out!
3 I can't *sell / smell* anything.
4 They *need / needed* more time.
5 I think they *want / wanted* to talk.
6 There are *thirty / thirteen* people in my class.
7 Alice *is / was* here.

8 The books *are / were* cheap.
9 I think there are some pears *and / or* grapes.
10 What *does / did* she say?
11 *That smile / That's a mile*.
12 We need more *sport / support*.
13 It's all in the *past / pasta* now.
14 Our *guests / guest* came late.

My score = _____/14

B2 Which word has a different number of syllables from the others? Circle it.

EXAMPLE   snakes   sheep   (foxes)   cats

1 likes   wants   talks   washes
2 wanted   walked   saved   brushed
3 chicken   chocolate   afternoon   different
4 about   around   asleep   asked
5 fourteen   forty   fortieth   hundred
6 builds   rebuild   builder   building
7 supermarket   waterfall   holiday   hairdresser
8 school   texts   over   sports

My score = _____/8

B3 All the words or expressions in each group have the same number of syllables. Circle the one with stress in a different place.

EXAMPLE   October   November   December   (January)

1 Saturday   holiday   tomorrow   yesterday
2 morning   fifty   fifteen   August
3 He told me.   I like it.   She finished.   Close the door.
4 Go to bed!   Don't worry!   What's the time?   Fish and chips.
5 table   tourist   tunnel   today
6 mistake   famous   become   remove
7 playground   shoe shop   first class   handbag
8 economics   economy   education   scientific
9 It isn't true.   I'll see you soon.   No, it isn't.   He's not at home.

My score = _____/9 × 2 = _____/18

B4
(D3)
Listen. Are the two expressions pronounced exactly the same on the recording, or is there a difference? Write S for *same* or D for *different*.

EXAMPLE
some of each   summer beach ....D........

1 some of you   summer view ....

2 stopped aching   stop taking ....

3 Mary knows   Mary's nose ....

4 Alaska   I'll ask her ....

5 burnt a cake   burnt the cake ....

6 greet guests   Greek guests ....

7 want to talk   wanted to talk ....

8 I've locked it   I blocked it ....

9 what's past   what's passed ....

10 a bitter fruit   a bit of fruit ....

My score = _____/10

Total score for Section B = _____/50

Section C   Conversation

C1
(D4)
Listen. Which sentence do you hear? Tick (✓) **a** or **b**.

EXAMPLE
a Was that the question he asked? ✓
b 'Was that the question?' he asked.

1 a We walked carefully downstairs. It was dark.
  b We walked carefully. Downstairs it was dark.

2 a I saw her clearly. She was hungry.
  b I saw her. Clearly, she was hungry.

3 a The word he said was right.
  b The word he said was 'right'.

4 a It was cold last night. The roads were icy.
  b It was cold. Last night, the roads were icy.

5 a 'Who?' said Martin.
  b Who said 'Martin'?

6 a What she said was good.
  b What she said was, 'Good'.

7 a Let's go home later. We can have a pizza.
  b Let's go home. Later we can have a pizza.

My score = _____/7

C2
D5
Listen. You will only hear the response. Which one is it? Tick (✓) **a** or **b**.

EXAMPLE

a – The train leasves at eleven fifteen.
– No it doesn't, it leaves at twelve fifteen.

b – The train leaves at twelve fifty.
– No it doesn't, it leaves at twelve fifteen. ✓

1 **a** – Where are you from?
– North Africa.

b – Which part of Africa are you from?
– North Africa.

2 **a** – Do you have any brothers or sisters?
– Yes, two brothers.

b – You have some brothers, don't you?
– Yes, two brothers.

3 **a** – Would you like anything to drink?
– I'd like red wine, please.

b – Would you like red or white?
– I'd like red wine, please.

4 **a** – Malaga's in the south of Italy.
– No it isn't, it's in the south of Spain.

b – Malaga's in the north of Spain.
– No it isn't, it's in the south of Spain.

5 **a** – Let's go tomorrow.
– It's closed tomorrow.

b – When is it closed?
– It's closed tomorrow.

6 **a** – What's upstairs?
– Menswear is upstairs.

b – Where's menswear?
– Menswear is upstairs.

7 **a** – We had to stay in a five-star hotel.
– How awful for you!

b – We spent two days in the airport.
– How awful for you!

8 **a** – I got an A in the exam!
– Well done!

b – I've crashed the car again.
– Well done!

My score = ____/8

C3
D6
Listen. How does the speaker sound? Circle the best alternative. Note that the punctuation is not written, so you must decide just from the pronunciation.

EXAMPLE

Nice day isn't it

The speaker sounds as if he/she...

... *is /* (*isn't*) asking a question

1 She plays a lot of instruments piano guitar	... *is / isn't* going to continue the list.
2 Well that is truly amazing	... *is / isn't* really amazed.
3 You're coming here tomorrow	... *is / isn't* asking a question.
4 Oh, thank you very much	... *does / doesn't* really mean it.
5 Next to the supermarket	... *is / isn't* asking a question.
6 I got up had a shower and got dressed	... *is / isn't* going to continue the list.
7 Oh really how interesting	... *is / isn't* really interested.
8 You're from Brazil aren't you	... *is / isn't* asking a question.
9 I think that's my bag	... *is / isn't* sure about it.
10 Yes it's quite good	... *is / isn't* going to say 'but...'

My score = ____/10

Total score for Section C = ____/25 × 2 =____/50

D3 Guide for speakers of specific languages

Note: It has not been possible to include all languages in this section.

Arabic

From Section A *Letters and sounds* (Units 1–20), you could leave out these units:
2, 4, 5, 14, 18, 20
From Section D *Sound pairs*, it would probably be useful for you to do these sound pairs:
4, 13, 14, 23, 28, 35, 36, 37, 40, 41, 44, 45, 46, 48

Chinese

From section A *Letters and sounds* (Units 1–20), you could leave out these units:
14, 19, 20
From Section D *Sound pairs*, it would probably be useful for you to do these sound pairs:
1, 2, 3, 10, 14, 15, 19, 23, 28, 31, 33, 34, 35, 37, 38, 39, 40, 41, 43, 44, 45, 50

Dravidian languages e.g. Tamil

From Section A *Letters and sounds* (Units 1–20), you could leave out these units:
6, 10, 11, 12
From Section D *Sound pairs*, it would probably be useful for you to do these sound pairs:
3, 10, 12, 14, 17, 19, 23, 28, 30, 31, 34, 35, 40, 45, 48

Dutch

From Section A *Letters and sounds* (Units 1–20), you could leave out these units:
15, 20
From Section D *Sound pairs*, it would probably be useful for you to do these sound pairs:
1, 7, 10, 13, 15, 17, 19, 20, 26, 31, 32, 33, 34, 37, 38, 39, 40, 44, 45

Farsi

From Section A *Letters and sounds* (Units 1–20), you could leave out these units:
3, 4, 5, 6, 8, 9, 12
From Section D *Sound pairs*, it would probably be useful for you to do these sound pairs:
1, 9, 10, 12, 14, 19, 23, 24, 25, 35, 38, 48

French

From Section A *Letters and sounds* (Units 1–20), you could leave out these units:
3, 4, 5, 6, 8, 9, 14, 15, 20
From Section D *Sound pairs*, it would probably be useful for you to do these sound pairs:
1, 2, 3, 4, 10, 15, 17, 19, 21, 28, 31, 33, 34, 35, 37, 39, 40, 41, 44, 45

German

From Section A *Letters and sounds* (Units 1–20), you could leave out these units:
11, 15, 20
From Section D *Sound pairs*, it would probably be useful for you to do these sound pairs:
1, 5, 15, 17, 28, 31, 33, 34, 37, 38, 39, 40

Greek

From Section A *Letters and sounds* (Units 1–20), you could leave out these units:
5, 8, 9, 13, 17, 20
From Section D *Sound pairs*, it would probably be useful for you to do these sound pairs:
1, 2, 3, 8, 10, 11, 12, 14, 17, 19, 23, 31, 32, 41, 44, 46, 47, 48

Italian

From Section A *Letters and sounds* (Units 1–20), you could leave out these units:
6, 8, 9, 10, 12, 13, 14, 19
From Section D *Sound pairs*, it would probably be useful for you to do these sound pairs:
1, 2, 4, 10, 14, 17, 23, 28, 31, 34, 35, 37, 40, 45

Japanese

From Section A *Letters and sounds* (Units 1–20), you could leave out these units:
3, 6, 12, 20
From Section D *Sound pairs*, it would probably be useful for you to do these sound pairs:
2, 6, 9, 17, 24, 25, 27, 29, 32, 33, 36, 43, 46, 48, 49, 50

Korean

From Section A *Letters and sounds* (Units 1–20), you could leave out these units:
10, 15, 20
From Section D *Sound pairs*, it would probably be useful for you to do these sound pairs:
1, 9, 10, 12, 14, 17, 19, 23, 26, 28, 29, 30, 31, 32, 33, 34, 35, 37, 40, 45, 46, 50

Malay / Indonesian

From Section A *Letters and sounds* (Units 1–20), you could leave out these units:
13, 15, 16, 20
From Section D *Sound pairs*, it would probably be useful for you to do these sound pairs:
1, 10, 19, 23, 28, 30, 31, 32, 34, 35, 37, 40, 44, 45

Polish

From Section A *Letters and sounds* (Units 1–20), you could leave out these units:
8, 18
From Section D *Sound pairs*, it would probably be useful for you to do these sound pairs:
1, 3, 10, 17, 26, 28, 31, 32, 33, 34, 35, 36, 39, 40, 41, 44, 45, 46, 47, 48

Portuguese

From Section A *Letters and sounds* (Units 1–20), you could leave out these units:
8, 20
From Section D *Sound pairs*, it would probably be useful for you to do these sound pairs:
1, 2, 3, 8, 10, 19, 23, 28, 31, 33, 34, 35, 36, 40, 46, 48, 49

Russian

From Section A *Letters and sounds* (Units 1–20), you could leave out these units:
4, 8, 11, 15, 20
From Section D *Sound pairs*, it would probably be useful for you to do these sound pairs:
1, 3, 10, 12, 14, 17, 21, 23, 24, 25, 26, 27, 28, 32, 33, 34, 38, 40, 41, 46, 47, 48

Scandinavian languages

From Section A *Letters and sounds* (Units 1–20), you could leave out these units:
6, 8, 15, 20
From Section D *Sound pairs*, it would probably be useful for you to do these sound pairs:
1, 10, 15, 16, 18, 31, 33, 35, 38, 39, 42, 45, 46

South Asian languages e.g. Hindi, Urdu, Bengali, Gujarati

From Section A *Letters and sounds* (Units 1–20), you could leave out these units:
15, 18
From Section D *Sound pairs*, it would probably be useful for you to do these sound pairs:
1, 4, 7, 17, 22, 28, 30, 32, 34, 35, 38, 40, 45, 46, 47

Spanish

From Section A *Letters and sounds* (Units 1–20), you could leave out these units:
17, 20
From Section D *Sound pairs*, it would probably be useful for you to do these sound pairs:
2, 3, 9, 10, 12, 14, 19, 21, 23, 24, 25, 26, 27, 28, 29, 34, 35, 40, 41, 42, 44, 45, 46, 47, 48, 49

Swahili

From Section A *Letters and sounds* (Units 1–20), you could leave out these units:
4, 8, 15, 20
From Section D *Sound pairs*, it would probably be useful for you to do these sound pairs:
1, 2, 3, 4, 9, 10, 13, 14, 17, 19, 21, 23, 28, 32, 33, 34, 35, 40, 41, 45, 50

Thai

From Section A *Letters and sounds* (Units 1–20), you could leave out these units:
3, 6, 10, 11, 15, 18, 19
From Section D *Sound pairs*, it would probably be useful for you to do these sound pairs:
3, 5, 6, 17, 30, 31, 33, 34, 35, 36, 38, 40, 45, 50

Turkish

From Section A *Letters and sounds* (Units 1–20), you could leave out these units:
4, 9, 16
From Section D *Sound pairs*, it would probably be useful for you to do these sound pairs:
1, 5, 11, 17, 19, 28, 34, 35, 38, 45, 47, 48, 49

West African languages

From Section A *Letters and sounds* (Units 1–20), you could leave out these units:
8, 10, 11, 12, 20
From Section D *Sound pairs*, it would probably be useful for you to do these sound pairs:
1, 2, 3, 9, 10, 12, 14, 17, 19, 22, 23, 28, 31, 34, 35, 37, 40, 45, 48, 50

Sound pairs

If you have problems in hearing the difference between individual sounds in Section A of the book, you will be directed to one of the exercises in this section.

or

Look in D3 *Guide for speakers of specific languages*, find the sound pairs recommended for speakers of your language, and do these.

In order to remember which sound pairs you have done, put a tick in the boxes. If you have completed it but you still find it difficult, tick 'visited'. If you are sure you know it, tick 'understood'. If you have recorded yourself saying the words correctly, tick 'recorded'.

D7 Sound pair 1: /æ/ and /e/

For more on these sounds, see Units 2, 6.

man – men	had – head
gas – guess	sad – said

Listen to the words in the box.

Listen. The speaker will say two words from the box.
If you hear the same word twice, write S (same).
If you hear two different words, write D (different).

1 .... 2 .... 3 .... 4 .... 5 .... 6 .... 7 ....

Listen. Circle the word you hear.

8 *bad / bed*
9 *dad / dead*
10 *sat / set*
11 *marry / merry*
12 Talk to the *man / men*.

visited	
understood	
recorded	

D8 Sound pair 2: /æ/ and /ʌ/

For more on these sounds, see Units 2, 18.

ran – run	cat – cut
match – much	sang – sung

Listen to the words in the box.

Listen. The speaker will say two words from the box.
If you hear the same word twice, write S (same).
If you hear two different words, write D (different).

1 .... 2 .... 3 .... 4 .... 5 .... 6 .... 7 ....

Listen. Circle the word you hear.

8 *fan / fun*
9 *cap / cup*
10 *rang / rung*
11 She's got a *cat / cut* on her arm.
12 *He's sung / He sang* in public.

visited	
understood	
recorded	

D9 Sound pair 3: /æ/ and /ɑː/

For more on these sounds, see Units 2, 14.

Listen to the words in the box.

(Note: In accents where the R is pronounced, these are not minimal pairs.)

hat – heart	had – hard
match – March	pack – park

Listen. The speaker will say two words from the box. If you hear the same word twice, write S (same). If you hear two different words, write D (different).

1 ....   2 ....   3 ....   4 ....   5 ....   6 ....   7 ....

Listen. Circle the word or phrase you hear.

8 *cat / cart*
9 *match / March*
10 *had a / harder* problem
11 He always *packs / parks* slowly.
12 She put her hand on her *hat / heart*.

visited	
understood	
recorded	

D10 Sound pair 4: /eɪ/ and /e/

For more on these sounds, see Units 2, 6.

Listen to the words in the box.

main – men	weight – wet
late – let	pain – pen

Listen. The speaker will say two words from the box.
If you hear the same word twice, write S (same).
If you hear two different words, write D (different).

1 ....   2 ....   3 ....   4 ....   5 ....   6 ....   7 ....

Listen. Circle the word you hear.

8 *gate / get*
9 *paper / pepper*
10 *waste / west*
11 What would happen if we *fail / fell*?
12 I've got a *pain / pen* in my hand.

visited	
understood	
recorded	

D11 Sound pair 5: /eɪ/ and /eə/

For more on these sounds, see Units 2, 14.

Listen to the words in the box.

(Note: In accents where the R is pronounced, these are not minimal pairs.)

way – wear	pays – pears
they – there	stays – stairs

Listen. The speaker will say two words from the box. If you hear the same word twice, write S (same). If you hear two different words, write D (different).

1 ....   2 ....   3 ....   4 ....   5 ....   6 ....   7 ....

Listen. Circle the word or phrase you hear.

8 *they / their*
9 *stays / stairs*
10 *hey / hair*
11 I don't want *to pay / a pear*.
12 There's *no way / nowhere* to go.

visited	
understood	
recorded	

D12 ## Sound pair 6: /eə/ and /ɑː/

For more on these sounds, see Unit 14.

Listen to the words in the box.

fare – far	stairs – stars
bear – bar	care – car

Listen. The speaker will say two words from the box.
If you hear the same word twice, write S (same). If you hear
two different words, write D (different).

1 .... 　 2 .... 　 3 .... 　 4 .... 　 5 .... 　 6 .... 　 7 ....

Listen. Circle the word you hear.

8 *fare / far*
9 *bare / bar*
10 *cares / cars*
11 I don't think it's *fair / far*.
12 We slept under the *stairs / stars*.

visited	
understood	
recorded	

D13 ## Sound pair 7: /ɑː/ and /ɔː/

For more on these sounds, see Units 14, 19.

Listen to the words in the box.

farm – form	part – port
bar – bore	star – store

Listen. The speaker will say two words from the box.
If you hear the same word twice, write S (same). If you hear
two different words, write D (different).

1 .... 　 2 .... 　 3 .... 　 4 .... 　 5 .... 　 6 .... 　 7 ....

Listen. Circle the word you hear.

8 *farm / form*
9 *park / pork*
10 There are thousands of *stars / stores*.
11 You can visit any *part / port*.
12 I don't think it's *far / four*.

visited	
understood	
recorded	

D14 ## Sound pair 8: /eə/ and /ɪə/

For more on these sounds, see Units 6, 14.

Listen to the words in the box.

hair – here	fair – fear
chairs – cheers	bear – beer

Listen. The speaker will say two words from the box.
If you hear the same word twice, write S (same).
If you hear two different words, write D (different).

1 .... 　 2 .... 　 3 .... 　 4 .... 　 5 .... 　 6 .... 　 7 ....

Listen. Circle the word you hear.

8 *where / we're*
9 *dare / dear*
10 *chairs / cheers*
11 *hair / hear*
12 There's something in the *air / ear*.

visited	
understood	
recorded	

D15 Sound pair 9: /ʌ/ and /ɑː/

For more on these sounds, see Units 14, 18.

Listen to the words in the box.

(Note: In accents where the R is pronounced, some of these are not minimal pairs.)

come – calm	much – March
duck – dark	cut – cart

Listen. The speaker will say two words from the box. If you hear the same word twice, write S (same). If you hear two different words, write D (different).

1 .... 2 .... 3 .... 4 .... 5 .... 6 .... 7 ....

Listen. Circle the word you hear.

  8 *hut / heart*
  9 *much / March*
10 *duck / dark*
11 *cut / cart*
12 Try to *come / calm* down.

visited	
understood	
recorded	

D16 Sound pair 10: /ɪ/ and /iː/

For more on these sounds, see Units 6, 11.

Listen to the words in the box.

hit – heat	rich – reach
chip – cheap	live – leave

Listen. The speaker will say two words from the box. If you hear the same word twice, write S (same). If you hear two different words, write D (different).

1 .... 2 .... 3 .... 4 .... 5 .... 6 .... 7 ....

Listen. Circle the word or phrase you hear.

  8 *chip / cheap*
  9 *fit / feet*
10 He doesn't want to *live / leave*.
11 Can you *fill / feel* it?
12 Do you want *to sit / a seat*?

visited	
understood	
recorded	

D17 Sound pair 11: /iː/ and /ɪə/

For more on these sounds, see Unit 6.

Listen to the words in the box.

knee – near	be – beer
he – here	tea – tear

(Note: In accents where the R is pronounced, these are not minimal pairs.)

Listen. The speaker will say two words from the box. If you hear the same word twice, write S (same). If you hear two different words, write D (different).

1 .... 2 .... 3 .... 4 .... 5 .... 6 .... 7 ....

Listen. Circle the word you hear.

  8 *we / we're*
  9 *knee / near*
10 *pea / pier*
11 *feed / feared*
12 Who is *he / here*?

visited	
understood	
recorded	

D18 Sound pair 12: /e/ and /ɜː/

For more on these sounds, see Units 6, 19.

Listen to the words in the box.

(Note: In accents where the R is pronounced, these are not minimal pairs.)

head – heard	west – worst
bed – bird	feather – further

Listen. The speaker will say two words from the box. If you hear the same word twice, write S (same). If you hear two different words, write D (different).

1 .... 2 .... 3 .... 4 .... 5 .... 6 .... 7 ....

Listen. Circle the word you hear.

8 *ten / turn*
9 *lend / learned*
10 *Jenny / journey*
11 That's a nice *bed / bird*.
12 This is the *west / worst* side.

visited	
understood	
recorded	

D19 Sound pair 13: /ɪ/ and /e/

For more on these sounds, see Units 6, 11.

Listen to the words in the box.

did – dead	lift – left
sit – set	bill – bell

Listen. The speaker will say two words from the box.
If you hear the same word twice, write S (same).
If you hear two different words, write D (different).

1 .... 2 .... 3 .... 4 .... 5 .... 6 .... 7 ....

Listen. Circle the word you hear.

8 *miss / mess*
9 *bill / bell*
10 *will / well*
11 Who dropped the *litter / letter*?
12 You should take the *lift / left*.

visited	
understood	
recorded	

D20 Sound pair 14: /ɒ/ and /əʊ/

For more on these sounds, see Unit 16.

Listen to the words in the box.

want – won't	cost – coast
not – note	shone – shown

Listen. The speaker will say two words from the box.
If you hear the same word twice, write S (same).
If you hear two different words, write D (different).

1 .... 2 .... 3 .... 4 .... 5 .... 6 .... 7 ....

Listen. Circle the word you hear.

8 *not / note*
9 *rob / robe*
10 *goat / got*
11 They *want / won't* sleep.
12 The *cost / coast* is clear.

visited	
understood	
recorded	

D21 Sound pair 15: /ɒ/ and /ʌ/

For more on these sounds, see Units 16, 18.

lock – luck	shot – shut
gone – gun	not – nut

Listen to the words in the box.

Listen. The speaker will say two words from the box.
If you hear the same word twice, write S (same).
If you hear two different words, write D (different).

1 .... 2 .... 3 .... 4 .... 5 .... 6 .... 7 ....

Listen. Circle the word or phrase you hear.

8 *not / nut*
9 *lock / luck*
10 They *shot / shut* the door.
11 This shirt has a horrible *collar / colour.*
12 Did you see *they're gone / their gun?*

visited	
understood	
recorded	

D22 Sound pair 16: /əʊ/ and /uː/

For more on these sounds, see Units 16, 18.

show – shoe	toe – two
blow – blue	soap – soup

Listen to the words in the box.

Listen. The speaker will say two words from the box.
If you hear the same word twice, write S (same).
If you hear two different words, write D (different).

1 .... 2 .... 3 .... 4 .... 5 .... 6 .... 7 ....

Listen. Circle the word you hear.

8 *soap / soup*
9 *rule / roll*
10 There's water in my *boat / boot.*
11 He went to the north *pool / pole.*
12 We *grow / grew* strawberries.

visited	
understood	
recorded	

D23 Sound pair 17: /əʊ/ and /ɔː/

For more on these sounds, see Units 16, 19.

coat – caught	low – law
boat – bought	woke – walk

Listen to the words in the box.

Listen. The speaker will say two words from the box.
If you hear the same word twice, write S (same).
If you hear two different words, write D (different).

1 .... 2 .... 3 .... 4 .... 5 .... 6 .... 7 ....

Listen. Circle the word you hear.

8 *so / saw*
9 *low / law*
10 *coal / call*
11 It's a new *bowl / ball.*
12 I *woke / walk* in the morning.

visited	
understood	
recorded	

🎧 **D24** ## Sound pair 18: /əʊ/ and /aʊ/

For more on these sounds, see Units 16, 20.

Listen to the words in the box.

| no – now blows – blouse |
| phoned – found tone – town |

Listen. The speaker will say two words from the box.
If you hear the same word twice, write S (same).
If you hear two different words, write D (different).

1 _____ 2 _____ 3 _____ 4 _____ 5 _____ 6 _____ 7 _____

Listen. Circle the word or phrase you hear.

  8 *know* / *now*
  9 *blows* / *blouse*
10 It isn't *a load* / *allowed*.
11 I don't want *to show her* / *a shower*.
12 Tim *phoned* / *found* her.

visited	
understood	
recorded	

🎧 **D25** ## Sound pair 19: /ʊ/ and /uː/

For more on these sounds, see Unit 18.

Listen to the words in the box.

| full – fool pull – pool |
| look – Luke |

Listen. The speaker will say two words from the box.
If you hear the same word twice, write S (same).
If you hear two different words, write D (different).

1 _____ 2 _____ 3 _____ 4 _____ 5 _____ 6 _____ 7 _____

Listen. Circle the word or phrase you hear.

  8 *Luke* / *look*
  9 *full* / *fool*
10 *pull* / *pool*
11 *Should I?* / *shoe dye*
12 The *butcher* / *boots you* saw.

visited	
understood	
recorded	

🎧 **D26** ## Sound pair 20: /ʌ/ and /ʊ/

For more on these sounds, see Unit 18.

Listen to the words in the box.

| luck – look bucks – books |

Listen. The speaker will say two words from the box.
If you hear the same word twice, write S (same).
If you hear two different words, write D (different).

1 _____ 2 _____ 3 _____ 4 _____

Listen. Circle the word you hear.

  5 *bucks* / *books*
  6 *luck* / *look*

visited	
understood	
recorded	

(D27) Sound pair 21: /ʌ/ and /ɜː/

For more on these sounds, see Units 18, 19.

Listen to the words in the box.

(Note: In accents where the R is pronounced, some of these are not minimal pairs.)

shut – shirt	suffer – surfer
such – search	ton – turn

Listen. The speaker will say two words from the box. If you hear the same word twice, write S (same). If you hear two different words, write D (different).

1 ....   2 ....   3 ....   4 ....   5 ....   6 ....   7 ....

Listen. Circle the word or phrase you hear.

  8 *but / Bert*
  9 *hut / hurt*
10 *under / earned a*
11 *suffer / surfer*
12 It looks like the butcher's *shut / shirt*.

visited	
understood	
recorded	

(D28) Sound pair 22: /ʌ/ and /e/

For more on these sounds, see Units 6, 18.

Listen to the words in the box.

won – when	study – steady
butter – better	nut – net

Listen. The speaker will say two words from the box. If you hear the same word twice, write S (same). If you hear two different words, write D (different).

1 ....   2 ....   3 ....   4 ....   5 ....   6 ....   7 ....

Listen. Circle the word or phrase you hear.

  8 *but / bet*
  9 *study / steady*
10 *won / when*
11 He shot *a gun / again*.
12 This one's *butter / better*.

visited	
understood	
recorded	

(D29) Sound pair 23: /ɔː/ and /ɒ/

For more on these sounds, see Units 16, 19.

Listen to the words in the box.

short – shot	order – odder
sport – spot	port – pot

(Note: In accents where the R is pronounced, some of these are not minimal pairs.)

Listen. The speaker will say two words from the box. If you hear the same word twice, write S (same). If you hear two different words, write D (different).

1 ....   2 ....   3 ....   4 ....   5 ....   6 ....   7 ....

Listen. Circle the word or phrase you hear.

  8 *short / shot*
  9 *order / odder*
10 *sport / spot*
11 *water ski / what a ski*
12 There's coffee in the *port / pot*.

visited	
understood	
recorded	

Sound pair 24: /ɜː/ and /ɪə/

For more on these sounds, see Units 6, 19.

Listen to the words in the box.

| bird – beard | her – hear |
| were – we're | fur – fear |

Listen. The speaker will say two words from the box.
If you hear the same word twice, write S (same).
If you hear two different words, write D (different).

1 ....   2 ....   3 ....   4 ....   5 ....   6 ....   7 ....

Listen. Circle the word you hear.

8 *bird / beard*
9 *were / we're*
10 *fur / fear*
11 I can't see if it's *her / here*.
12 He has a black *bird / beard*.

visited	
understood	
recorded	

Sound pair 25: /ɜː/ and /eə/

For more on these sounds, see Units 14, 19.

Listen to the words in the box.

| her – hair | fur – fair |
| were – where | bird – bared |

(Note: In accents where the R is pronounced,
some of these are not minimal pairs.)

Listen. The speaker will say two words from the box. If you hear the same word twice, write S (same). If you hear two different words, write D (different).

1 ....   2 ....   3 ....   4 ....   5 ....   6 ....   7 ....

Listen. Circle the word you hear.

8 *were / where*
9 *stir / stair*
10 *bird / bared*
11 I can't see if it's *her / hair*.
12 It isn't *fur / fair*.

visited	
understood	
recorded	

Sound pair 26: /ɜː/ and /ɔː/

For more on these sounds, see Unit 19.

Listen to the words in the box.

| worked – walked | shirt – short |
| burn – born | bird – bored |

(Note: In accents where the R is pronounced,
some of these are not minimal pairs.)

Listen. The speaker will say two words from the box. If you hear the same word twice, write S (same). If you hear two different words, write D (different).

1 ....   2 ....   3 ....   4 ....   5 ....   6 ....   7 ....

Listen. Circle the word you hear.

8 *bird / bored*
9 *sir / saw*
10 *shirt / short*
11 You weren't *first / forced* to do it.
12 We *worked / walked* all day.

visited	
understood	
recorded	

D33 Sound pair 27: /ɜː/ and /ɑː/

For more on these sounds, see Units 14, 19.

hurt – heart	heard – hard
further – father	firm – farm

Listen to the words in the box.

Listen. The speaker will say two words from the box.
If you hear the same word twice, write S (same).
If you hear two different words, write D (different).

1 .... 2 .... 3 .... 4 .... 5 .... 6 .... 7 ....

Listen. Circle the word you hear.

  8 *fur / far*
  9 *hurt / heart*
10 *further / father*
11 The question wasn't *heard / hard*.
12 She owned a *firm / farm*.

visited	
understood	
recorded	

D34 Sound pair 28: /b/ and /p/

For more on these sounds, see Unit 3.

bill – pill	cubs – cups
back – pack	big – pig

Listen to the words in the box.

Listen. The speaker will say two words from the box.
If you hear the same word twice, write S (same).
If you hear two different words, write D (different).

1 .... 2 .... 3 .... 4 .... 5 .... 6 .... 7 ....

Listen. Circle the word you hear.

  8 *bill / pill*
  9 *bush / push*
10 The soldiers lay on their *backs / packs*.
11 They tied the *robe / rope* round his neck.
12 There's a *bear / pear* in that tree.

visited	
understood	
recorded	

D35 Sound pair 29: /b/ and /v/

For more on these sounds, see Units 3, 8.

best – vest	bet – vet
cupboard – covered	

Listen to the words in the box.

Listen. The speaker will say two words from the box.
If you hear the same word twice, write S (same).
If you hear two different words, write D (different).

1 .... 2 .... 3 .... 4 .... 5 .... 6 .... 7 ....

Listen. Circle the word or phrase you hear.

  8 *bet / vet*
  9 *They've ached / They baked* all day.
10 *summer beach / some of each*
11 *Say 'boil' / Save oil.*
12 *I brushed it / I've rushed it.*

visited	
understood	
recorded	

D36 ## Sound pair 30: /p/ and /f/

For more on these sounds, see Units 3, 8.

Listen to the words in the box.

pull – full	copy – coffee
wipe – wife	supper – suffer

Listen. The speaker will say two words from the box.
If you hear the same word twice, write S (same).
If you hear two different words, write D (different).

1 .... 2 .... 3 .... 4 .... 5 .... 6 .... 7 ....

Listen. Circle the word or phrase you hear.

 8 *pool / fool*
 9 *pine / fine*
10 He was driving *past / fast*.
11 *a nicer pear / a nice affair*
12 a change of *pace / face*

visited	
understood	
recorded	

D37 ## Sound pair 31: /s/ and /z/

For more on these sounds, see Unit 4.

Listen to the words in the box.

place – plays	Sue – zoo
rice – rise	east – eased

Listen. The speaker will say two words from the box.
If you hear the same word twice, write S (same).
If you hear two different words, write D (different).

1 .... 2 .... 3 .... 4 .... 5 .... 6 .... 7 ....

Listen. Circle the word you hear.

 8 *ice / eyes*
 9 *sip / zip*
10 They *race / raise* horses here.
11 What's wrong with your *niece / knees* today?
12 I just want some *peace / peas* please.

visited	
understood	
recorded	

D38 ## Sound pair 32: /s/ and /ʃ/

For more on these sounds, see Units 4, 12.

Listen to the words in the box.

same – shame	self – shelf
fist – fished	sell – shell

Listen. The speaker will say two words from the box.
If you hear the same word twice, write S (same).
If you hear two different words, write D (different).

1 .... 2 .... 3 .... 4 .... 5 .... 6 .... 7 ....

Listen. Circle the word you hear.

 8 *sign / shine*
 9 *mass / mash*
10 I didn't *save / shave* for years.
11 They didn't *suit / shoot* him.
12 They sat on the *seat / sheet*.

visited	
understood	
recorded	

D39 Sound pairs 33: /s/ and /θ/, /z/ and /ð/

For more on these sounds, see Units 4, 17.

sink – think	worse – worth
bays – bathe	closed – clothed

Listen to the words in the box.

Listen. The speaker will say two words from the box.
If you hear the same word twice, write S (same).
If you hear two different words, write D (different).

1 .... 2 .... 3 .... 4 .... 5 .... 6 .... 7 ....

Listen. Circle the word you hear.

  8 *sing / thing*
  9 *breeze / breathe*
10 That's a funny *sort / thought*.
11 Her *mouse / mouth* seems to be smiling.
12 Are they *closed / clothed* yet?

visited	
understood	
recorded	

D40 Sound pair 34: /d/ and /t/

For more on these sounds, see Unit 5.

hard – heart	road – wrote
dune – tune	die – tie

Listen to the words in the box.

Listen. The speaker will say two words from the box.
If you hear the same word twice, write S (same).
If you hear two different words, write D (different).

1 .... 2 .... 3 .... 4 .... 5 .... 6 .... 7 ....

Listen. Circle the word you hear.

  8 *said / set*
  9 *down / town*
10 I forgot the *code / coat*.
11 It's a very *wide / white* beach.
12 She started *riding / writing* young.

visited	
understood	
recorded	

D41 Sound pairs 35: /t/ and /θ/, /d/ and /ð/

For more on these sounds, see Units 5, 17.

tree – three	boat – both
breed – breathe	dough – though

Listen to the words in the box.

Listen. The speaker will say two words from the box.
If you hear the same word twice, write S (same).
If you hear two different words, write D (different).

1 .... 2 .... 3 .... 4 .... 5 .... 6 .... 7 ....

Listen. Circle the word you hear.

  8 *tree / three*
  9 *day / they*
10 I don't want your *tanks / thanks*!
11 That's what I *taught / thought*!
12 They couldn't *breed / breathe* very well.

visited	
understood	
recorded	

(D42) ## Sound pairs 36: /t/ and /tʃ/, /d/ and /dʒ/

For more on these sounds, see Units 5, 12.

Listen to the words in the box.

| art – arch | what – watch |
| paid – page | head – hedge |

Listen. The speaker will say two words from the box.
If you hear the same word twice, write S (same).
If you hear two different words, write D (different).

1 .... 2 .... 3 .... 4 .... 5 .... 6 .... 7 ....

Listen. Circle the word you hear.

8 *taught / torch*
9 *aid / age*
10 It's a tropical *beat / beach*.
11 He took the *coat / coach* all the way to London.
12 It went over my *head / hedge* into the next garden.

visited	
understood	
recorded	

(D43) ## Sound pair 37: /f/ and /v/

For more on these sounds, see Unit 8.

Listen to the words in the box.

| leaf – leave | half – halve |
| safer – saver | ferry – very |

Listen. The speaker will say two words from the box.
If you hear the same word twice, write S (same).
If you hear two different words, write D (different).

1 .... 2 .... 3 .... 4 .... 5 .... 6 .... 7 ....

Listen. Circle the word or phrase you hear.

8 *that sofa / that's over*
9 This is where we *lift / lived*.
10 That's quite a *few / view*!
11 Ask your *wife's / wives'* friends.
12 a current *affair / of air*

visited	
understood	
recorded	

(D44) ## Sound pair 38: /v/ and /w/

For more on these sounds, see Units 8, 10.

Listen to the words in the box.

| vet – wet | veil – whale |
| invite – in white | verse – worse |

Listen. The speaker will say two words from the box.
If you hear the same word twice, write S (same).
If you hear two different words, write D (different).

1 .... 2 .... 3 .... 4 .... 5 .... 6 .... 7 ....

Listen. Circle the word or phrase you hear.

8 *made of air / made aware*
9 Which is *verse / worse*?
10 It's next to the *vine / wine*.
11 It's in the *vest / west*.
12 *half a weight / half of eight*

visited	
understood	
recorded	

Sound pairs 39: /f/ and /θ/, /v/ and /ð/

For more on these sounds, see Units 8, 17.

Listen to the words in the box.

| fin – thin | deaf – death |
| loaves – loathes | van – than |

Listen. The speaker will say two words from the box.
If you hear the same word twice, write S (same).
If you hear two different words, write D (different).

1 .... 2 .... 3 .... 4 .... 5 .... 6 .... 7 ....

Listen. Circle the word or phrase you hear.

8 *first / thirst*
9 I got these *free / three* gifts.
10 It's a *fort / thought.*
11 *What some of us / What's a mother's* first thought.
12 I don't know *Eva / either.*

visited	
understood	
recorded	

Sound pair 40: /g/ and /k/

For more on these sounds, see Unit 9.

Listen to the words in the box.

| goat – coat | glass – class |
| dog – dock | pig – pick |

Listen. The speaker will say two words from the box.
If you hear the same word twice, write S (same).
If you hear two different words, write D (different).

1 .... 2 .... 3 .... 4 .... 5 .... 6 .... 7 ....

Listen. Circle the word you hear.

8 The *gap's / cap's* too small.
9 His *bag / back* was broken.
10 Did you see the *ghost / coast*?
11 There was a *guard / card* by the door.
12 Is it *gold / cold*?

visited	
understood	
recorded	

Sound pair 41: /h/ and / /

For more on this sound, see Unit 10.

Listen to the words in the box.

| hill – ill | hold – old |
| hear – ear | hall – all |

Listen. The speaker will say two words from the box.
If you hear the same word twice, write S (same).
If you hear two different words, write D (different).

1 .... 2 .... 3 .... 4 .... 5 .... 6 .... 7 ....

Listen. Circle the word you hear.

8 *hate / eight*
9 *heart / art*
10 You can smell it in the *hair / air.*
11 She lost her *hearing / earring.*
12 They aren't *heating / eating* it properly.

visited	
understood	
recorded	

D48 ## Sound pair 42: /j/ and /dʒ/

For more on these sounds, see Units 10, 12.

Listen to the words in the box.

use – juice	your – jaw
yoke – joke	yet – jet

Listen. The speaker will say two words from the box.
If you hear the same word twice, write S (same).
If you hear two different words, write D (different).

1 .... 2 .... 3 .... 4 .... 5 .... 6 .... 7 ....

Listen. Circle the word or phrase you hear.

8 *yet / jet*
9 *until you lie / until July*
10 I don't see the *yoke / joke.*
11 Did you see *yours / Jaws?*
12 What's the *use / juice?*

visited	
understood	
recorded	

D49 ## Sound pairs 43: /h/ and /ʃ/, /h/ and /f/

For more on these sounds, see Units 8, 10, 12.

Listen to the words in the box.

hip – ship	hot – shot
horse – force	hate – fate

Listen. The speaker will say two words from the box.
If you hear the same word twice, write S (same).
If you hear two different words, write D (different).

1 .... 2 .... 3 .... 4 .... 5 .... 6 .... 7 ....

Listen. Circle the word you hear.

8 I think the *holder's / shoulder's* broken.
9 You have to *hold / fold* it there.
10 I can't sleep with this *heat / sheet.*
11 I don't think it's *hair / fair.*
12 The boss *hired / fired* me.

visited	
understood	
recorded	

D50 ## Sound pair 44: /tʃ/ and /ʃ/

For more on these sounds, see Unit 12.

Listen to the words in the box.

cheap – sheep	chair – share
watch – wash	witch – wish

Listen. The speaker will say two words from the box.
If you hear the same word twice, write S (same).
If you hear two different words, write D (different).

1 .... 2 .... 3 .... 4 .... 5 .... 6 .... 7 ....

Listen. Circle the word you hear.

8 *choose / shoes*
9 *chair / share*
10 I tried to *catch / cash* the cheque.
11 But there aren't any *chips / ships!*
12 You'll have to *watch / wash* the baby.

visited	
understood	
recorded	

D51 Sound pair 45: /tʃ/ and /dʒ/

For more on these sounds, see Unit 12.

Listen to the words in the box.

chin – gin	rich – ridge
chain – Jane	H – age

Listen. The speaker will say two words from the box.
If you hear the same word twice, write S (same).
If you hear two different words, write D (different).

1 ....   2 ....   3 ....   4 ....   5 ....   6 ....   7 ....

Listen. Circle the word you hear.

  8 *chose / Joe's*
  9 *cheap / jeep*
10 I dreamt of enormous *riches / ridges.*
11 Hair-loss starts with *H / age.*
12 I don't think it's in *tune / June.*

visited	
understood	
recorded	

D52 Sound pairs 46: /ts/ and /tʃ/, /dz/ and /dʒ/

For more on these sounds, see Unit 12.

Listen to the words in the box.

cats – catch	mats – match
raids – rage	aids – age

Listen. The speaker will say two words from the box.
If you hear the same word twice, write S (same).
If you hear two different words, write D (different).

1 ....   2 ....   3 ....   4 ....   5 ....   6 ....   7 ....

Listen. Circle the word you hear.

  8 *arts / arch*
  9 *aids / age*
10 *eats / each*
11 *Watch / What's* the time! / ?
12 They suffered the *raids / rage* of the bandits.

visited	
understood	
recorded	

D53 Sound pairs 47: /tr/ and /tʃ/, /dr/ and /dʒ/

For more on these sounds, see Units 12, 13.

Listen to the words in the box.

trees – cheese	train – chain
draw – jaw	drunk – junk

Listen. The speaker will say two words from the box.
If you hear the same word twice, write S (same).
If you hear two different words, write D (different).

1 ....   2 ....   3 ....   4 ....   5 ....   6 ....   7 ....

Listen. Circle the word you hear.

  8 *trips / chips*
  9 *drunk / junk*
10 The *train / chain* isn't moving.
11 There's something in the *trees / cheese.*
12 It's in the lower *drawer / jaw.*

visited	
understood	
recorded	

Sound pair 48: /n/, /ŋ/ and /ŋk/

D54

For more on these sounds, see Unit 15.

Listen to the words in the box.

thin – thing	sinner – singer
thing – think	singing – sinking

Listen. The speaker will say two words from the box.
If you hear the same word twice, write S (same).
If you hear two different words, write D (different).

1 .... 2 .... 3 .... 4 .... 5 .... 6 .... 7 ....

Listen. Circle the word or phrase you hear.

8 *hand / hanged*
9 *win / wing*
10 *Robin Banks / robbing banks*
11 I *ran / rang* home yesterday.
12 They're *singing / sinking*.

visited	
understood	
recorded	

Sound pairs 49: /m/ and /n/, /m/ and /ŋ/

D55

For more on these sounds, see Unit 15.

Listen to the words in the box.

some – sun	smack – snack
game – gain	some – sung

Listen. The speaker will say two words from the box.
If you hear the same word twice, write S (same).
If you hear two different words, write D (different).

1 .... 2 .... 3 .... 4 .... 5 .... 6 .... 7 ....

Listen. Circle the word or phrase you hear.

8 *term / turn*
9 *mice / nice*
10 The *son warned / sun warmed* me.
11 It's *mine / nine* already!
12 You have to *swim / swing* to the left.

visited	
understood	
recorded	

Sound pair 50: /l/ and /r/

D56

For more on these sounds, see Unit 13.

Listen to the words in the box.

light – write	lock – rock
alive – arrive	flight – fright

Listen. The speaker will say two words from the box.
If you hear the same word twice, write S (same).
If you hear two different words, write D (different).

1 .... 2 .... 3 .... 4 .... 5 .... 6 .... 7 ....

Listen. Circle the word you hear.

8 They *played / prayed* for the team.
9 It wasn't *long / wrong*.
10 They *glow / grow* in the dark.
11 There were *flies / fries* all around my burger.
12 I'll *collect / correct* it tomorrow.

visited	
understood	
recorded	

D5 Sentence stress phrasebook

You will speak more fluently if you say some very common expressions with a fixed pronunciation, like a single word. The expressions below are grouped according to their stress pattern.

Listen and repeat.

D57 oOo

Good morning.
Good evening.
Excuse me!
How are you?
You're welcome.
I'd love to.

D58 OoO

What's your name?
What's the time?
Thanks a lot.
Close the door.
Yes, of course.
Come and see!
Don't forget.

D59 oOoO

A piece of cake.
The shop was closed.
It's time to go.
I spoke to John.
A cup of tea.

D60 OoOo

See you later!
Just a moment.
Pleased to meet you.
Where's the station?

D61 OOo

No problem!
Don't worry.
Keep quiet!
Please help us.
Who told you?

D62 OOoo

How much is it?
How far is it?
What time is it?
What day was it?

D63 OooO

What do you do?
Where are you from?
Where do you live?
Where were you born?
When does it leave?
How do you do?
What do you want?

D64 ooOo

Can you help me?
Do you like it?
Are you coming?
Was it raining?
There's a problem.

D65 ooOoO

Would you like a drink?
Do you want to come?
Is it time to go?
Is it far from home?

D6 Glossary

accent An accent is the way the people of a place pronounce their language. For example, people in London and Sydney both speak English, but they have different accents.

auxiliary verb An auxiliary verb is a verb which does not have a meaning by itself; it helps the grammar of the sentence. For example, in *Do you like music?*, *do* is an auxiliary verb.

C In this book, the symbol C means consonant sound.

careful speech / fast speech People pronounce sentences differently when they speak carefully. For example, you may use careful speech when you are talking in public or reading aloud. But in normal conversation you would use fast speech.

consonant sound A consonant sound is a sound we make by obstructing the flow of air from the mouth.

contraction A contraction is a short form of an auxiliary verb in writing. For example, *are* is contracted to *re* in *they're*.

emphasising Emphasising in speech is like underlining in writing; we use it to make one word stand out as more important than the others. We can emphasise words by pronouncing them louder, longer and/or higher.

minimal pair If two words are pronounced nearly the same, but they have just one sound different, they are a minimal pair. For example, in the pair *ship* /ʃɪp/ and *sheep* /ʃiːp/, only the second sound is different.

native speaker If you are a native speaker of a language, that language is your first language, the language which you learnt as a young child.

phonemic symbol A phonemic symbol is a letter which represents a sound. For example, the first sound in *shoe* is represented by the phonemic symbol /ʃ/.

rhyme Two words rhyme if they have the same final vowel or vowel and consonant sounds. For example, *go* rhymes with *show* and *hat* rhymes with *cat*.

sentence stress Sentence stress is the pattern of strong and weak syllables in a sentence. For example, the sentence *How do you do?* is normally said with this sentence stress pattern: OooO (the first and last syllables strong, the second and third syllables weak).

sound A sound is the minimum segment of the pronunciation of a word. For example, the word *this* has three sounds: /θ/, /ɪ/ and /s/.

stress pattern The pattern of strong and weak syllables in a word or sentence is its stress pattern. In this book, stress patterns are represented by big and small circles. For example, the stress pattern of the word *pronunciation* is oooOo.

syllable A syllable is a word or part of a word that has one vowel sound. It may also have one or more consonant sounds. For example, *ago* has two syllables. The first syllable is just one vowel sound. The second syllable is a consonant sound followed by a vowel sound.

tone   A tone is the way your voice goes up or down when you say a sentence. This can change the meaning of the sentence.

unstressed   An unstressed syllable is one which is not pronounced strongly.

V   In this book, the symbol V means vowel sound.

voice   Many pairs of consonant sounds are similar, but one of them is voiced and the other is not. For example, /d/ is similar to /t/, but /d/ is voiced and /t/ is not. A consonant is voiced when there is vibration in the throat.

vowel sound   A vowel sound is a sound we make when we don't obstruct the air flow from the mouth in speaking.

weak vowels   Unstressed syllables often contain a weak vowel. The most common weak vowel is /ə/. This is the first vowel sound in *about*, for example. The vowel /ɪ/ is also sometimes weak, in the second syllable of *orange*, for example.

word stress   Word stress is the pattern of strong and weak syllables in a word. For example, the word *decided* has three syllables and the second one is pronounced more strongly. So *decided* has this word stress pattern: oOo.

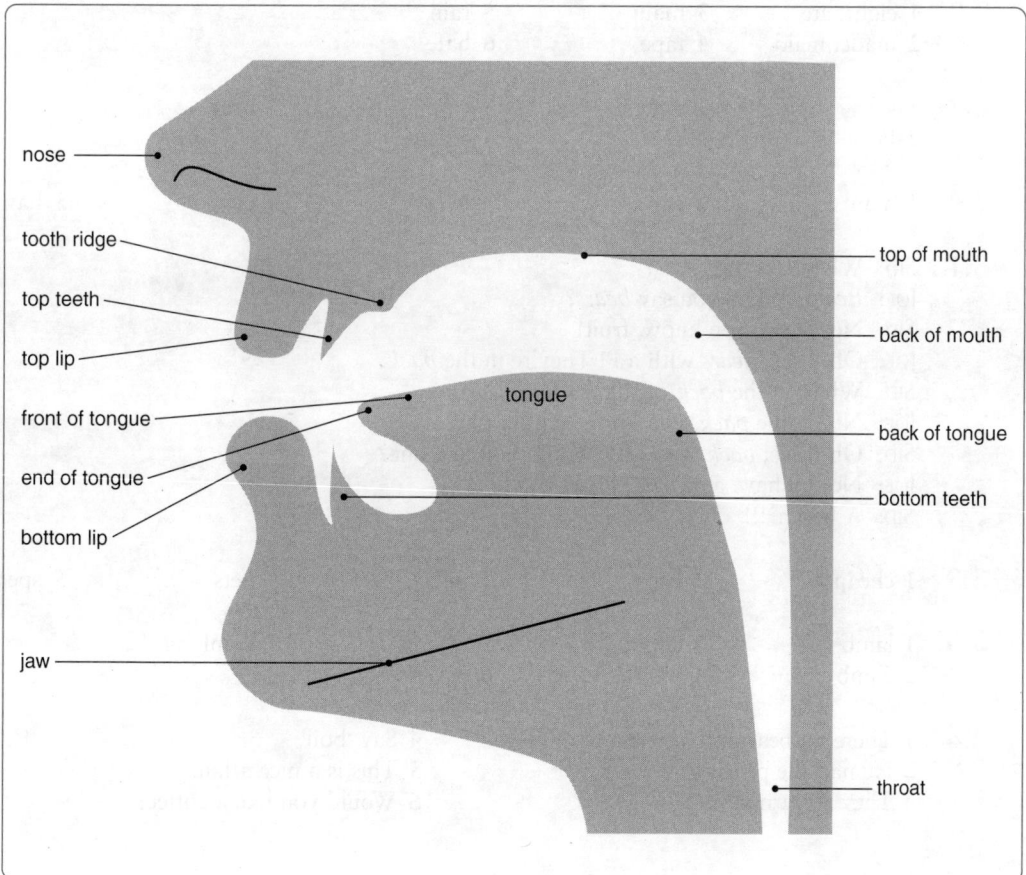

- nose
- tooth ridge
- top teeth
- top lip
- front of tongue
- end of tongue
- bottom lip
- jaw
- tongue
- top of mouth
- back of mouth
- back of tongue
- bottom teeth
- throat

Key

1.1 Last *week*, I *sent* my *son* Jamie to the shops to *buy some* food. He got a *piece* of *meat* and *two pears*. On the *way* home, the bag broke. The food fell onto the *road* and got dirty. In the end, Jamie *threw* the food in the bin.

1.2
1 dog   CVC
2 rabbit   CVCVC
3 frog   CCVC

4 gorilla   CVCVCV
5 snake   CCVC
6 bee   CV

1.3
1 Phil the fox A
2 Mary the canary B
3 Ida the spider B
4 Claire the bear B

5 Polly the parrot A
6 Deborah the zebra B
7 Myrtle the turtle B
8 Kitty the cat A

1.4 The answers depend on your own first language. See Section D3 for more information about this.

2.1

/eɪ/	/æ/
cake table baby train eight	hat hand cat map rat

2.2
1 eight, ate
2 made, maid

3 main
4 tape

5 rain
6 hate

2.3
1 salt
2 far

3 watch
4 said

5 care
6 square

7 heat

2.4
1 man
2 cap
3 heart
4 pen
5 hay

3.1
SID: Where are the *pears*?
JOE: *Bears*?!!! Did you say *bears*?
SID: No, *pears*, you know, fruit!
JOE: Oh, I see, *pears* with a P! They're in the *pack*.
SID: What, in the *back* of the truck?
JOE: No, in the *pack*, you know, with a *P*!
SID: Oh, I see, *pack* with a P! Would you like one?
JOE: No, I'll have a *peach*, please.
SID: A beach?!!!

3.2
1 cheap
2 back
3 pill
4 pets
5 speak

3.3
1 lamb
2 climb
3 cupboard
4 photo
5 receipt
6 psychology
7 combing

3.4
1 There's a bear in that tree.
2 He had the peach to himself.
3 They've earned it.
4 Say 'boil'.
5 This is a nice affair.
6 Would you like a coffee?

4.1

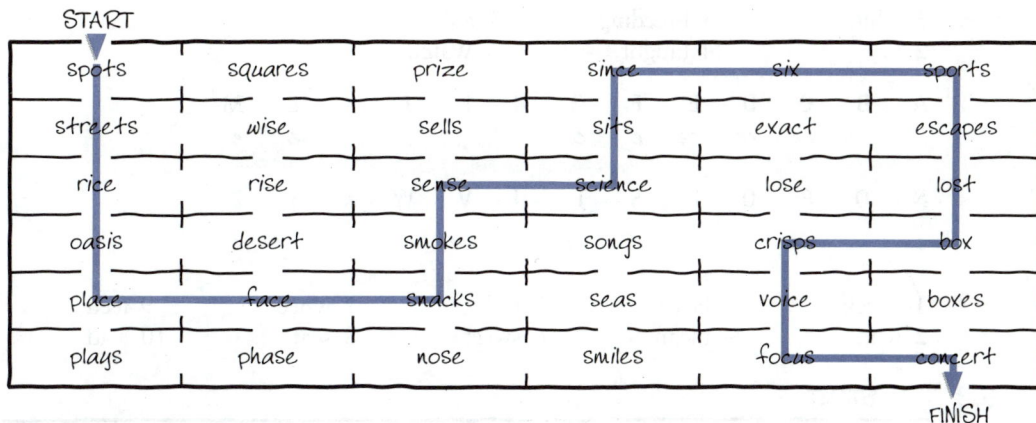

4.2 SID: Alice's *niece* is nice.

JOE: *Are* nice, Sid. Plural. Her *knees are* nice.

SID: I'm not talking about her *knees*, I'm talking about her *niece*!

JOE: Oh, I see, *niece* with a C.

SID: That's right. She has nice *eyes*.

JOE: How can *ice* be nice? It's too cold.

SID: Not *ice*, you fool! *Eyes*: E-Y-E-S!

4.3 1 I'm not going to (advise) you, you never take my *advice*.

2 Your tooth is *loose*. You'll (lose) it if you're not careful.

3 The shop's very *close* to home, and it doesn't (close) till late.

4 I can't (excuse) people who drop litter. There's no *excuse* for it.

4.4

1 prize	3 suit	5 think
2 he's at	4 saved	6 clothed

5.1 There was a young lady called Kate,

Who always got out of bed *late*.

The first thing she *said*

When she lifted her *head*

Was 'I thought it was better to *wait*.'

There was a young waiter called Dwight,

Who didn't like being *polite*.

If you asked him for *food*,

He was terribly *rude*

And invited you out for a *fight*.

5.2

1 built, build	3 sent, send	5 white, wide
2 try, dry	4 hurt, heard	6 down, town

5.3 1 whistle   2 needed   3 listen   4 ended   5 soften

Note that where there are two Cs at the end of a verb in the past tense, the –ed is pronounced /t/, e.g. walked /wɔːkt/, liked /laɪkt/. See Unit 25.

5.4
1 whiter	3 breeding	5 aid
2 dry	4 taught	6 Watch

6.1

A	B	C	D	E	F	G	H	I	J	K	L	M
	ee	ee	ee	ee	e	ee					e	e

N	O	P	Q	R	S	T	U	V	W	X	Y	Z
e		ee			e	ee		ee		e		e

6.2
1 cheek	3 beat	5 feel	7 wheel	9 feed
2 read	4 mean	6 sweet	8 seat	10 lead

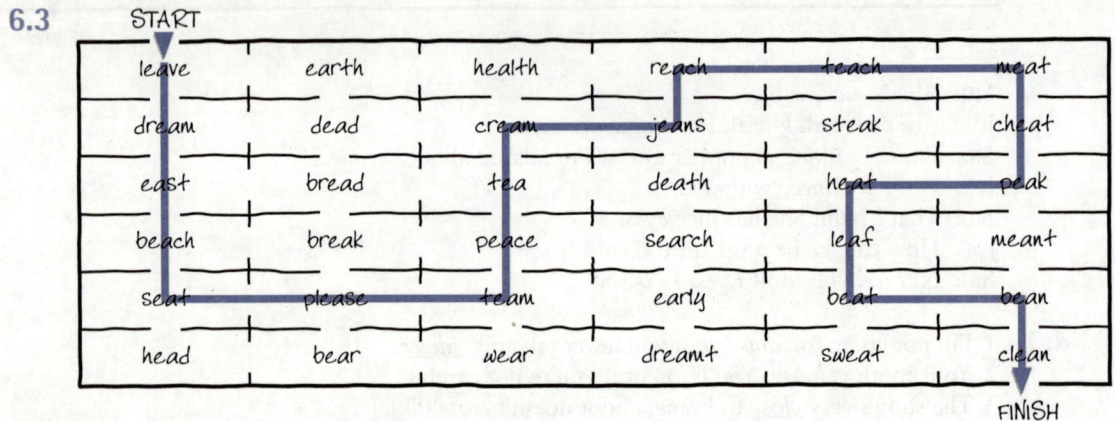

6.3

START

leave	earth	health	reach	teach	meat
dream	dead	cream	jeans	steak	cheat
east	bread	tea	death	heat	peak
beach	break	peace	search	leaf	meant
seat	please	team	early	beat	bean
head	bear	wear	dreamt	sweat	clean

FINISH

6.4
1 men	3 beer	5 bird
2 pain	4 leave	6 left

7.1
pasta   faster
Rita   metre
daughter   water

7.2
1 from Canada to China	5 a question and an answer
2 The parrot was asleep.	6 a woman and her husband
3 The cinema was open.	7 a pasta salad
4 the photographer's assistant	

7.3

vowel in weak syllable = /ə/	vowel in weak syllable = /ɪ/
woman collect asleep salad letter sofa quarter	orange return market begin visit teaches needed peaches women

7.4
1 women	3 manager's	5 waiter's	7 officer's	9 drive
2 address	4 teaches	6 dancer's	8 away	10 races

8.1   1 3   2 4   3 2   4 4   5 4

8.2 SID: My *wife's* left me.
JOE: Your *wives* left you? How many *wives* did you have, Sid?
SID: One wife. And now she has left me.
JOE: Oh, I see, *wife's* with an F, not *wives* with a V!
SID: That's right! Yes, she took the *van* and drove off.
JOE: What did she want the *fan* for?
SID: I said *van*, you know, a kind of vehicle.
JOE: Oh, I see: *van* with a V, not *fan* with an F!

8.3

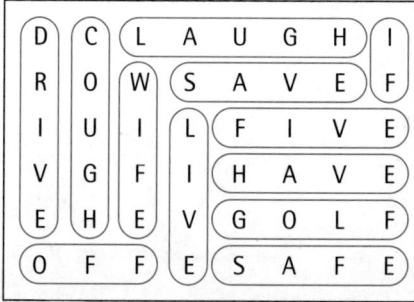

8.4
1 thief's	3 copy	5 verse
2 view	4 vote	6 free

9.1
1 up cup
2 aim game, came
3 ache cake
4 round ground, crowned
5 old gold, cold
6 lime climb
7 air care
8 all call
9 rate great, crate
10 ill kill

9.2   1 bigger   2 six   3 ache   4 rocks   5 queue

9.3 SID: Hey, there's the monster!
JOE: That's just a *log*.
SID: Yes, it's *Loch* Ness.
JOE: No, not *Loch*. I mean *log*, you know, from a tree!
SID: I've never seen a tree with a *lock*.
JOE: No, not a *lock* that you open with a key; a *log* with a G!

9.4   1 coast   2 glasses   3 bag   4 coat

10.1
1 worth
2 hear, year
3 your, wore
4 win
5 hate, weight, wait
6 wise
7 hall, wall
8 weighed
9 hill, will
10 heart
11 while
12 heat, wheat
13 wake
14 high, why
15 hold

10.2
1 under   3 who   5 honest
2 whole   4 untie   6 write

10.3

1 Your uniform used to be yellow. /j/
    j   j   j   j

2 Haley's horse hurried ahead. /h/
    h   h   h   h

3 This is a quiz with twenty quick questions. /w/
             w   w   w   w   w

4 We went to work at quarter to twelve. /w/
  w   w   w   w   w

5 New York University student's union. /j/
      j   j   j   j   j

6 The hen hid behind the hen house. /h/
        h   h   h   h   h

7 Which language would you like to work in? /w/
    w   w   w   w

10.4

1 heart	3 vest	5 juice
2 earring	4 aware	6 sheet

11.1

words with the vowel /aɪ/	words with the vowel /ɪ/
wife wine wide light life line lime mice mine mile mite night nice nine fight fine file time sight side site quite (and also ... lice might mime Nile tight tile tide)	will wish win mill fit fill fish tin sit sin quit (and also ... wit lit nit fin till sill quill)

11.2

A: Why did Jim hit Bill?   /aɪ/ 1 /ɪ/ 4
B: Well, Jim's a guy who likes a fight.   /aɪ/ 3 /ɪ/ 1
A: But Bill's twice his size.   /aɪ/ 2 /ɪ/ 2
B: Yeah, that's why Jim got a black eye and a thick lip. /aɪ/ 2 /ɪ/ 3
A: And Bill's got a big smile.   /aɪ/ 1 /ɪ/ 2
B: That's right.   /aɪ/ 1 /ɪ/ 0

11.3

1 might time	3 lip pill	5 pitch chip	7 dice side
2 lick kill	4 kiss sick	6 tick kit	8 lights style

11.4

1 live	2 feel	3 letter	4 lift

12.1

contains /dʒ/	contains /ʃ/	contains /tʃ/
Belgian German Japanese	Welsh Russian Polish Turkish French	Dutch Chinese Chilean

12.2 SID: It's fish and *chips* for lunch, Joe!
JOE: *Ships*!? I can't eat *ships*, they're too big!
SID: I said *chips*, you know, fried potatoes!
JOE: Oh, I see, *chips* with a CH, not *ships* with an SH.
SID: That's right. You're a genius, Joe!
JOE: Was the fish expensive, Sid?
SID: No, it was *cheap*.
JOE: *Jeep*!? You bought a *Jeep*?
SID: No, *cheap*, the opposite of expensive.
JOE: Oh, I see, *cheap* with a CH, not *Jeep* with a J!

12.3
1 which chair
2 match cheers
3 watch chat
4 stage joked
5 catch chickens
6 change jackets

12.4
1 watch	3 shave	5 What's
2 ridges	4 use	6 trees

13.1
1 late, rate	3 rare, lair	5 lend	7 leg
2 rose, rows	4 learn	6 lie, rye	8 reach

13.2 I worked *late* that day and I didn't *arrive* home until 10 o'clock. I was very wet because of the *rain*. Then, to my *surprise*, my key didn't fit in the *lock*. So I looked closely at my keys and saw that they were the *wrong* ones. I had left my house keys at work. So I got back on my motorbike and *rode* back to the office to *collect* them. I got home really tired, so I went to bed, *read* for half an hour, switched off the *light* and went to sleep.

13.3
1 court	2 folk	3 hair	4 should	5 artist

13.4
1 supplies	2 correct	3 flight	4 cheese	5 drawer

14.1

words with the vowel /ɑː/	words with the vowel /eə/
bar far dart star start car card cart calm half hard chart (and also... bard balm fart calf hart char)	bare rare dare fair stair square care hair chair (and also... fare stare hare)

14.2 SID: This is a great life, with no worries or *cares*!
JOE: It would be nice if we had *cars* though, Sid.
SID: I didn't say *cars*, I said *cares*!
JOE: Oh, I see. Not *cars*, as in traffic, but *cares* with an ES at the end!
SID: That's right. I've always loved sleeping under the *stars*.
JOE: But why? There's hardly any space under the *stairs*!
SID: No, not *stairs*, *stars*! You know, little lights in the sky.
JOE: Oh, *stars*! I thought you said *stairs*, that people walk up!

14.3 1 Am 3 Am 5 Am 7 Eng
2 Eng 4 Am 6 Eng

14.4 1 heart 3 far 5 beer
2 no way 4 part 6 come

15.1 /m/ = 19 /n/ = 11 /ŋ/ = 5

15.2

START

sing	think	thick	strong	wrong	rung
sign	uncle	unless	drug	strange	comb
thanks	angry	signal	drank	English	finger
anxious	angel	single	monkey	money	young
language	tongue	skiing	skin	came	ink
lounge	danger	band	dream	swim	wing

FINISH

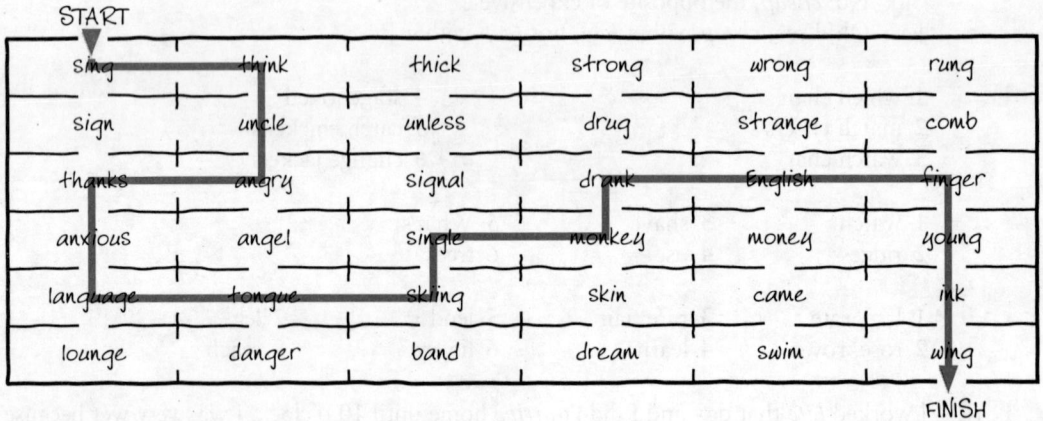

15.3 SID: Hey, Joe, your coat is very worn.
JOE: No, it isn't *warm*. I always feel cold in this coat.
SID: No, not *warm*! I said *worn*, with an N!
JOE: Oh, *worn* with an N!
SID: Yes, the cloth is *thin*.
JOE: What do you mean "the cloth is *thing*"?
SID: No, *thin* with an N at the end, not *thing* with a G at the end!

15.4 1 Robin 2 ran 3 swim 4 son warned 5 sinking

16.1

words with /əʊ/	words with /ɒ/
cold both road show snow roll joke coat	shop song want rock what wash

16.2

1 come	3 love	5 cloth	7 lost
2 most	4 cow	6 word	

16.3   1 A–B   2 B–A   3 A–B   4 B–A   5 A–B

16.4   1 coast   2 shut   3 boat   4 woke   5 found

17.1

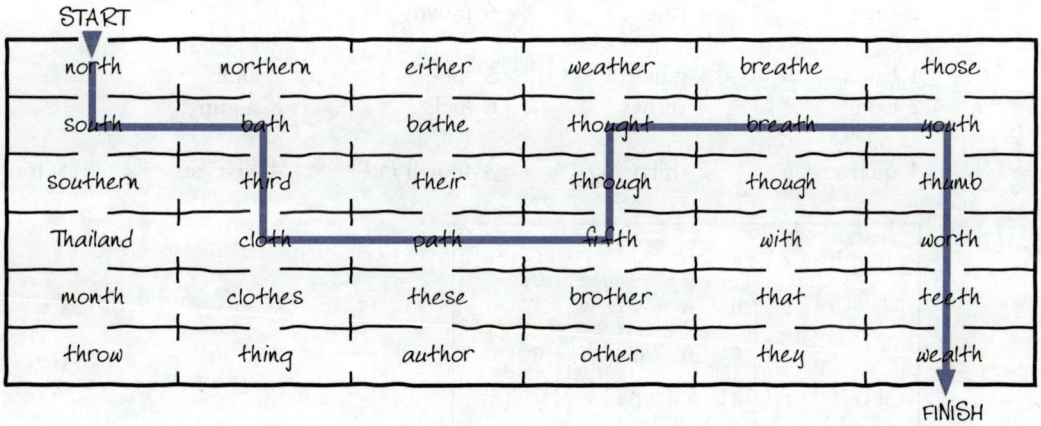

17.2
Arthur had a *brother*
And he didn't want *another*.
And of the brothers, *neither*
Wanted sisters *either*.
The last thing on this *earth*
They wanted was a *birth*.
So Arthur's mother *Heather*
Got them both *together*,
And told them all good *brothers*
Should learn to share their *mothers*.

17.3

1 bath	3 thin	5 thought
2 through	4 thick	6 death

17.4

1 use	3 Free	5 breeding
2 taught	4 clothed	6 These are

18.1

/ʌ/	/uː/
studied London summer months pub lunches much	school two June food true too

18.2

1 month, June	3 won, Cup	5 full, moon
2 son, brother	4 juice, good	6 wood/would, would/wood

18.3

1 book	3 does	5 group	7 south
2 rude	4 rule	6 move	

18.4

1 cat	3 gun	5 'pool'	7 shut
2 calm	4 shows	6 luck	8 a gun

19.1

1 quarter /ɔː/	2 thirty /ɜː/	3 fourth /ɔː/	4 first /ɜː/	5 fourteen /ɔː/

19.2

Words with /ɜː/	Words with /ɔː/
bird turn heard word her girl	ball sort more course war saw law all

19.3

1 A		3 B		5 A		7 A		9 B	
2 B		4 A		6 B		8 B			

19.4

1 far		3 walk		5 pot		7 her	
2 worst		4 shut		6 beard		8 walked	

20.1

1 boys /ɔɪ/, bows /aʊ/	4 point /ɔɪ/	7 hour /aʊ/
2 noise /ɔɪ/	5 how /aʊ/	8 flower /aʊ/
3 found /aʊ/	6 boil /ɔɪ/	9 enjoy /ɔɪ/

20.2

/ɔɪ/ (4 words)	/aʊ/ (6 words)
enjoy noisy points choice	down town loud shout out around

20.3

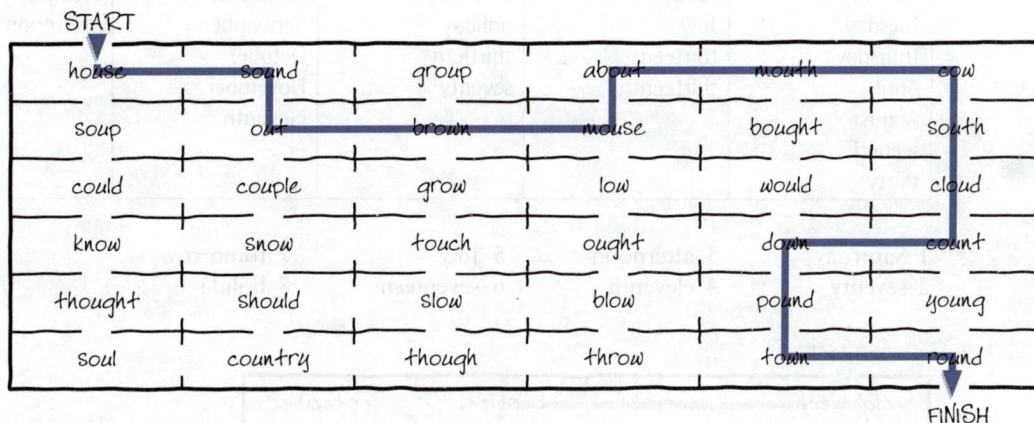

20.4

1 toy	2 Good boy	3 found	4 tone

21.1

1 syllable	2 syllables	3 syllables
aunt	doctor	grandfather
cook	sister	officer
dad	teacher	passenger
	uncle	

21.2

1 bought CVC	6 laugh CVC
2 eyes VC	7 two CV
3 key CV	8 youth CVC
4 day CV	9 weigh CV
5 through CCV	10 rhyme CVC

21.3

1 /deɪ/ = day	/eɪd/ = aid		4 /tiː/ = tea	/iːt/ = eat	
2 /nəʊ/ = no	/əʊn/ = own		5 /meɪ/ = may	/eɪm/ = aim	
3 /peɪ/ = pay	/eɪp/ = ape		6 /seɪ/ = say	/eɪs/ = ace	

21.4 The correct number of syllables is:

interesting	Ooo	*3 syllables*		vegetables	Ooo	*3 syllables*
restaurant	Oo	*2 syllables*		chocolate	Oo	*2 syllables*
Wednesday	Oo	*2 syllables*		general	Oo	*2 syllables*
different	Oo	*2 syllables*		lovely	Oo	*2 syllables*

Note that in some words you can almost hear the missing syllable.

21.5 1 Walt·er walked to·wards the wait·er. = *8 syllables*
2 Bett·y bought a bett·er bit of butt·er. = *10 syllables*
3 The fat cat sat on the vet's wet hat. = *9 syllables*

22.1

Oo	oO	Ooo	oOo	ooO
Monday	today	Saturday	tomorrow	seventeen
Tuesday	July	holiday	September	afternoon
Thursday	thirteen	thirtieth	October	
April	thirteenth	seventy	November	
August			eleventh	
second				
thirty				

22.2
1 Saturday	3 afternoon	5 July	7 tomorrow
2 seventy	4 eleventh	6 seventeen	8 holiday

22.3

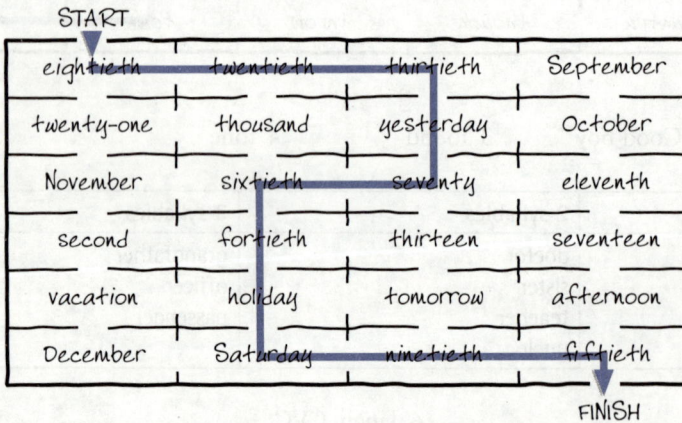

22.4
1 17	3 50	5 30
2 14th	4 1916	6 80

23.1

1 oOo	*tomato*	<u>Close the door.</u>	He told me.	I like it.
2 ooO	*afternoon*	Does he drive?	Were you cold?	<u>What happened?</u>
3 oOo	*December*	It's open.	<u>They arrived.</u>	They listened.

23.2

OooO	oOoO	OoO	OoOo
What do you want?	The bus was late.	Come and look.	Close the window.
Give me a call.	The water's cold.	Where's the car?	Nice to see you.
What did she say?	It's cold and wet.	What's the time?	Phone and tell me.

23.3 Can't Pete drive?
Doesn't Oscar listen?
Can't you make Jennifer talk to you?

23.4

| 1 B | 2 B | 3 A | 4 B | 5 A | 6 A |

24.1

1 lie	fly	5 lime	climb
2 lock	clock	6 late	plate
3 rain	train	7 route	fruit
4 key	ski		

24.2

1 back	black	6 pay	play / pray
2 fight	flight / fright	7 two	true
3 fat	flat	8 say	stay / slay
4 go	glow / grow	9 sin	skin / spin
5 pain	plain / plane	10 send	spend

24.3

1 glass	3 fright	5 stream	7 plane
2 play	4 tooth	6 stay	8 smell

24.4

1 B	3 A	5 A	7 B
2 A	4 B	6 B	8 A

25.1

1 field	feel / feed	5 shelf	shell / chef
2 change	chain	6 wealth	well
3 six	sick	7 guest	guess / get
4 build	bill / bid	8 wild	while / wide

25.2 A: OK, first question. What's the eighth month in the year?
B: It's August.
A: Correct! Second question. What's the highest mountain on Earth?
B: Mount Everest.
A: Correct again! Mount Everest! Next question: Which city is furthest east in Europe: Athens, Brussels or Budapest?
B: Is it Budapest, or perhaps Brussels?
A: No, it isn't. It's Athens. OK, last question. What's the biggest land animal in the world?
B: The elephant.
A: Very good! Three out of four correct, that's seventy-five percent!

25.3
1 I *think old* cars are better.
2 The *bank ought* to be open by now.
3 I *think all* the time.
4 These big cars *hold eight* people.
5 Did he *film other* kinds of movies too?
6 Three people have *six eyes*.
7 If you took aspirins, your head *wouldn't ache*.

25.4

1 cook	3 didn't	5 guess	7 pasta
2 helper	4 learnt	6 burnt	8 mix

26.1

1 b	3 g	5 d	7 f
2 c	4 a	6 e	

26.2

1 syllable O	sings goes gets comes sees pulls
2 syllables Oo	watches dances kisses washes closes pushes

26.3
1 *Hands* up!
2 There are many different *kinds* of whale.
3 My favourite *subject's* chemistry.
4 The *wind's* very strong today.

26.4

1 bird	3 arms	5 car	7 bag	9 class
2 guests	4 song	6 books	8 shop	10 boxes

27.1

1 h	3 g	5 i	7 j	9 b
2 e	4 c	6 a	8 f	10 d

27.2

1 syllable O	walked washed helped phoned danced asked
-ed = extra syllable Oo	hated needed waited wasted tasted ended

27.3

O O O	OoOoOo (-ed = extra syllable)
Ken **cooked** lunch. Fred **phoned** friends. Marge **mixed** drinks. Will **watched** films.	Karen **counted** money. Stella **started** singing. Alice **added** sugar. Sheila **shouted** loudly.

27.4

1 walked	3 laugh	5 hated	7 needed
2 want	4 danced	6 help	8 paint

28.1 1 How did you *react* when you saw the *actor* coming in?
2 The *writer* decided to *rewrite* the whole book.
3 The *painter* tried to *repaint* this part of the picture.
4 We asked the *printer* to *reprint* the whole document.
5 The *viewer* will be able to *review* this programme tomorrow.
6 They had to *replay* the match after a *player* was hurt.

28.2

1 answer	4 guitar	7 shampoo
2 mistake	5 complete	8 reason
3 copy	6 promise	

28.3

1 progressed = oO	progress = Oo
2 import = oO	export = Oo
3 protest = Oo	rebelled = oO
4 desert = Oo	contrast = Oo
5 produce = oO	objects = Oo

29.1

Oo	Ooo	Oooo
bookshops shoe shops snack bars something playground handbag	*anything* post office hairdresser's everything hamburger sports centre swimming pool credit card	*shopping centre* travel agent's supermarket

29.2 The following should be circled.

1 second hand	4 short-sighted
2 old fashioned	5 half price
3 hand made	6 first class

29.3

1 a Yes, I have.	3 a Yes, I have.
2 b No, I haven't.	4 a Yes, I have.

30.1 1 believer, believable, unbelievable, unbelieving
2 enjoyable, unenjoyable, enjoyment
3 careful, carefully, careless, carelessness, carer, caring, uncaring

30.2

Oo	nation, clinic, public
oOo	relation, romantic, discussion
ooOo	population, scientific, pessimistic
oooOo	communication, pronunciation, investigation
ooooOo	identification
oooooOo	telecommunication

30.3
1 introduction ooOo
2 basic Oo
3 economic ooOo
4 description oOo
5 romantic oOo
6 competition ooOo

7 optimistic ooOo
8 celebration ooOo
9 diplomatic ooOo
10 operation ooOo
11 explanation ooOo
12 decision oOo

31.1
1 personality ooOoo
2 university ooOoo
3 publicity oOoo
4 majority oOoo

5 nationality ooOoo
6 reality oOoo
7 humanity oOoo
8 electricity ooOoo

31.2

Oo	Ooo	oOoo	ooOoo	ooOo
physics history nation	chemistry geography	economy geology photography	sociology nationality	*economics* mathematics

31.3 My favourite subjects at school were sciences, especially *chemistry* and *biology*. I've always been good with numbers, so I was good at *mathematics*. I didn't really like the social science subjects like *sociology* and *history*, and that's strange because when I went to university I did *geography*.

31.4
1 civilisation
2 biology

3 personality
4 legalisation

5 author

32.1
1 Sorry!
2 Go straight on!

3 Run!
4 Don't move!

5 Don't worry!

32.2
1 Smile!
2 Look out!
3 Go away!

4 Don't look down!
5 Sorry!

32.3
1
Don't sleep! *Stay* awake!
Get dressed! Don't *be* late!

2
Stand still! Stay there!
Don't move! *Take* care!

3
Say please! Don't *be* rude!
Sit *down*! Eat your food!

33.1
1 OoO   2 OoooO   3 OO   4 OoooO   5 OoO

33.2
1 it   3 are   5 of   7 some
2 a   4 can   6 or   8 my

33.3
1 Eat *some* cheese. *1*
2 That *was the* man. *2*
3 What *was his* name? *2*
4 What for? *0*

5 Go *to the* shops. *2*
6 Go home. *0*
7 Turn *to the* right. *2*

33.4 **1**
Drink milk.
Drink *some* milk. / Drink *the* milk.
Drink *it with* milk.
Drink *some of the* milk. / Drink *it with the* milk. / Drink *it with some* milk.

2
Turn right.
Turn *it* right.
Turn *to the* right.
Turn *it to the* right.

34.1 *Possible answers:*

1 He read the book. / I read my book.
2 We sang a song. / You sang that song.
3 They drank some milk. / It drank the milk.
4 We ate our lunch. / She ate some lunch.

34.2
1 Can you give *it* to *them* please?
2 Did *you* meet *their* daughter, Catherine?
3 I don't think *he* likes *her*.
4 What did *she* say to *them*?
5 Where did *she* buy *her* guitar?
6 What's *his* mother's name?
7 Where are *your* parents from?
8 **We** bought presents for *our* children.

34.3
1 He's <u>buying</u> <u>pres</u>ents for them.
2 They're <u>opening</u> their <u>presents</u>.
3 They'll <u>thank</u> him for the <u>presents</u>.
4 He'll <u>thank</u> her for the <u>money</u>.

34.4
1 We've done it
2 I'll ask him
3 I'll see you
4 He's gone to
5 I'll tell her

35.1 There (are) a lot of books in the picture. Some of them (are) on the desks and some (are) on the shelves. There are some trees outside the windows. The windows (are) open. There are some pens on one of the desks.

35.2
1 a	3 a	5 b	7 a
2 b	4 b	6 b	

35.3
1 are	3 was	5 are	7 was	9 are
2 was	4 were	6 are	8 is	10 were

35.4
1 are	3 is	5 was	7 was	9 was
2 were	4 are	6 was	8 are	10 are

36.1
1 Where *do they* live?
2 What *did she* say?
3 Where *will they* work?
4 What *did you* see?
5 Where *have they* gone?
6 Who *did we* meet?
7 Where *will he* sit?
8 When *will it* end?
9 Where *have you* been?
10 Who *has she* asked?

36.2   1 Where do you live? OooO
2 Where do you work? OooO
3 Are you married? ooOo
4 What does he teach? OooO
5 Where does he teach? OooO
6 Where did you meet him? OoooOo
7 When did you get married? OoooOo

36.3   1 Who have / Who've you told?
2 What did he say?
3 When do you start?
4 Where has / Where's he gone?
5 How do you do?

37.1

oOoO	oOoOo	oOooO	oOooOo
a bowl of soup a pot of tea	a jar of honey a bag of apples	a bottle of wine a carton of milk	a packet of biscuits a kilo of carrrots

37.2   1 and   3 for   5 and   7 a   9 for
2 an   4 of   6 to   8 some   10 of

37.3   1 *it's* time *for* lunch
2 *some* egg *and* chips
3 *the* bag *of* nuts
4 *to* drink *and* eat
5 *to* cook *some* rice
6 *as* fast *as* that
7 *a* meal *for* two
8 *the* box *of* food
9 *some* fish *or* meat

37.4   1 We had a nice cup *of* tea.
2 I don't want *to* go out tonight.
3 I need a *drink of* water.
4 We *cooked a* chicken.
5 He can't *cook a* meal.
6 Have *an ice-cream*!
7 Come in *and* sit down.

38.1   1 felt *able*
2 *no* new
3 *cooks* take
4 see *new*
5 *faced* old
6 *a* notion
7 *stop* turning
8 escape *terror*
9 men *cheer*
10 learnt '*yes*'

38.2   1 ~~Known uses~~ good news, as they say.   *No news is*
2 Have you ~~phone jaw~~ parents this week?   *phoned your*
3 I've never ~~her July~~ before.   *heard you lie*
4 I think I ~~fell train~~; let's go inside.   *felt rain*
5 These ~~ship steak~~ cars across the river.   *ships take*
6 They ~~join does~~ for dinner.   *joined us*
7 We ~~stop choosing~~ the typewriter when we got the computer.   *stopped using*

38.3   There was ‿ an ‿ old man called Greg,
Who tried to break ‿ open an ‿ egg.
He kicked ‿ it ‿ around,
But fell ‿ on the ground,
And found that he'd broken ‿ a leg.

39.1 1 TOM /tiːʲəʊʷem/
      2 BEN /biːʲiːʲen/
      3 ERIN /iːʲɑːʳaɪʲen/

      4 TANIA /tiːʲeɪʲenaɪʲeɪ/
      5 ROSIE /ɑːʳəʊʷesaɪʲiː/

39.2 1 blue‿w and grey
      2 me‿j and you
      3 why‿j or where

      4 her‿r or you
      5 away‿j or here

39.3 1 Are yo<u>u into</u> golf? *winter*
      2 He has hair over th<u>e ears</u>. *years*
      3 It's starting t<u>o ache</u>. *wake*
      4 I'm not su<u>re I'd</u> agree with you. *ride*
      5 She has a shower <u>each</u> morning. *reach*

      6 It's quarter t<u>o eight</u> already. *wait*
      7 <u>Do I</u> owe you anything? *why*
      8 Her <u>eyes</u> are a strange colour. *rise*
      9 You should know better at you<u>r age</u>! *rage*

40.1 1 **a** sum
        b sung
      2 **a** beach
        b beak
      3 **a** coke
        b coach
      4 **a** cheek
        b cheap

40.2 1 (arc) art
      2 (tribe) tried
      3 (ache) eight
      4 (wing) win
      5 (lime) line
      6 (bag) bad

40.3 1 I got this cup by *winning the game*.
      2 I'll have to warm my *hands*.
      3 Her heart broke when *he left her*.
      4 It's the last term before *the holidays*.

41.1 1 ~~noose~~ news
      2 ~~art~~ heart
      3 ~~den~~ then
      4 ~~tank~~ thank
      5 ~~robin~~ robbing
      6 ~~look~~ luck
      7 ~~old~~ hold

41.2 **1**
A: Can I help you?
B: Yes, I'd like to see … I'm sorry, *how* do you pronounce this name?
A: O'Shaughnessy. Doctor O'Shaughnessy.
B: Yes, I'd *like* to see Doctor O'Shaughnessy, please.

2
A: My name's Mark.
B: *Sorry*, Mike, you say?
A: No, Mark. M-A-R-K.
B: Oh, I see. You don't *pronounce* the R?
A: No, not in my accent.

3
A: My surname's Vaugn.
B: Sorry, could you *repeat* that, please?
A: Vaugn.
B: Vaugn? How do you *spell* that?
A: V-A-U-G-N.
B: Oh yes, I've seen that name before!

41.3   3 Sorry, could you repeat that, please?
      2 Sorry, I don't understand.
      1 How do you pronounce that?
      4 Can you speak more slowly, please?

42.2   1 There was nothing inside / It was empty.
      2 We walked carefully downstairs / It was dark.
      3 I watched him / Silently he opened the drawer.
      4 The rain didn't stop the next day / It just carried on.
      5 The weather was hot / At the weekend it was 40 degrees.
      6 I saw her clearly / She was hungry.
      7 It was cold / Last night the roads were icy.

42.3
Name:	Martin Britton
Address:	Flat 6
	98 Carlowe Road
	Middleton
Postcode:	DG16 H39
Telephone:	691 2281
email:	mbrit@jetcom.uk

43.1   1 a It was a small car / with a red stripe along the side.
         b ~~It was a small car with a red / stripe along the side.~~
      2 a Do you want chicken and chips / or fish and salad?
         b ~~Do you want chicken / and chips or fish and salad?~~
      3 a ~~Derek can wear the most / expensive suit but he never looks smart.~~
         b Derek can wear the most expensive suit / but he never looks smart.

43.2   1 Take your boots and ski suit / and a dress and some nice shoes for the evenings.
      2 Take a hat and sunglasses and T-shirts / and an umbrella in case it rains.
      3 Take a smart suit and a shirt and tie / and some casual clothes for the weekend.
      4 Take your camera and some good walking shoes / and a towel and bathing costume for
         the beach.

43.3   A man wanted to buy his wife a new dress /
      because it was her birthday / so he went to a
      department store / and looked around / and he
      was looking for about an hour / but he
      couldn't decide / and finally this shop assistant
      came / and asked if he needed help / he said he
      was looking for a dress / and the shop assistant
      asked / is it for you sir?

44.1   1 B is looking in a business appointments book.
      2 B is doing a mental calculation.
      3 B is checking in a personal diary.
      4 B is looking in a wallet.

44.2 **1** I don't really have much time to ehm ::: to listen to music •
       2 Yeah, I love Brazilian music, people like Gal Costa •••
       3 She plays quite a lot of instruments, piano, guitar •••
       4 Dad's really into classical music, you know, specially Mozart •
       5 I started the piano when I was, let's see, ehm ::: fifteen •

44.3 I didn't go to the concert because I lost my ticket. Well no, I didn't actually lose it, it was in my jeans pocket, you see, and I put it in the washing machine. So anyway, I went to the door of the theatre and they said it was no good.

45.1 **1** Her computer fell on the floor and she lost all her data.
       2 He asked for a glass of water with lemon and ice.
       3 She's got a place at university.

45.2 **1** Well   **2** anyway   **3** Well   **4** anyway

46.1 It's really cold in Montana sometimes. Your beard and moustache get full of ice and you feel the air freeze, in your nose and mouth.

46.2 Debbie   you know
       Kimberly   kind of
       Greg   like

46.3 We don't <u>like</u> have coffee breaks, <u>I mean</u> we just <u>like</u> get
a coffee or tea and <u>sort of</u> <u>like</u> take it back to our desks,
<u>you know</u>, but it's <u>kind of</u> dangerous 'cause, <u>I mean</u>, people
sometimes <u>like</u> knock the drink over the computer, <u>you know</u>.

46.4 **1** I don't think these are the men, <u>*you know*</u>.
       2 I've taught you everything *you know*.
       3 Do you know the place *I mean*? It's just over there.
       4 She's not the one. <u>*I mean*</u>, she's too tall.
       5 They're *like* wild animals.
       6 This is, <u>*like*</u>, Arctic weather.

47.1

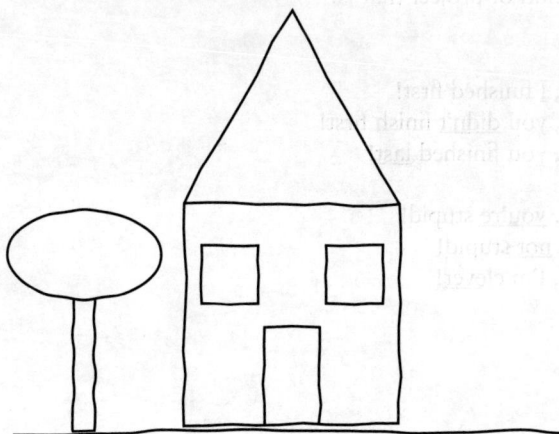

47.2 1 Take a piece of paper and a pen. 4 Draw a triangle on top of the square.
2 Draw a line across the page. 5 Draw some windows and a door.
3 On top of that line, draw a square. 6 Draw a tree to the left of the house.

47.3 1 Check that everything looks *right* and then send it.
2 Click here so you get a new page. <u>OK,</u> and now write the title at the top.
3 Make sure you save that *OK* and now close the program.
4 You will see the icon on the *right* of your screen.
5 Open the program, <u>*right*</u> and now start a new document.
6 I think it's ready *now* you can switch it on

48.1 1 **a** What she said was good. 1
b What she said was 'Good!' 2

2 **a** He said, 'Linda was married.' 2
b He said Linda was married. 1

3 **a** That's the thing she said. 2
b 'That's the thing,' she said. 1

4 **a** He wrote a letter to the president. 1
b He wrote 'A letter to the president'. 2

5 **a** I don't know what I thought. 2
b 'I don't know what,' I thought. 1

6 **a** She says, 'What she thinks is right.' 1
b She says what she thinks is right. 2

7 **a** 'Who?' wrote Julius Caesar. 2
b Who wrote *Julius Caesar*? 1

8 **a** Who said 'Martin'? 1
b 'Who?' said Martin. 2

48.2 So I say to Claire 'Where's David, Claire?' and she says 'Oh, he's staying at home
to do his homework,' and of course I thought, 'Oh no he's not!' Because I saw him,
you see, going into the café with Lorraine and I said, 'Hi David!' and he went
completely red, and Lorraine said, 'We're doing a school project together,' and
I thought, 'Oh yes, I know what kind of project that is!'

49.1 1

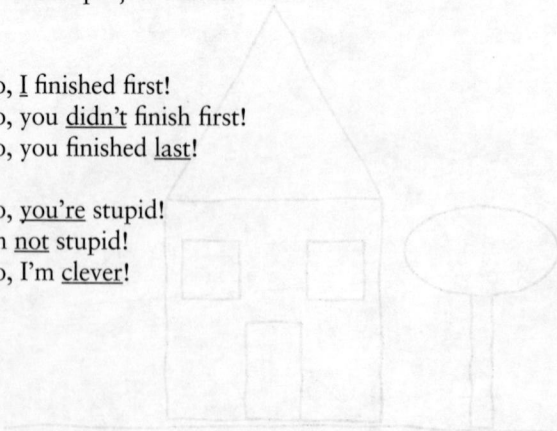

A: I finished first. B: No, <u>I</u> finished first!
B: No, you <u>didn't</u> finish first!
B: No, you finished <u>last</u>!

2

A: You're stupid! B: No, <u>you're</u> stupid!
B: I'm <u>not</u> stupid!
B: No, I'm <u>clever</u>!

49.2 A: I won't pass.
B: You <u>will</u> pass.
A: <u>You'll</u> pass.
B: I don't know.
A: You won't <u>fail</u>.
B: I <u>might</u> fail.
A: <u>I</u> will fail.
B: The exam's not hard.
A: It's <u>very</u> hard.
B: But not <u>too</u> hard.
A: Too hard for <u>me</u>.
B: But you're very clever!
A: <u>You're</u> the clever one.
B: Yes, I suppose you're right.

50.1 1 It's cold ... <u>very</u> cold.
2 It's a bag ... a <u>plastic</u> bag.
3 My name's Bond ... <u>James</u> Bond.
4 It's in Asia ... <u>central</u> Asia.
5 He's a composer ... a <u>French</u> composer.

50.2 A: It's very quiet.
B: <u>Too</u> quiet.
A: I think something's <u>wrong</u>.
B: <u>Very</u> wrong.
A: I don't <u>like</u> it.
B: I don't like it at <u>all</u>.
A: Let's get <u>out</u> of here.
B: Let's get out <u>fast</u>!

50.3 1 a <u>Near</u> Milan, yes.
2 a I'm a graphic <u>designer</u>.
3 a Yes, a very nice <u>flat</u>.
4 a Well, I'm learning <u>French</u>.
5 a Yes, I <u>lived</u> there for a year.
6 a Yes, two <u>brothers</u>.
7 a I like <u>jazz</u> and <u>classical</u>.

1 b Near <u>Milan</u>, yes.
2 b I'm a <u>graphic</u> designer.
3 b Yes, a <u>very</u> nice flat.
4 b Well, I'm <u>learning</u> French.
5 b Yes, I lived there for a <u>year</u>.
6 b Yes, <u>two</u> brothers.
7 b I like jazz <u>and</u> classical.

51.1 1 A: A black coffee please.
B: Sorry, do you want milk with your coffee?
A: No, a <u>black</u> coffee, please.

2 A: What's your nationality?
B: Well, my wife's an American citizen.
A: Yes, but what's <u>your</u> nationality, sir?

3 A: What time is it?
B: Well, the clocks changed last night ...
A: So what time <u>is</u> it then?

51.2 **1** a–1, b–2   **2** a–1, b–2   **3** a–2, b–1   **4** a–1, b 2

52.1 **1** A: I'd like a salad please.
B: A <u>mixed</u> salad or a <u>Greek</u> salad?
A: What's the difference?
B: Well, a <u>mixed</u> salad has <u>tuna</u> and a <u>Greek</u> salad has <u>cheese</u>.

2 A: I'd like to stay two nights please.
B: Do you want <u>full</u> board or <u>half</u> board?
A: What's the difference?
B: <u>Full</u> board includes <u>all</u> meals and <u>half</u> board includes just <u>breakfast</u> and <u>dinner</u>.

3 A: We'd like a room for two please.
B: Would you like <u>standard</u> or <u>deluxe</u>?
A: What's the difference?
B: <u>Standard</u> has a <u>mountain</u> view and <u>deluxe</u> has a <u>sea</u> view.

52.2 **1** a–2, b–1   **2** a–2, b–1

52.3 **1** b–a   **2** a–b   **3** b–a

53.1 **1** b   **2** b   **3** b   **4** a

53.2 **1** A: No, the <u>bath</u>room!
2 A: No, he's <u>retired</u>!
3 A: No, a book<u>shelf</u>.
4 A: No, I said <u>im</u>possible!
5 A: No, <u>down</u>stairs!

54.A If a person who has a bad quality accuses you of having that same bad quality, you can reply 'Look who's talking!'

If somebody tell you their plan, and the plan is very unlikely to succeed, you can reply "You'll be lucky!"

54.1 **1** ◣   **2** ◢   **3** ◣   **4** ◢

The meaning of the expressions in this exercise is:

You must be joking. – If someone makes a suggestion and you think it is a very bad idea, you can say this.

Chance would be a fine thing. – If someone is telling you about something you would like to do if you had the opportunity, you can say this.

Go for it! – When someone is about to start a performance, you can encourage them by saying this.

Give me a break. – If you achieve something in difficult circumstances and someone nevertheless complains about it, you can say this.

54.2 **1** a – Who? ◣   **3** a – Yes? ◢
  b – Who? ◢   b – Yes. ◣
2 a – What? ◣   **4** a – When? ◣
  b – What! ◢   b – When? ◢

54.3 1 a   2 b   3 a   4 b

55.1

1

A: When?
B: Tomorrow.
A: When? ✔
B: Tomorrow.
A: Tomorrow? ✔
B: Yes, tomorrow.

2

A: Which way?
B: Left.
A: What? ✔
B: Left.
A: In front of the shop? ✔
B: Yes.

55.2

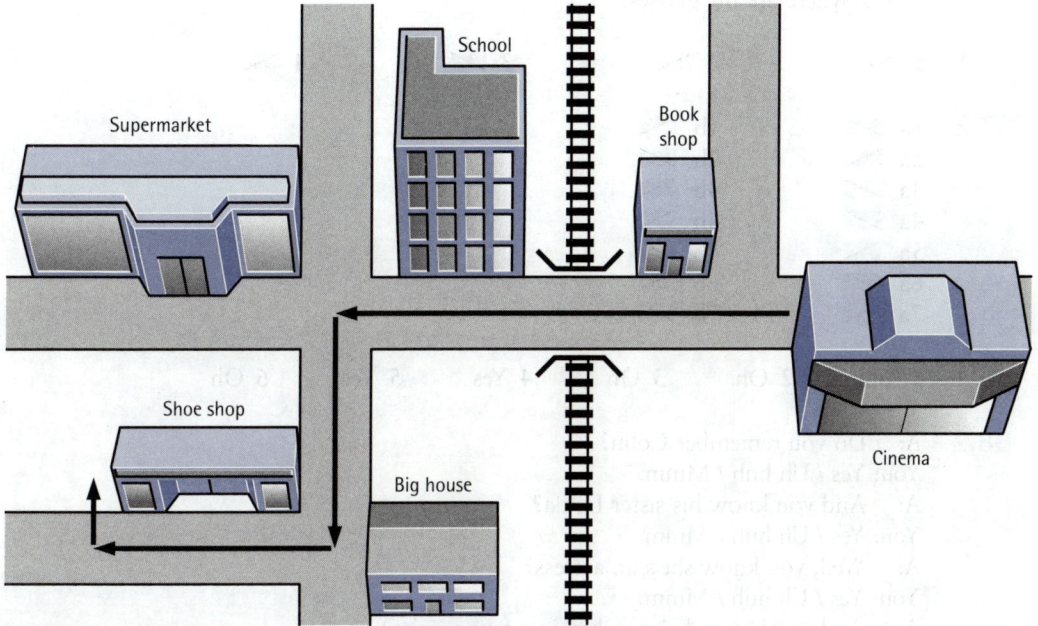

55.3

1 Right at the lights (?)
2 Next to the supermarket (?)
3 It's this one (.)
4 It's opposite the school (?)

5 It's a long way (.)
6 Under the bridge (.)
7 Take the next left (?)

56.1

1 Have you been to America?
2 What do you study?
3 What time is it?
4 Are you over eighteen?

5 Can you drive?
6 Where's he going?
7 Do you like it?

56.2

1 <u>Where</u> in Cuba?

2 And what's your <u>name</u>?

3 Where <u>do</u> you live?

4 What do you <u>study</u>?

5 When <u>will</u> you finish?

56.3
1 a Do you have any <u>children</u>?
   b Do <u>you</u> have any children?
2 a What's your <u>first</u> language?
   b What's <u>your</u> first language?
3 a What do you do on <u>Sundays</u>?
   b What do you <u>do</u> on Sundays?
4 a … <u>why</u> did he do it?
   b … why did <u>he</u> do it?
5 a … where <u>are</u> my glasses?
   b … where are <u>my</u> glasses?

57.1 1 ◣   2 ◣   3 ◤   4 ◤

57.2
1a ◤		1b ◣
2a ◣		2b ◤
3a ◤		3b ◣
4a ◤		4b ◤
5a ◣		5b ◤
6a ◤		6b ◣
7a ◣		7b ◤

58.1 1 Yes   2 Oh   3 Oh   4 Yes   5 Yes   6 Oh

58.2
A: Do you remember Colin?
You: Yes / Uh huh / Mmm.
A: And you know his sister Linda?
You: Yes / Uh huh / Mmm.
A: Well, you know she's an actress?
You: Yes / Uh huh / Mmm.
A: And you know she's worked in a few movies?
You: Yes / Uh huh / Mmm.
A: And you know she was making another movie in Australia?
You: Yes / Uh huh / Mmm.
A: Well, a spider bit her and she's very sick!
You: *Oh, that's terrible!*
A: Yeah, it's terrible, isn't it!

58.3 1 Oh, really!   2 Oh, really.   3 Oh, really!   4 Oh, really.

59.1
1 It's nice .
2 We're quite good .
3 Yes, it is, but…
4 I don't know .
5 Yes .
6 He does, but…
7 She likes you .
8 They're friendly, but…
9 Not bad .

59.2 1 disagreeing   2 disagreeing   3 agreeing

59.3
1 How's your headache? It isn't getting worse, is it? ↗
2 Those flowers are lovely, aren't they? ↘
3 You haven't seen my glasses anywhere, have you? ↗
4 Torsen's a great player, isn't he? ↘
5 I'm not sure. He was from Brazil, wasn't he? ↗
6 I can't quite remember. You need 40 points to win, don't you? ↗
7 Tennis is so boring, isn't it? ↘
8 She isn't a very good swimmer, is she? ↘
9 I'm not sure. It starts at nine, doesn't it? ↗
10 It wasn't a very interesting game, was it? ↘

60.1

people they like	people they don't like
Anne Kathleen	Jeremy Gail Tim

60.2 *Possible answers*

A: The beach was quite nice.
You: *Nice? It was absolutely fantastic!*
A: The weather was good.
You: *Good? It was brilliant!*
A: The nightlife was OK.
You: *OK? It was amazing!*

A: The shops were nice.
You: *Nice? They were brilliant!*
A: The people were OK.
You: *OK? They were absolutely fantastic!*
A: The flight was good.
You: *Good? It was brilliant!*

60.3
1 a Brilliant! →
  b Brilliant! ⤴
2 a Well done! ⤴
  b Well done! →
3 a Amazing! →
  b Amazing! ⤴
4 a Delicious! ⤴
  b Delicious! →
5 a Excellent! ⤴
  b Excellent! →

Section D   Reference

The phonemic alphabet

D1.1
1 *For writing:* pencil paper <u>pen</u> notebook
2 *In the office:* <u>desk</u> fax computer telephone
3 *Body parts:* neck head hand <u>leg</u>
4 *Farm animals:* <u>hen</u> pig sheep cow
5 *Colours:* green blue <u>red</u> black
6 *Verbs:* <u>get</u> take give go
7 *Numbers:* seven <u>ten</u> three five

D1.2

tʃ	eə	ɪ	ŋ	g	l	ɪ	ʃ
m	k	w	e	s·	tʃ	ə	n
ɪ	k	n	j	uː	z	b	s
k	w	k	əʊ	s	f	r	ɪ
s	ɪ	w	ʃ	k	j	iː	k
t	k	aɪ	ə	uː	uː	ð	s
e	dʒ	t	n	l	tʃ	z	θ
dʒ	uː	s	ʃ	uː	ə	ð	əʊ

D1.3   **1 Long vowel crossword**

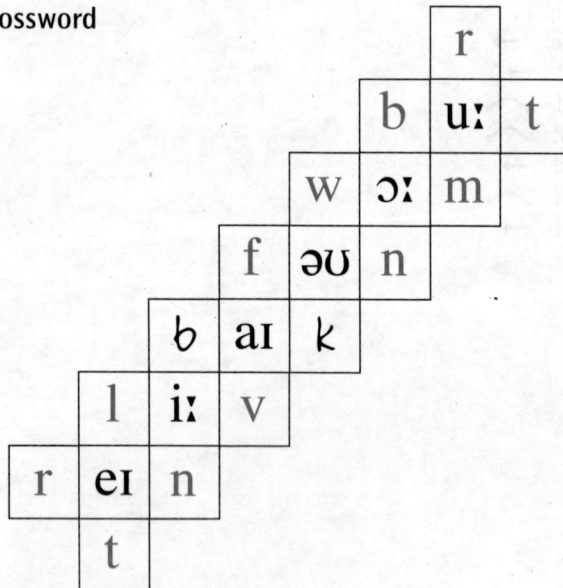

r
b uː t
w ɔː m
f əʊ n
b aɪ k
l iː v
r eɪ n
t

2 Short vowel crossword

```
                        p
                    l   ʊ   k
                f   ɪ   t
            k   ʌ   p
        g   ɒ   n
    p   e   t
h   æ   t
    k
```

3 Vowels before R crossword

```
                        ɔ
                    b   ɪə   d
                h   eə   z
            h   ɜː   z
        k   ɑː   d
    p   ɔː   t
        t
```

D1.4
1 jumping
2 washing
3 using
4 bathing
5 singing
6 thinking
7 playing

D1.5

	ɔɪ	ɔː	ɪə	eə	aɪ	iː
w		wore		wear	why	we
f		four	fear	fair		
d		door	deer	dare	die	
p		pour	pier	pair	pie	pea
t	toy		tear		tie	tea
b	boy	bore	beer	bear	buy	be
h			here	hair	high	he
ʃ				share	shy	she

D1.6

h	æ	m	b	ɜː	g	ə	s
p	r	f	b	r	e	d	t
æ	aɪ	ɪ	tʃ	ɪ	p	s	r
s	s	ʃ	m	iː	t	ɒ	ɔː
t	k	æ	r	ə	t	r	b
ə	ʌ	n	j	ə	n	ɪ	r
t	ə	m	ɑː	t	əʊ	n	ɪ
b	ə	n	ɑː	n	ə	dʒ	z

hamburger   bread   chips   meat
carrot   onion   tomato   banana
pasta   rice   fish   orange
strawberries

D1.7

k	d	ɒ	k	t	ə	n
ʊ	d	r	aɪ	v	ə	ɜː
k	p	eɪ	n	t	ə	s
m	ə	k	æ	n	ɪ	k
f	e	n	dʒ	ə	n	ɪə
ɑː	v	r	aɪ	t	ə	g
m	e	s	ɪ	ŋ	ə	ɑː
ə	t	w	eɪ	t	ə	d

doctor   driver   painter   mechanic
engineer   writer   singer   waiter
cook   nurse   farmer   vet
guard

D1.8

1

r	aɪ	m
aɪ	■	aɪ
t	aɪ	t

2

t	ɔː	k
ɔː	■	ɔː
l	ɔː	z

3

w	ɒ	t
ɒ	■	ɒ
ʃ	ɒ	p

4

k	ʌ	m
ʌ	■	ʌ
t	ʌ	tʃ

5

b	æ	k
æ	■	æ
t	æ	p

6

b	ʊ	ʃ
ʊ	■	ʊ
k	ʊ	d

7

p	eɪ	n
eɪ	■	eɪ
dʒ	eɪ	l

8

j	e	t
e	■	e
s	e	l

9

r	əʊ	t
əʊ	■	əʊ
l	əʊ	n

Key

D2 Pronunciation test

Section A Letters and sounds

A1
1 want
2 care
3 soup
4 most
5 blood
6 rude
7 bread

A2
1 lamb
2 receipt
3 listen
4 hour
5 half
6 calm
7 here

A3
1 came
2 cake
3 late
4 rose/rows
5 wait/weight
6 size/sighs
7 hi/high
8 bear/bare
9 burn

A4
1 pen
2 cut
3 feel
4 west
5 coat
6 fair
7 women
8 office's
9 vet
10 price
11 suit
12 code
13 wine
14 back
15 hair
16 wash
17 singing
18 collect

Section B Syllables, words and sentences

B1
1 glass
2 truth
3 smell
4 need
5 wanted
6 thirteen
7 is
8 were
9 and
10 does
11 That's a mile
12 support
13 pasta
14 guests

B2
1 washes
2 wanted
3 afternoon
4 asked
5 fortieth
6 builds
7 supermarket
8 over

B3
1 tomorrow
2 fifteen
3 Close the door.
4 Don't worry!
5 today
6 famous
7 first class
8 economy
9 No, it isn't.

B4
1 S
2 S
3 D
4 S
5 D
6 S
7 D
8 D
9 S
10 S

Section C Conversation

C1
1 a
2 b
3 a
4 a
5 b
6 b
7 a

C2
1 b
2 b
3 a
4 a
5 a
6 b
7 a
8 a

C3
1 is
2 isn't
3 is
4 does
5 isn't
6 isn't
7 isn't
8 is
9 is
10 is

D4 Sound pairs

Sound pair 1

1 S	2 S	3 D	4 S	5 S	6 S	7 S
8 bad	9 dead	10 sat		11 merry	12 men	

Sound pair 2

1 S	2 S	3 D	4 S	5 D	6 S	7 D
8 fun	9 cap	10 rang		11 cut	12 He's sung	

Sound pair 3

1 S	2 D	3 S	4 D	5 D	6 S	7 D
8 cat	9 match	10 harder		11 parks	12 hat	

Sound pair 4

1 D	2 S	3 S	4 S	5 D	6 D	7 D
8 gate	9 pepper	10 west		11 fail	12 pain	

Sound pair 5

1 S	2 D	3 D	4 S	5 D	6 S	7 D
8 their	9 stairs	10 hey		11 a pear	12 nowhere	

Sound pair 6

1 S	2 D	3 S	4 S	5 D	6 S	7 S
8 far	9 bare	10 cars		11 fair	12 stars	

Sound pair 7

1 D	2 S	3 D	4 S	5 S	6 D	7 S
8 form	9 park	10 stores		11 part	12 four	

Sound pair 8

1 S	2 D	3 S	4 D	5 D	6 S	7 S
8 where	9 dare	10 cheers		11 hear	12 air	

Sound pair 9

1 S	2 D	3 S	4 S	5 D	6 D	7 S
8 heart	9 much	10 dark		11 cart	12 come	

Sound pair 10

1 S	2 D	3 D	4 S	5 S	6 S	7 S
8 cheap	9 fit	10 live		11 feel	12 to sit	

Sound pair 11

1 D	2 S	3 S	4 D	5 S	6 D	7 S
8 we're	9 knee	10 pier		11 feed	12 here	

Sound pair 12

1 S	2 D	3 S	4 S	5 S	6 D	7 S
8 turn	9 learned	10 Jenny	11 bird		12 west	

Sound pair 13

1 D	2 S	3 S	4 D	5 S	6 D	7 S
8 mess	9 bill	10 will	11 letter		12 left	

Sound pair 14

1 S	2 S	3 S	4 D	5 D	6 D	7 D
8 note	9 rob	10 goat	11 won't		12 cost	

Sound pair 15

1 D	2 S	3 D	4 S	5 S	6 D	7 S
8 not	9 luck	10 shut	11 collar		12 they're gone	

Sound pair 16

1 S	2 S	3 S	4 D	5 D	6 D	7 D
8 soup	9 rule	10 boot	11 pole		12 grow	

Sound pair 17

1 D	2 S	3 D	4 S	5 S	6 S	7 D
8 saw	9 low	10 call	11 bowl		12 walk	

Sound pair 18

1 D	2 S	3 D	4 S	5 S	6 D	7 S
8 know	9 blouse	10 allowed	11 a shower		12 phoned	

Sound pair 19

1 S	2 S	3 D	4 D	5 S	6 S	7 D
8 Luke	9 fool	10 pool	11 shoe dye		12 butcher saw	

Sound pair 20

1 S	2 D	3 D	4 S	5 books	6 luck

Sound pair 21

1 D	2 S	3 S	4 S	5 D	6 D	7 D
8 but	9 hurt	10 earned a	11 suffer		12 shut	

Sound pair 22

1 S	2 D	3 S	4 S	5 D	6 S	7 D
8 bet	9 steady	10 won	11 again		12 butter	

Sound pair 23

1 S	2 S	3 D	4 D	5 D	6 S	7 S
8 short	9 odder	10 spot		11 water ski		12 port

Sound pair 24

1 S	2 D	3 D	4 D	5 D	6 S	7 S
8 beard	9 we're	10 fur		11 her		12 bird

Sound pair 25

1 D	2 D	3 S	4 S	5 S	6 S	7 D
8 where	9 stir	10 bared		11 hair		12 fur

Sound pair 26

1 S	2 S	3 S	4 D	5 D	6 S	7 D
8 bored	9 sir	10 short		11 first		12 walked

Sound pair 27

1 D	2 S	3 S	4 D	5 D	6 S	7 D
8 far	9 heart	10 further		11 hard		12 firm

Sound pair 28

1 S	2 S	3 D	4 D	5 D	6 S	7 D
8 bill	9 push	10 packs		11 robe		12 bear

Sound pair 29

1 S	2 S	3 S	4 D	5 D	6 D	7 S
8 vet	9 They've ached	10 some of each	11 Say 'boil'			12 I've rushed it

Sound pair 30

1 S	2 D	3 D	4 S	5 S	6 S	7 S
8 fool	9 pine	10 past		11 a nicer pear		12 face

Sound pair 31

1 S	2 D	3 S	4 S	5 D	6 S	7 D
8 eyes	9 sip	10 raise		11 niece		12 peace

Sound pair 32

1 S	2 D	3 D	4 D	5 S	6 S	7 S
8 sign	9 mash	10 save		11 shoot		12 seat

Sound pairs 33

1 D	2 S	3 D	4 S	5 S	6 D	7 D
8 thing	9 breeze	10 thought		11 mouse		12 closed

Key

Sound pair 34

1 S   2 S   3 D   4 D   5 D   6 S   7 D
8 said   9 town   10 coat   11 wide   12 writing

Sound pairs 35

1 S   2 D   3 D   4 S   5 D   6 D   7 D
8 tree   9 they   10 thanks   11 taught   12 breathe

Sound pairs 36

1 S   2 S   3 D   4 D   5 D   6 S   7 D
8 torch   9 aid   10 beat   11 coach   12 hedge

Sound pair 37

1 D   2 S   3 D   4 S   5 D   6 D   7 S
8 that's over   9 lived   10 few   11 wife's   12 of air

Sound pair 38

1 D   2 D   3 S   4 D   5 S   6 S   7 D
8 made aware   9 verse   10 wine   11 vest   12 half a weight

Sound pairs 39

1 D   2 D   3 D   4 S   5 D   6 S   7 S
8 thirst   9 free   10 thought   11 What some of us   12 either

Sound pair 40

1 S   2 D   3 S   4 D   5 D   6 D   7 D
8 gap's   9 back   10 ghost   11 card   12 gold

Sound pair 41

1 S   2 S   3 D   4 D   5 S   6 D   7 S
8 eight   9 heart   10 hair   11 earring   12 heating

Sound pair 42

1 D   2 D   3 S   4 D   5 S   6 S   7 D
8 jet   9 until July   10 yoke   11 yours   12 juice

Sound pairs 43

1 S   2 D   3 S   4 D   5 D   6 S   7 S
8 holder's   9 fold   10 sheet   11 hair   12 fired

Sound pair 44

1 D   2 S   3 S   4 D   5 S   6 D   7 S
8 shoes   9 chair   10 cash   11 chips   12 watch

Sound pair 45

1 D	2 D	3 S	4 S	5 S	6 S	7 D
8 Joe's		9 cheap	10 riches		11 H	12 tune

Sound pairs 46

1 D	2 S	3 S	4 D	5 S	6 D	7 D
8 arch		9 aids	10 each		11 Watch	12 rage

Sound pairs 47

1 S	2 S	3 D	4 S	5 D	6 D	7 S
8 chips		9 drunk	10 train		11 trees	12 jaw

Sound pair 48

1 D	2 S	3 D	4 S	5 S	6 S	7 D
8 hanged		9 win	10 robbing banks	11 ran		12 sinking

Sound pairs 49

1 S	2 S	3 D	4 D	5 D	6 D	7 S
8 turn		9 mice	10 son warned	11 mine		12 swing

Sound pair 50

1 D	2 S	3 S	4 D	5 S	6 S	7 D
8 prayed		9 wrong	10 glow		11 fries	12 collect

Acknowledgements

I would like to thank the following reviewers in different parts of the world who helped with feedback and piloting during the development of this project:
Zaina Aparecida Abdalla Nunes, São Paulo, Brazil
Tim Bromley, Bath, UK
Elise Brun, Orsay, France
Katie Head, Cambridge, UK
Martin Hewings, Birmingham, UK
Kathy Keohane, Stockport, UK
Magdalena Kijak, Krakow, Poland
Jennifer Jenkins, London, UK
Elizabeth de Lange, Beckum, Germany
David Marson, Colchester, UK
Matthew Norbury, Edinburgh, UK
Andrea Paul, Melbourne, Australia
David Perry, Valencia, Spain
Tony Robinson, Cambridge, UK
Sylvie Rolfe, Sydney, Australia
Diane Slaouti, Manchester, UK
Rastislav Sustarsic, Lubljana, Slovenia
Robin Walker, Oviedo, Spain
Max Walsh, Colchester, UK

I would like to thank Noirin Burke for her faith. Many thanks too to Alyson Maskell and Frances Amrani for their editorial care and initiative.

I also owe special thanks to the excellent IATEFL publication "Speak Out"*, many of whose contributors may recognise their influence in one part or another of this book.

*The newsletter of the pronunciation special interest group.

Mark Hancock 2003

Illustrations by Martin Aston, Kathy Baxendale, Jo Blake, Nick Duffy, Tony Forbes, Phil Healey and David Shenton.

Cover design by Dunne and Scully

Designed and typeset by Kamae Design, Oxford.